THEY CHOSE PEACE

Daniel Kumbon

Enga Province
Papua New Guinea

Copyright © Daniel Kumbon 2025

All rights reserved. No part of this book may be reproduced or transmitted in any form or by any means, electronic or mechanical, including photocopying, recording or by any information storage and retrieval system, without prior written permission of the Publisher below. The Australian Copyright Act 1968 allows one chapter only, or 10% of this book, whichever is the greater, to be photocopied by any educational institution for its educational purposes provided that the educational institution (or body that administers it) has given a copyright notice to the Copyright Agency (Australia) under the Act.

The Author reserves his moral rights.

Paperback ISBN: 978-1-7638456-2-6

First Published in 2025 by
First Nations Writers Festival International Limited
T/as First Nations Publishers

A Registered Charity (ABN 79 655 932 979)

2/53 Junction St, Nowra NSW 2540, Australia
Phone: +61 491 851 353

Email: firstnationswritersfestival@gmail.com
Web: www.firstnationswritersfestival.org

FB: www.facebook.com/firstnationswritersfestival.com

Cover Design: Busybird Publishing

Typeset: Busybird Publishing

Line Edited: Anna Borzi AM 2025

Printed and bound in Australia by IngramSpark

A memoir is a slice of real life from *one person's emotional truth* or perspective, what one person remembers may be different from what another person remembers. *This book was written by memory, and mine is imperfect. Also used are past notes, records, publications and the interviews of others present. I've done my best to be faithful to my experiences, and when possible, have consulted others who were also present during that time.*

Papua New Guinea

Coping With Personal Loss &
Reporting Conflict All My Life
in My Beloved Enga Province,
Papua New Guinea

PREFACE

In February, 2025, Prime Minister James Marape went to Australia in search of historical records of Papua New Guinea. This was in preparation for the celebration of 50 years of political independence later in the year. I was glad he did, because I was using old patrol reports in this book.

The old records were generously supplied to me by Jim Fenton 92, a former Kiap (patrol officer) with the Australian colonial administration.

He was the first Kiap to settle permanently at the new Kandep patrol post in 1960, a part of the Western Highlands District and administered from Mt Hagen. Jim Fenton sent me the priceless records a week or so earlier before the prime minister visited Australia.

Jim Fenton had transferred from Telefomin in what is now West Sepik Province. Some copies of his reports were about the three years he lived in Kandep. I believe he has more reports from other districts he served in PNG.

When you think of it, all Kiaps who worked in Papua New Guinea prior to independence kept patrol reports. If stacked on top of each other, they could reach the heights of Mt Wilhelm[1]. The reports are a treasure trove of information, and so valuable for future generations.

Transcripts or scanned copies of all the original reports should be collected and stored in all the libraries in the country. The material should also be stored electronically for easy access by anyone interested in Papua New Guinea's recent past, especially the time of the Australian Colonial Administration. The reports are very important because Kiaps worked in close consultation with local people from every region of the country.

---

1 - Mount Wilhelm (German: Wilhelmsberg) is the highest mountain in Papua New Guinea at 4,509 metres (14,793 ft).

On his Australian trip, Prime Minister James Marape said such information would be gathered as part of PNG's 50th anniversary celebrations. I am not sure if he included patrol reports by all of the former Kiaps, living or dead.

The PM said such information will be compiled into study resources for schools and used to create documentaries for radio and television, especially for people born before independence and beyond.

He made the statement after he visited the Australian Broadcasting Corporation's archives in Sydney where he viewed some of the historical video footage. His decision is of significant importance.

The government must find ways to collect copies of all of the patrol reports from all of the former patrol officers who lived and worked in PNG. The written words are as important as the video recordings.

Some former Kiaps have written books about their experiences in PNG. Graham Hardy, who came to Wabag in 1954, wrote 'Over the Hills and Far Away' after he retired. He gave me full permission to use one whole chapter concerning a patrol he made into Maramuni in one of my own books. I noticed there were no reports as such anywhere in Wabag. I am glad I recorded his patrol report before he died on 24 August, 2024.

I took a copy of my book to the National Library in Port Moresby and deposited it at the PNG Section, hoping future generations could have access to it. Hardy's book and other books by patrol officers, missionaries, businessman and planters should also be traced, purchased and copies placed in all the libraries in the country.

Prime Minister James Marape visited the Australian Governor General Her Excellency the Honorable Sam Mostyn AC, where they engaged in discussions on the deep historical ties and shared future of both nations.

"I affirmed that our relationship with Australia is a valued and foundational one, dating back to Papua New Guinea's attainment of sovereignty in 1975. Since then, Australia has stood with us every step of the way, contributing significantly to our progress during the past 49 years as we approach our 50th anniversary of independence," he said.

Mr. Marape acknowledged that Australia's ties with PNG extend far beyond 1975, with strong historical, economic, and security co-operation dating back to the colonial era. He said Australia has been a key partner in

PNG's development long before independence and remains committed to its progress.

A key highlight of the discussion was Marape's invitation to the Governor General to attend a special 50th anniversary event in Papua New Guinea dedicated to honoring women and girls.

This landmark event scheduled within PNG's 50th anniversary celebrations would call upon men and boys in the country to formally recognise and celebrate the contributions of women in PNG.

"The Governor General is a strong advocate for women's rights, with a distinguished background as a business woman and community leader, and she has graciously accepted the invitation."

"She commended PNG on its progress and reiterated Australia's continued commitment to supporting our development and aspirations," Marape said.

He reflected on his visit to the Australian Broadcasting Corporation (ABC) archives as an emotional and deeply moving experience as he explored historical recordings and documents capturing PNG's journey to independence.

The ABC, which has had a presence since the late 1940s, played a significant role in shaping PNG's early media landscape, contributing to the foundation of the National Broadcasting Commission (NBC) in 1973.

"I want to thank the ABC for granting me access to its archives, which contain a treasure trove of historical materials: photographs, transcripts, video footage, and audio recordings dating back to the 1940s," he said.

Among the many records he encountered, the highlight was hearing the full recording of former Australian Prime Minister Gough Whitlam's speech on PNG's Independence Day on September 16, 1975.

"Listening to Whitlam's words on the first day of our independence was profoundly moving. His message about the shared destiny of our two nations and the principles of sovereignty and self-determination still resonates strongly today, especially as we prepare to mark 50 years of independence," he said.

He was committed to ensuring that these historical records were integrated into educational materials so future generations will understand the struggles and sacrifices that led to PNG's independence. He placed emphasis on creating documentaries for radio and television for schools so that all Papua New Guineans – especially our youth born in the 1980s and beyond – never take our sovereignty for granted.

The patrol reports from all of the Kiaps who ever lived and worked in PNG should also be collected and brought into the country and kept for future generations. The central place to store them should be at the National Archives in Waigani in the nation's capital. There were hardly any patrol reports or old photographs deposited there.

I use samples of Jim Fenton's work in this book. It shows how important and interesting the work he did in Kandep, in what is now Enga province. I accorded him the honor to write the Foreword to ensure his enduring words about such an interesting period of PNG's history, should remain with us forever.

Daniel Kumbon
Wabag
25 January, 2025

FOREWORD

I first met Daniel Kumbon some years ago when he was attending a Writers Festival in Brisbane. Daniel is an internationally known PNG journalist and author, having published several books relating to the history and progress of his beloved country, particularly the spectacular highlands region where the formidable Enga people reside.

Daniel is an Engan with an intricate knowledge of the customs and social fabric of this tribal group. This book is a historical record of devastation and great personal loss and the breakdown in social cohesion and lawlessness which prevails today in the country of his birth.

I deem it a privilege that Daniel has asked me to write the foreword to his latest book published to coincide with the 50th Anniversary year of Papua New Guinea's attainment of independence from the Australian colonial administration.

The importance of this book lies in his knowledge of the social, economic and political issues affecting his Enga people from the early colonial days to the present.

My association with Daniel goes back 65 years to the colonial era when he was a small boy living in his village and I was a young Patrol Officer charged with the establishment of a Patrol Post at, in what was then termed "uncontrolled territory" due to the age old norm of tribal warfare, which Daniel so aptly describes, and which now, in this 50th year of independence, has descended into uncontrolled chaos with the introduction of modern weapons, widespread death and destruction of property, displacement and immeasurable suffering. A far cry from the peaceful and progressive attitude of the Kandep people when independence was granted in 1975.

At my advanced age I am a living link to the introduction of the colonial administration in Daniel's homeland. It saddens me to observe the current situation and I commend Daniel for recording these events in the hope that it informs the present and future generations of their past ancestors' place in the history of their beautiful and bountiful country.

All those expatriates who lived and worked in PNG prior to independence, no matter in what capacity, to this day have strong and enduring affection for its people and their welfare.

I know that those, who like myself, that are left from the early times have memories that are etched in their minds forever. I would like to conclude this foreword to Daniel's book with a verse that reflects the nostalgia we have for those never to be repeated years.

> *The great mountain ranges with rivers that run raging*
> *The country beneath us folds and falls as we fly in the dusk*
> *A once young Kiap who for years now has been aging*
> *Leaving behind memories that will turn into dust.*
>
> *May this country remember these men who once ventured*
> *Into the hidden places where most would not go.*
> *And there on a ridge line calling aloud to the mountains*
> *Is a Kiap with his carriers and policemen who are still on patrol.*

Jim Fenton
Brisbane
2025

INTRODUCTION

Twenty years ago, Resident Judge, Justice Moses Jalina warned that crime and corruption in high places would tear the country apart while a complacent people stood by and watched.

He implied that in some other country, a nation-wide revolution or military coup would have overthrown successive governments which continued to mismanage and plunder the rich resources of the country. He warned that PNG was travelling fast towards self-destruction.

Justice Moses Jalina made the bold statement during Legal Year celebrations in early 2007 in Wabag town. He said Papua New Guinea will face disastrous consequences within the next 10-20 years if people continued to be complacent—if they continued to think everything was going to be all right.

"People are thinking everything is okay," Jalina said. "But in 10-20 years-time, PNG will not be the same. Police are just watching crimes being committed."

"The media", he said, "was full of stories on allegations of corruption in high places. But it does not lead to any changes—nobody has taken any action. But in places like Australia and other free democracies, once corruption is exposed in the media, law enforcement agencies take immediate action to arrest the culprits and bring them to justice."

"Here, police are not arresting law breakers. Un-roadworthy vehicles are allowed to be driven around. They are not arresting them," he said.

The judge told the Provincial Police Commander not to allow uniformed policemen to drive unscrupulous foreigners around and to check that they, the police, were not being bribed.

He appealed to the people to become whistle blowers and make police aware of crimes committed so that arrests can be made and free our country of crime and deep-rooted corruption.

He warned, in words to the effect, that if people just stood by and allowed foreigners to consort with the police force, Papua New Guineans will end up losers. As the Ela Motors advertisement says, "When the going gets tough, the tough get going. And when the going gets tough, the tough foreigners will pack up and leave. You and I will remain."

He said all this in the presence of Deputy Chief Justice, Sir Salamo Injia, Mt Hagen Resident Judge, Justice Allen David, Governor Peter Ipatas and other dignitaries.

Governor Peter Ipatas supported the judge, asserting that the people had indeed become complacent. And the national government had failed the country in addressing serious crime and tribal warfare.

"I just don't know how this country is surviving when I see law and order breaking down everywhere," he said. "To fight crime, Enga has done its part to recognise Village Court officials, established the National Court in Wabag and promised to support Legal Year celebrations in the province each year."

Ipatas has been calling continuously on the national government to bring in Australian federal police to help local police control tribal warfare and other serious crime so rampant in the province.

The law-and-order situation, especially tribal warfare, is worse than ever. While the Legal Year celebrations were being celebrated, young men were killed in two tribal wars a couple of kilometers down the road.

People were calling for an urgent State-of-Emergency operation to stop the two tribal wars involving high-powered guns resulting in up to 20 men being killed in a matter of days.

One of the fights was an ongoing conflict between the Ambulin and Wapukin tribes which saw more than 10 men killed in recent days. It had started in October, 2002 bringing the death toll to more than 120.

At least two women were reportedly raped—one, the wife of a government worker living at Birip PTB Camp belonging to the National Works Department.

The second fight between the Anjin and Langap tribes resulted in seven deaths.

These fights drastically affected the education of hundreds of children attending Pina Catholic Mission Primary School and the Highland Lutheran International School.

HLIS students and staff were forced to evacuate to Kumul Lodge when fighting between the Wapukin and Ambukin intensified on the edges of the school boundaries.

At least one teacher was nearly injured by a stray bullet. A few policemen were able to provide some protection and prevented further harm to staff, students and destruction to school property.

Concerned parents wrote to the Internal Security Minister, The Deputy Prime Minister, Inter-government Relations Minister and the Governor requesting a special task force or a unit from the State of Emergency operations in the Southern Highlands to come and protect staff, students and property at the schools.

"Innocent lives are under threat, including those of school children," they wrote. "We sincerely request intervention by transferring a unit from Mendi or alternatively, declare a separate state of emergency."

There was a state-of emergency operating in place to counter serious crime in the neighboring Southern Highlands province.

A detachment was deployed to Wabag and the situation calmed down for a while.

What was complex and frightening was that the two fights were well planned coordinated battles because several tribes from Wabag town to Akom formed allegiances over the years calling themselves the 'Nakau Team – Nettle Team and Paipai Team – Destroyer Team.

People feared that if Birip, the only village remaining along the Wabag –Akom stretch of the Highlands Highway, was destroyed, there would be widespread criminal activity along the road.

But until now, 2025, the year PNG celebrates 50 years for its independence anniversary, Birip village has remained steadfast in upholding the law and maintaining neutrality even in the face of recent widespread fighting in the same area stretching to the Tsak Valley and down to Kuimimanda village. A peace treaty was finally signed in Port Moresby by representatives from the opposing sides after much time and resources had been exhausted.

Enga Nius[2], which reported on tribal warfare and other serious crime, ceased to exist a year later. No proper records were available locally. But the law-and-order situation never improved. The use of high-powered guns spread to almost all parts of the province. A proper record has not been kept of the total number of people killed in all the tribal wars fought since the scourge resurfaced in Enga province soon after independence.

The costs of destruction to both public and private property ran into billions and billions of kina. Imagine all the vehicles, workshops, shops, government offices, schools, health facilities and homes that have gone up in flames in fifty years!

The only time the people of Enga ever enjoyed peace, harmony and freedom of movement was during the late 1950s – 1970s when the Australian colonial government was in full control and enforced an iron-clad rule.

I know because I have lived it – the peace and progress, then the pain, personal loss and suffering. As a student at the University of Papua New Guinea, we Enga students tried to address tribal warfare in our 1996 Year Book, a copy of which is now in the PNG Section of the National Library.

In this book, I do not mention mass killings in the mining township of Porgera, much death, suffering and destruction to property in all of the districts – Wapenamanda, Wabag, Laiagam, Kandep or Kompiam, but I do make mention of the few brave men who have attempted to stop the menace, appealing to the people to give up their destructive attitudes.

Nor, how I later lost my own lifetime investment following the 2022 national elections and how I averted a tribal war. This is my story really – my life and work as a journalist in my own province.

I am from here, live and work here. There was and is no other place that I can call home. I belong here.

It disheartens me to state again that high-powered guns have replaced bows and arrows. Politically-induced fights have become hard to control for the poorly-resourced armed forces of the state – the police and army combined. Traditional rules of tribal warfare were not observed. Houses were burnt down with people inside. Bus-loads of people were ambushed

---

2 - Enga News

on the main highways, and people were killed indiscriminately. People who possessed guns became warlords.

Enga province is part of PNG. One of the major resource projects in the country – Porgera gold mine, operates in the province. The people's actions affected the whole country. The bulk of peace-loving citizens desperately needed outside support. Maybe, the Red Cross needs to come to the province and rehabilitate all the traumatised people. Tribal war, killing and destruction continued to be a vicious circle.

On a positive note, I, my two councilors and my tribesmen did our part to avert a tribal war when my property was destroyed for no apparent reason in 2023. We knew human life is more precious than property which can be replaced.

1

CHOOSING PEACE

'Peace cannot be achieved through violence, it can only be attained through understanding.'
Ralph Waldo Emerson

On The Verge of Tribal War

I didn't know whether to cry or to cut my hands off. I had completely lost my property – my lifetime investment, to a horde of thugs. My people had just killed a man in retaliation. I could not blame them. It was a provoked spur of the moment reaction.

The situation quickly turned into a daytime nightmare. Blood had been spilled. In all likelihood there would be full-scale tribal war. I knew the mayhem that would follow. Many more people would die and property would be destroyed on a grand scale. Women and children would be displaced. Immense suffering would follow.

I also knew what the end result would be. Compensation would be paid, equating precious human life with a display of wealth – pigs and cash. How crazy and absurd.

No, I didn't want that to happen. I have spent a lifetime reporting tribal warfare in my beloved province with a heavy heart. I have seen gory images of headless bodies, burnt out ruins of expensive homes and property, sad faces of displaced families, homeless widows and orphans full of tears. The scenes flashed across my troubled mind.

I couldn't sleep that night. How could I stop the impending fight? I was far from home seeking medical treatment for a stress-related illness. Doctor Kuranda David had warned me to avoid stressful situations. But this was a situation impossible to ignore. It concerned me. I was the centre of attention, the main character in a Hollywood-style blockbuster.

On this night, Monday 20 March 2023, I did not sleep. I kept tossing and turning on a large double bed in a lodge at Rainbow Estate in Port Moresby.

My people had killed a man late that afternoon after some members of the Imma tribe had destroyed my property on the Kandep government station. If there was still daylight, and if my people had not withdrawn under cover of the descending darkness, more lives could have been wasted.

I longed to know why my property had been destroyed, forcing my people to face the inevitable tribal war? The clock was ticking fast to the break of dawn. The fight would start any moment. I couldn't do anything. I was mentally crushed and physically weak. I was far from home and with no consolation from anybody in Port Moresby. The news hadn't yet spread on social media.

I thank God for that great man of history, Alexander Graham Bell for inventing the telephone. I had in my hands a mobile phone with which I could easily speak with my two Aimbarep Pumbuti councillors – Cr Yapi Pasul and Cr Bus Pyaso.

My wife, Julie and some relatives had phones. Talking with them at least eased some tension.

They had informed me of the situation as they withdrew from the conflict zone. But I couldn't reach them now in the night. The Digicel signal does not reach my village, maybe because it is nestled directly beneath Mt Kondo which probably deflected the signal. Those manning the frontline at Kombolos village could not use their phones.

There was nothing I could do. The closest target the Imma would aim for was Kombolos village. My own village, Kondo, was about 10 kilometres away. The first member of parliament, our tribal leader – the late Nenk Pasul MBE – was born there. That afternoon, men had been deployed to stand guard in case of sneak attacks during the night.

Fighting rules had changed in Enga province. Homes had already been burned with occupants trapped inside. In olden times, the attackers would wait in ambush. The first person to come outside was shot with arrows. They were fair: the victim was given a chance to escape. The faces of victims were spared for their loved ones to see before burial. But now they were disfigured beyond recognition. There was too much hatred in the province.

My mind was cluttered with all sorts of thoughts. My tribe was drawn to a conflict that we did not initiate. I kept tossing and turning, thinking hard in that room waiting impatiently for dawn to break.

It was mental torture: a nightmare! Every second seemed an eternity. I was hungry. I hadn't eaten. My eyes were red from lack of sleep. It seemed as if I was naked, without soul, and with no strength to stand up. The Angel of Death was knocking at my door.

The only sensible thing to do was to get on my knees and pray to God Almighty. I prayed for Divine intervention to allow the storm to pass.

But then I felt a mix of shame and guilt. I had made a mockery of the Christian faith. I was baptised twice in two different Christian church denominations. I quit attending church after realising my mistake. But yet I prayed.

Soon, the sweet little voices of tiny birds began to sing. Dawn was breaking. The uninterrupted free flow of melodies soothed my troubled mind. Humans were but one species of the animal kingdom. These tiny birds were part of that kingdom. They have always been free to sing in the morning, flying from tree to tree searching for food.

All the while, my people waited tensely in the cold to face death itself up at Kombolos village.

But God gave us the ability to adjust, think and choose what was right. Today was a new day. I had to face it. I made myself another cup of coffee.

I hadn't finished that coffee when my phone rang. It was Cr Yapi Pasul. He said he was with some of our tribal leaders and wanted to make a proposal. Like me, they hadn't slept either.

"Can we send word to the Kambrip Yanagin people that we will pay immediate compensation for the men killed yesterday. If they refuse our offer, then that will be it. But at least we must initiate peace before an arrow is fired.

"I am with Cr Bus Pyaso, Buka Nokop Mas and others standing here. What do you think?" he said.

"That is great. It's a good idea. Who else will make such decisions on behalf of the tribe in situations like this? You have to make critical decisions on behalf of the tribe. Pigs and cash are things of this earth. We can pay the compensation. Send word to the Kambrip Yanagin people" I said.

"Good. That's all we wanted to hear. We are going now before they attack us. We must move fast."

The moment Cr Yapi Pasul switched off his phone, I got on my knees and thanked God. I knew he had heard my plea. The Lord had planted the peace proposal in the minds of my two councillors.

They had vehicles with them and they drove immediately to Gin village to relay the message of peace.

One of our own tribal villages, Tumbil is sandwiched between those two Kambrip villages. I have traditional land at Tumbil village.

It was possible that the Kambrip Yanagin would easily allow the Imma to attack us from their village. Tension built up again in that room in Port Moresby as I waited for news from home – good or bad.

Relatives Demand Cash to Buy Guns, Ammunition & Hire Mercenaries

Our people guarding Kombolos village were unaware of the peace proposal. They were restless and on edge. The attack could come any minute. They realised they had no guns. Their bows and arrows would be useless against superior weaponry. They felt insecure on the front line.

They rang me and demanded money from me to buy guns, ammunition, hire mercenaries and for their supply of buai and smokes.

I told them I had spoken with our two councillors earlier that morning regarding a ceasefire. We all had to wait to hear of the outcome.

But they still kept pestering me. They wanted cash straight away. I reminded them I was in Port Moresby because I was sick. What did they expect me to do – hire a helicopter, load it with guns and land it on Mt Kondo?

Still, they persisted and demanded money. I was dealing with village people. They were stubborn to the core. Fed-up, I blocked the particular number. Later, I discovered a nasty text message on my phone accusing the Kumbon family of involving them in the conflict without making available the means to protect and defend themselves.

'We need money and guns now to feel confident and gain strength. What do you want us to do? Tell us right now,' read part of the text message. But when had I informed them that I was ready to fund a tribal war? Only some politicians and businessmen funded tribal wars these days. They seemed to be the people with cash and supplied guns to rural communities very easily.

My relatives didn't understand the complexities of tribal warfare: the cost and pain that follows and the time it consumes. They had no experience in fighting, to rally support, pay compensation or deliver public speeches to hold the alliance together during a fight. Or to handle the situation with sensitivity till the conflict ended. It needed skill and wisdom to pay adequate compensation to ensure the problem was buried for good.

The relatives who pestered me were toddlers when our tribe fought the last two battles in the early 1980s a couple of years after independence. We paid compensation for all those that had been killed or wounded. Tribal war is a time consuming, wasteful enterprise – unlike peace which is a life-sustaining necessity which people should maintain.

My tribe had been at peace for 31 years, since the completion of compensation payments for deaths in the last two wars. We were now suddenly confronted with this unprovoked mess.

I was ready to tell my tribesmen to escape with their lives to neighbouring villages. Let the enemy come in freely and destroy our villages as they did to my property. They would not dig up the soil and carry it away. We can go back and rebuild.

The late Inspector Peter Pyaso, the Mobile Unit Squad 9 commander in the province and I had always been telling our people not to go and fight in other people's tribal wars. If they died, nobody should go and join in that fight to take revenge. Their own lives were important.

Unfortunately, Inspector Peter Pyaso was killed by Lakain tribesmen when he went to stop a tribal war at remote Lapalama in Kompiam district in 1992. He left a big vacuum in both the police hierarchy in Enga province and in our village at Kondo. I needed him now.

He could have intervened to prevent a tribal war, make arrests or opt for peace. The Imma Lutheran Church Bishop, late Philipo Paiakae was his uncle. After his funeral, we had given the traditional compensation or Laita to Bishop Paiakae. But Inspector Peter Pyaso was gone and so was his uncle, the bishop.

We had lost nearly two dozen able-bodied men from all the Aimbarep Pumbuti major clans in the two fights we had been involved in. Now, not many elders were left who could advise the younger generation about the consequences of tribal war and instruct them to avoid nasty situations that would lead to war. With the traditional Hausman, or houses for men only, gone, all the men were sleeping in their family homes. Children grew up without the essential instructions from elders in the Hausman.

In 1982, just before my tribe was involved in the second of the two fights, I started work as press officer to Danely Tindiwi – the first Premier of Enga province. Prior to that I was a broadcast officer with Radio Western Highlands, one of the provincial radio stations run by the National Broadcasting Commission.

The late Inspector Peter Pyaso also transferred to Wabag police station from Kerowagi in Simbu province. We used our hard-earned cash to help pay compensation for some of the deaths in the fights. Our relatives expected us to buy the largest pigs. We did so without complaint.

Our aim was to free our people. We warned them we would never help them again if they instigated fresh conflicts.

But wars fought in that period were totally different. Bows and arrows, spears and wooden shields were used. Now, high-powered guns – M16s, AK47s AR15s were bought in the black market or hired, resulting in an unprecedented number of casualties on both sides of inter-tribal conflicts.

To compound the situation, the police force in Enga was stretched. Tribal warfare was widespread in the province. Even the deployment of PNG defence force personnel did not help. Tribal warriors owned the same types of guns as the security forces. The death toll kept mounting as thick smoke covered the landscape from burning villages and property worth billions of kina. No district was free of tribal feuds and general lawlessness.

The government was concentrating police operations on Porgera. The country needed the gold mine to operate. The economy was in a poor state, coupled with widespread corruption in high places. Living standards had fallen, causing public servants to live below the poverty line.

That was the situation I was confronted with as an unattached public servant. My relatives in the village did not understand the serious problems faced by the country. Maybe they thought I was enjoying life in Port Moresby.

I am sure that if I hadn't taken the medication prescribed to me by my doctor, I could have developed serious stress-related complications. I was lucky, I was in Port Moresby. I was able to absorb and handle the situation by phone with my two councillors and local leaders back home.

It turned out that the person killed was a student at Kandep High School. He was the son of Kambrip Kunias from Yanagin village. The Kambrip Yanagin and Kambrip Gin tribesman were our traditional allies in politics and in war.

Nenk Pasul's mother was from the major Kambrip tribe. They had been supporting Nenk, to win and become the first elected member for Kandep Open in the House of Assembly in forthcoming provincial government elections.

I knew Kunias very well. He had multiple wives – four of them from four major clans in my own Ambarep Pumbuti tribe. The Aimbarep girls all gave him many sons. The one killed was from his wife from the Southern Highlands.

I felt confident that the remaining sons would accept our peace proposal.

It was customary that once a man was killed in tribal war, the relatives had the power to allow the fight to continue, to take revenge or opt for compensation payment.

Usually, compensation was paid first by the tribe on whose side a person was killed. That side is called 'sangalis' in our local Enga language. But we, the 'yourwaip'- the other side wanted to pay first. We didn't want more unnecessary killings to occur.

I was glad my two councillors rang me early that Tuesday morning. I waited to hear what the Kambrip Yanagin relatives would say about the peace proposal. I hoped they would accept it. I did not wish to see my tribe create enemies with our former ally.

The Peace Offer

For over 40 years, I've been reporting crime, especially tribal warfare, the most deadly and destructive pastime of my people in Enga province. We live in the central highlands of Papua New Guinea. The neighbouring highlands provinces do engage in tribal warfare – but not as viciously intense as in Enga province.

I never thought the threat of tribal war would ever reach me personally, one that would involve my whole Aimbarep Pubuti tribe.

One can earn a fortnightly salary, own a business or kill a pig and share it with whom he wished. Your tribesmen would keep their distance unless invited. They keep busy with their own lives most of the time.

But when you are attacked, when members of your family are harassed or your property is destroyed, they will instantly react and rally support around you. They will even act independently to attack the culprits without seeking prior approval. That's the nature of tribalism, how criminals are harboured and how people die unnecessarily.

The Imma tribesman had violated our tribal pride and dignity. The property was mine. But my tribesmen took pride in my accomplishments. If the majority agreed to fight, everybody would get involved with no complaints and count the losses afterwards. That was the situation with which I was confronted.

Everybody knew that my property, on state land, had been destroyed by Imma tribesmen. Nothing was left but the photographs in my laptop and the memory of all that hard work we had put in will remain with us. My plan to settle there in retirement was shattered.

My country celebrates 50 years of independence on 16 September 2025. But there is no reason for me and my family to be happy about it. Three attempts to get assistance from the government's Small and Medium sized Enterprise, SME program failed.

However, I am an independent sort of person – unlike the leaders and public servants who were accused of abusing government power, misleading people and thriving on corruption at the expense of ordinary people. Some were suspected of supplying guns used in almost all of the tribal wars in the province. But like the late judge Moses Jalina said, a complacent people stood helplessly on the sidelines hoping that everything will be fine.

I'm from the old school – the one where village elders firmly instructed us, the youth, in the Hausman to accomplish things with our own two hands. The Hausman was a man only house where the menfolk lived and discussed important tribal matters. It was where youth were instructed on how to conduct their lives from youth to adulthood.

We were instructed to respect our elders and visitors who came to our homes and to help our parents – fetching water, collecting firewood and looking after pigs.

I developed my property based on that teaching – with my own two hands. I built a store, a permanent home, three bush material houses, a cook house and the fencing with trees I had planted in the 1960s and early 1970s while a student at Kandep primary 'T' School. I took home seedlings that forestry officials gave away free of charge. They encouraged people to plant them. I was that sort of boy.

On that black Monday, the Imma tribesman poured onto my property without warning. They destroyed everything completely. They had dismantled my two permanent buildings and carried every piece of timber, corrugated iron roofing, louvres, iron posts and plywood away. Only the cement floor of the store remained.

My wife and Monica, one of my two sisters, and her family had fled to nearby Paruli, my wife's village. They took nothing with them.

Monica recognised some of the attackers. They were members of the Imma tribe – maternal cousins, uncles and political supporters of Alfred Manase, the former member for Kandep. She pleaded with them to stop.

She was married to one of Alfred Manase's Wasant tribesman from Pulya village. Even when she mentioned Alfred's name, her lone voice was drowned by the gleeful shouts, singing and laughter as tree after tree was cut down.

This was the second time my sister and her six children had to escape from a life-threatening situation. In 2022, she had fled with her children from Andokoe in the Wage census division. An election-related tribal war had flared up between supporters of Manase and another candidate during the national elections.

My sister's persistent pleas that the mob should desist were ignored and the Imma continued on with their destructive work. Somebody pushed her violently towards the Kandep-Mendi-road as if to show her the exit during a mad football stadium stampede. She walked away from the carnage choking in her own tears, her bewildered children following closely behind her. My wife had escaped to her village first. I tried to comfort them all by phone.

They were in mourning. They had been attacked without warning. If this was how innocent families in other parts of Enga province had suffered in all those tribal feuds, I must applaud them for bearing the kind of loss and pain my family suffered. A feeling of emptiness surrounds you.

Later, I had to hold a small funeral feast called a kumand to release my family from mourning. Then I took my wife to Port Moresby to recover from the ordeal.

When my relatives heard about the wanton destruction, they had mobilised and rushed to the scene and confronted the thugs in the afternoon.

There was a brief fight. The late Kambrip Kunias Poko's son was killed on the Imma side. My people withdrew from the scene as it was getting dark. The Imma tribesman continued on with their destructive work to the next day. To those who saw it, my area seemed as if a tsunami had passed through – all 2000 different species of trees, flowers, food gardens, everything had been levelled.

In the next few days, all the sweet potatoes had been dug up and the felled trees had been carried away by local communities. Some were sold to public servants and others in the small township.

Then local people deliberately allowed their goats, cows and pigs into the township to forage on the grass, insects and worms on my block. It seemed some people didn't want evidence to show that there had been buildings there and that people had lived in them.

It seemed as if they didn't want outsiders to live in the town anymore. But that's impossible. The town of Kandep is state land. Outside people will always live there unless the Kandep district headquarters was moved to a new location.

The Imma and Alitip people must honour their tribal leaders like Imma Muniakali, Mamb Mara, Alitip Wandi and others who had offered their lands to total strangers – Kiaps and missionaries to work and live among them.

While the colonial government established the district headquarters at the current location, the Lutheran missionaries established themselves at Kokas. The Apostolic church settled at Sawi. The Foursquare Church, Seventh Day Adventists, CAF – Christen Apostolic Fellowship came later to settle among them too.

Kandep Secondary School, Kandep Hospital, Kandep primary school, Andait Vocational Centre and several elementary schools also operate among them. No other location in Kandep has a concentration of such essential services like they do.

The Imma and Altip tribes must count themselves lucky that so many institutions were operating on their soil. They should refrain from stealing from those living among them, stage tribal wars on the Kandep government station, destroy or carry away equipment from the Kandep district office or destroy people's property like they did to mine.

They must not take advantage of a weak government that was incapable of containing tribal warfare and general lawlessness in the province. Kandep people must not jump on the band wagon and destroy our district.

Many of my people wanted to fight. but I and my two councillors had won them over. We had to wait on the relatives of the person killed to respond to our peace offer.

Black Monday: How My Property Was Destroyed, Resulting in Student Death

In Enga province, people die over trivial matters – such as when a fight erupted leading to tribal war after two people argued over who should play first at a snooker table.

Or when some children playing marbles in a certain village start an argument. Parents take sides and relatives join in, aggravating the situation further developing into war.

Or when two brothers killed each other with the same axe during an argument over who should get a pig at a compensation payout. One brother grabbed the rope tied to the pig's foreleg, the other tried to pull it away saying their sister should have the pig.

Instead of resolving the matter, the first brother pulled out his axe and planted it with full force into his brother's chest. He escaped to a house. The wounded brother chased after him with the axe still embedded in his chest and cornered him. With his last remaining strength, he pulled out the bloody axe and plunged it deep into his brother's abdomen. They both died from loss of blood. The two brothers, from one father and two different mothers, lay next to each other, motionless.

Another argument occurred in October, 1994. This time, two-brothers-in-law argued about who should get a particular pig. A fist fight escalated into tribal war drawing in seven different clans.

It spread, igniting six different fights stemming from that one argument between the brothers-in-law. Seventeen lives were lost over a wretched pig! How absurd it is that precious lives can be lost just like that.

My property, estimated as being worth up to K1.5million, developed over a 15-year period was wilfully destroyed in two days. It was good enough a reason to fight. The Kambrip Yanagin too, had reason to fight because the student was killed. But both sides opted for peace.

In the morning of that black Monday, the Imma people had tried to stop a team of technicians from installing a Digicel tower on the grounds of the Kandep district administrator's official residence.

The installation site is the same location where my daughter Jacinta Roa's family vehicle had been burned a year before, on the eve of the 2022 national elections. Her husband was the acting district administrator at the time.

Earlier that day, one team of Imma tribesmen unsuccessfully applied for bail to free a second suspect, Piso Nawe, one of their own men, from the Wabag police cells in relation to the truck rusting under the new Digicel Tower.

I have no connection with the Digicel tower installation or the vehicle. I am still baffled by the actions of the Imma tribesmen to wilfully destroy my property.

They hadn't given any chance to Elijah, the man renting my store, to pack his store-goods properly, load his power generator or pack up his belongings. They began tearing down the store while he was trying to salvage some of the store goods.

I'm not sure why they tried to involve me and my tribe. Why they were trying to stop development from taking place on the Kandep government station had nothing to do with me or my tribe. I wondered if they destroyed my property to provoke me and my people to start a tribal war! This would prevent police from arresting the remaining suspects in the burning of Mr Roa's Electoral Commission hired truck.

But the truck belonged to Mr Cleopas Roa, my daughter's husband. He was, at the time, deputy administrator of Provincial Affairs and Local Level Government in the Enga Administration and acting district administrator for Kandep.

When his truck was destroyed, Wabag police on electoral duties in Kandep collected all the information they could from witnesses. My daughter Jacinta was in the Kandep District Administrator's official residence. She saw the thugs climb over the fence into the premises. They surrounded her family vehicle while one person started a fire on the seats in the cabin. Eyewitnesses supplied the names to police.

They lodged a complaint at the Wabag police station with a list of about two dozen suspects. Most of them were from the Kanda major clan of the Imma tribe. They live on the north western peripheries of the small township of Kandep.

Roa is also married to the Imma people. He is their brother-in-law. His first wife and their first-born son live among her people. The son did casual work for educated elites of the Imma tribe.

The Imma Kanda people had no right to involve me in family affairs of my married daughter. In Engan tradition, when daughters marry, they leave their father's household for good.

But surely the Imma leaders, the village court magistrates, councillors and educated elites would not think I'd be that stupid to lead my people to a deadly war. Even the government's Kandep District Law and Order officer was from the Imma tribe. How could they not intervene in the initial stages?

No, fighting was not the answer. How could I, an educated person, one who has travelled the world, a senior public servant, one who has spent a lifetime reporting gory images of revenge killings, tribal war casualties, death and destruction all over the province, lead my people to certain death?

We have an obligation to respect and uphold the laws of this country.

The first two fights we had been involved in were provocations so they destroyed my property.

Now, my tribe had to honour the legacy left behind by the late Nenk Pasul MBE our tribal leader. He had encouraged us to keep the peace. We were proud of him, the first elected member for Kandep in the House of Assembly.

Nenk Pasul had assisted Jim Fenton, Ross Allen, Llyod Warr and other patrol officers to promote peace among the Kandep people. And in his capacity as member for Kandep, he intervened to stop many tribal fights.

I remember accompanying him with other members of our tribe to Poketamanda village in the Lai census division to stop a fight there. Cr Yangala was happy to see the Member of the House of Assembly go to his area to stop his people from fighting. That was after independence, before Papua New Guinea's first general elections in 1977.

That black Monday afternoon, my tribesmen went to Kandep government station to investigate why the Imma were destroying my property. They had first burned one of my cook houses and chopped down some of the trees.

Instead of trying to resolve the matter, the Imma engaged my people in a fight resulting in the death of the Kambrip student.

Seven of the deceased student's relatives had supported Alfred Manase during the 2022 national elections. When Don Polye won, four had gone to Port Moresby leaving the others behind among the Imma Kanda people. Don Polye is their own Kambrip tribesman.

Of the three who remained, one was later arrested in Wabag town in connection with the burning of Roa's vehicle.

On Tuesday March 14, 2023, a second suspect was arrested in relation to the arson case. He was Piso Nawe, an Imma Kanda tribesman.

Next day, the Imma tribesman gathered at the top end of the airstrip and went berserk. They demanded the immediate release of Piso Nawe in police custody in Wabag. Somebody made the false claim that 60 suspects had been reported to police in the burning of Mr Roa's vehicle.

Then, some of the Imma tribesman went and fired warning shots over my property. The gun used belonged to a young man named Andy from the Kambrip Peam major clan of Gin village.

Andy didn't know up to that point that he was related to me by blood. Gin Lyalae Samale, my cousin had failed to tell his son and grandchildren about his roots. The Hausman system of instructing the male youth was long gone.

One of my aunts, Tolya had married a man named Samale from Gin village. She gave birth to my cousin, Lyalae. Andy, the gunman, was the son of Andale, my cousin Lyalae's first born son between his second wife from Kiran village. He was embarrassed to learn these facts as they were revealed to him much later.

Six days later when the Imma started burning my property, Andy escaped with his gun to my Kondo village and joined my people there. Another nephew Stanley, one of Kunias Poko's sons, also joined my tribesmen with another modern gun. His mother was from Kimbalam village, one of four Aimbarep Pumbuti girls Kunias Poko had married. I received reports that there was an alarming build-up of firearms in my village ready for tribal war. Gunmen from Wage had climbed over a mountain range to my village.

Meanwhile in Port Moresby, early that Tuesday morning after I had talked with my two councillors, I received a phone call from Michael

Toke, one of my tribesmen, living in Port Moresby. He told me the four boys who had supported Alfred Manase did not want to fight against us. He asked me if he could give my number to them.

"Can I give your phone number to them? They want to speak to you in person" Michael asked.

"Of course. That's good. Give them my number, they are our nephews," I said.

That afternoon, Alex Andale rang me. He sounded urgent but not emotional. He spoke in a calm clear voice, one which emanated peace.

Before Alex continued, I told him straight that my people would pay immediate compensation. He was happy to hear that we also wanted peace. In fact, on Monday night, the night I did not sleep, he and his three brothers had told their own people back at Yanagin village not to fight.

I relayed the message to my people. I asked them to disband the arms build-up at my village. Cr Bus Pyaso collected cash from my people, bought some drinks, buai, cigarettes and sent them off.

Alex Andale is a community school teacher, the first educated person in the Kunias family. He is a level-headed young man who shares the same views as me that fighting is bad. The long-standing relationship between our two tribes had to remain intact. We agreed that fighting achieves nothing – only more unnecessary deaths. Credit goes to him for playing a key role in the peace negotiations.

The situation calmed down. My people who were in defensive positions at Kombolos withdrew to their homes to begin collecting pigs and cash to pay the compensation.

When Alex, Enos and the other two people went to Port Moresby, they went to live among Michael Toke and their other cousins and relatives from my tribe. We are blood. That made the peace process much easier.

Whatever ulterior motives the Imma Kanda may have had, backfired on them. When the second suspect from their tribe was later arrested, they could not bail him out. And when they failed to stop the technicians from installing the Digicel tower, I believe they vented their frustrations on my property.

God Almighty had heard my prayers. He had seen me struggle for genuine peace that sleepless night in the nation's capital.

The peace proposal offered early morning on Tuesday 21 March, 2023 by Cr Yapi Pasul, Cr Bus Pyaso and other leaders had to be endorsed by all the relatives of the deceased and accepted by the Kambrip Yanagin people before burial – as is the custom.

But attempts were made to derail the peace process. It seemed as if somebody really wanted a tribal war in the small township of Kandep.

Attempts to Derail Peace Process

My prayers answered, a peace process had commenced immediately after the young student had been killed. Alex Andale and the other three young men in Port Moresby told their relatives at Yanagin not to fight.

I realised it next day when Alex Andale told me how he had asked his people to stop considering taking revenge. The same idea had formed in the minds of my two councillors and village leaders to offer peace. This good news spread fast that both sides had opted for peace.

This decision was unique and unprecedented in Enga province. When blood was spilled or when somebody's property was totally destroyed, tribal war erupted abruptly in almost every case. Rarely will anybody take bodies of relatives killed in tribal wars to the hospital morgue.

In this instance, the body of the young man killed was brought, under PNG Defence Force army escort, to Wabag General Hospital for a post mortem.

Then attempts were made to arrest my two councillors. When police went to Kondo village to arrest him, Cr Bus Pyaso told them to go back to Kandep government station and see the unprovoked destruction done to the property. That was the reason that the young man was killed in a public fight.

Cr Bus Pyaso was the nephew of the late Inspector Peter Pyaso who had instructed him well to always keep the peace in our village. Our people had never involved themselves in any major conflict until now. His people were preparing to pay compensation when the police went to arrest him. The arresting officer left.

Cr Yapi Pasul was unfortunate. He was arrested in Mendi town by another group of policemen. He punched one of the policemen who attempted to force him into the Mendi police cells and take his mobile phone.

Somebody had falsely reported that Cr Yapi was driving a stolen vehicle hired to him by the Kandep District Development Authority. He was acting President of Kandep Local Level Government Council at the time.

Cr Yapi told the police to contact the owner in Mt Hagen and confirm that the registration papers in the vehicle were genuine. Instead of making a phone call, they told him to bail himself out. Which he did immediately with contributions from relatives in Mendi town.

He was forced to stay in a lodge in the town before he collected his vehicle the next day. They found nothing wrong with the vehicle and the papers were in order. He drove the vehicle away, but without his bail refund. Those who arrested him were nowhere to be seen.

On Friday 24 March 2024, Alex Andale flew to Wapenamanda to take his brother's body home from the Wabag hospital morgue. It had been taken there by the army.

On Saturday 25 March 2023, before they buried the body, Alex Andale and his Kambrip Yanagin people openly announced their intention not to fight, indicating they had accepted our peace proposal.

I felt grateful that Alex Andale and his brothers had kept their word. We also had to keep our promise and pay the compensation.

We didn't have to wait for the Imma tribe who had already paid their prepayment or bel kol of K1,000 cash and a pig. By custom, they had to pay full compensation first. But my tribe wanted to reverse traditional practices. Restoration of immediate peace was the priority.

Then at about 3am, in the early morning of Monday 10 July, one of the dry trees on my property was cut down. The invading Imma tribesman had left it standing because it was too big to cut down during the mayhem of that Black Monday.

By 7am, everything – branches and twigs had been carried away. Only the huge trunk was left. A list of suspects was provided to me – some of whom had blood ties with the Imma Kanda major clan.

I didn't want to pursue the matter.

Exactly two weeks later on Monday 24 July, Kenneth Andrew's lodge was burned to the ground by a group of tribal warriors from the Pakait tribe of Titip village in the Wage Census division. Two factions from the

Pakait tribe had fought over a piece of land. The other faction opposed it claiming the land did not belong to them. They fought, resulting in about 21 deaths.

Sixteen of those deaths were as a result of drowning. Early that morning they had crossed the Lai River on canoes. After they burned Kenneth Andrew's Guest House, without opposition from anybody at Nagulam village, they stayed on the airstrip for a while. Then some of their enemy who had escaped from the fighting at Titip to nearby Kokas village engaged them.

Some from the invading party were killed there on the government station. The rest were chased for about three kilometres into the Lai River. It appeared they didn't know how to swim. They went down as they were with their shoes, clothes and weapons. Divers from my Aimbarep tribe assisted in recovering the bodies and weapons.

Yet, Kenneth Andrew's people accused my tribe of organising and collaborating with their enemy side to burn the Guest House. But how could we? He and his people failed to reason that if we had wanted to, we could have burned it when my property was destroyed. We had the manpower. We wouldn't have required anybody, let alone people from Wage to cross the Lai River in canoes to help us. Instead of revenge, both the Kambrip Yanagin people and my tribe had opted for peace.

Kenneth Andrew is my son-in-law. His second wife, Priscilla is my niece, my brother Nathan's daughter. I had given him four large trees to mill timber, free of charge to build his Guest House. I gave him the trees because Priscilla has two sons, my bubus. How could I betray the little ones and organise their enemy to come and destroy property intended for my two bubus to inherit one day?

Priscilla's elder sister sent me a text saying she had rung me many times the day before to find out from me if it was true that Jacinta Roa, Cr Yapi Pasul and myself were involved in burning the Guest House.

"I rang you yesterday to ask you a very important question to truly hear from your mouth when I heard it straight from the Wage people calling your name, Jacinta and Cr Yapi Pasul in regard to the burning down of Priscilla's Guest House.

"I don't want to listen to gossip. I wish to hear it straight from you whether it's true that you, Daniel Kumbon was involved. You are our dad. How can you be involved?" she asked.

My niece, Alice was right. I am their daddy, Priscilla's dad. How could I be involved in burning down the guest house? It was a very disturbing accusation indeed. But we ignored it. The same intention to derail the peace process was evident here.

The fact remains that the Kambrip Yanagin student would not have died or my property destroyed had the Imma leaders taken responsibility for the arson of Roa's family truck from day one. After all, we are family.

As I've said, Kenneth Andrew and Cleopas Roa are my in-laws and Roa is Andrew's brother-in-law. Our families live next to each other at Premier Hill, Wabag town. I appealed to Andrew many times to resolve the arson case by either handing the culprits over to police or get his people to pay compensation to Roa.

Instead, he said he would take the matter to Governor Sir Peter Ipatas, Provincial Administrator, Dr Samson Amean and former Kandep MP Alfred Manase and ask them to do something about it.

I told him that his approach was wrong because the three leaders did not direct those culprits to burn Mr Roa's truck. It was burned on Saturday 9 July 2022 before ballot boxes were moved to Wabag for counting.

During counting, car loads of Alfred Manase supporters from the Imma tribe kept coming to Kennth Andrew's house at Premier Hill. On Tuesday 12 July some of the suspects in the arson case were seen going there too. No attempt was made to arrest them, hoping Mr Roa would be compensated.

After Don Polye was declared winner and after five months of arguing, Roa's family started making arrests. On 2 December 2022, Paul Kunias, a suspect in the arson case was caught in Wabag town. He was one of Kambrip Kunias Pok's sons. His mother is from my own village of Kondo.

I got phone calls and text messages from Paul Kunias to withdraw the charges and release him from police custody. He claimed he was innocent. I told him I had nothing to do with his arrest. The car was not mine.

Nor was I in Kandep when the incident occurred. I simply didn't know anything.

The Imma Kanda tribesman had fired warning shots over my property after he had been arrested. The gun was the one owned by Andy, the young man from Gin village who later defected to Kondo, his great grandmother's village.

In the new year, police arrested the second suspect Piso Nawe from the Imma Kanda major clan. He went to join Paul Kunias in the cells.

On Tuesday 16 January, Paul rang me again from the cells and said Piso burned Mr Roa's vehicle and he felt like murdering him. He then asked me to tell Jacinta to withdraw the charges against him. I told him to speak to Jacinta himself. I advised him, however, that he could turn state witness by testifying that Piso Nawe was the culprit, if what he said was the truth.

By now he had the phone numbers of Jacinta, her sister Susan and my son Jr. He kept ringing everybody, asking them to remove the charge. Even when he was taken to Baisu to await his court appearance, he kept ringing us. But who gave him our phone numbers remains a mystery. Were detainees allowed to keep their phones, have access to units or call people while awaiting trial?

Tension was building up on Tuesday 4 July 2023 in Wabag town. Paul Kunias and Piso Nawe were scheduled to appear in court the next day. They had been transported up from Baisu and held at the Wabag police cells.

The duo had spent nearly eight months in custody. Their relatives had come all the way from Kandep to see the outcome of the case. Among them was Paul's mother. Jacinta said she bought her refreshments because, like her, Paul's mum was from Kondo village. She was her auntie.

Minutes before they were to be taken to the court house, Paul Kunias rang me yet again. I was with Jacinta Roa and a Kambrip man named Jim from Yanagin village, one of Paul Kunias' own tribesman. He had come that morning from home with the rest of his people. Because he is related to us, Jim had come to be with us that day.

Paul Kunias requested that we withdraw the case. We told him yet again to turn state witness. That was the only way he could be released or given a lighter sentence. He forgot that Jacinta's family had lost a truck for no reason. They were eager to know why it was burned while parked in front of the official District Administrator's residence.

But when the duo defended themselves, Paul Kunias told the magistrate a different story. He claimed he was nowhere near the premises where the vehicle was burned.

While the court was still in session, the duo had somehow managed to cut loose the plastic handcuff binding their wrists together. They sprinted through the open door towards the high steel fence surrounding the court house. Piso was caught struggling to jump over the fence.

Paul, who jumped over the fence towards the post office, had to jump over another high fence. He managed to reach the main bus stop. But he was caught by a passing army vehicle before he hopped on a bus to freedom.

The next day the court sentenced them both to two years imprisonment for unlawfully escaping from the court house. It was hard to say whether somebody had advised them to escape or whether it was their own idea. It remains a mystery. But if Paul Kunias had a phone in the cells, then Lord knows who else he was contacting to seek advice, receive instructions or facilitate their escape.

On that Black Monday, when the Imma tribesman couldn't bail their man, Piso Nawe from police custody, they had descended on my property and started destroying it. That's when my relatives from Kondo village went to investigate and the student was killed in a brief fight.

I thank God for creating both day and night. The fight could have continued on if it wasn't for the night – that particular night which gave us enough time to think, pray and consult relatives by phone to find ways to stop the fight.

As the two served their two-year terms, the Roa family were advised to stop making more arrests. My tribe prepared to pay the compensation.

On Friday 31 March 2023, I published a major feature article in both dailies – the Post Courier and The National, detailing the wanton destruction of my property, the subsequent peace agreement and how my people were gathering pigs to pay the compensation.

And why the Kambrip Yanagin and my people had chosen peace over tribal war. The news reached the attention of some very important people. They were prepared to help us. Peace is what Enga desperately needed to free the masses from bondage of never-ending tribal war.

Important People Contribute Towards Compensation Payment

On Thursday, 13 April 2023, I went to see Provincial Administrator, Sanso Tsaka. He was very busy and I had to wait until 2pm when I was finally called to see him in his office. There sitting with him was Kenneth Andrew. He was surprised to see me.

Mr Andrew protested that he wasn't prepared to talk with me to discuss a sensitive issue. He said he wasn't the right person because, he was from the Wage Census division in Kandep. But the PA said this was the right moment and asked him to start our discussion with a prayer. When we ended our discussion, I prayed to God to bless our meeting and to ask that peace would be the result.

I left the office with three important pieces of information: that the Provincial Administrator, from his own pockets, would help both of us with 'coke[3]' when we were ready to pay compensation. But Kenneth Andrew said he was from the Wage Census division and not an Imma tribesman. He named other people who would be responsible for paying compensation for the deceased.

But I had been arguing with him to initiate a peace settlement from the start when Mr Roa's truck had been burned because he is a second generation Imma tribesman. His father was from Titip in the Wage area but had come to live among his uncles at Lungutenges village.

Mr Andrew built his lodge on land given to him by the main suspect in the police cells, Piso Nawe from Nagulam village. My brother and I had assisted him with four big trees to mill to build his lodge.

Kenneth Andrew figures prominently among the Imma people. He had been seen with Alfred Manase and other candidates and supporters on the day the truck was burned. Most of the suspects leading the

---

3 - Coca Cola

rampage were Imma Kanda clansman from Nangulam village. He knew them. They were his people. His lodge was built on their land.

He had organised the prepayment compensation or bel kol before the burial of the Kambrip Yanagin student who had been killed. Many people expected him to organise the main payment. I had mentioned him in my news feature too. But here in the Provincial Administrator's office, he said he was from Wage.

The first person to respond to my newspaper article was Grand Chief Sir Paul Kurai. He rang me from Australia and said he would come home and help me.

True to his word, he sent a text message on Friday 21 April asking me to see him at Ribito Hotel next day. As we talked over breakfast, Sir Paul looked at me strongly to perhaps detect any guilt on my face. I had to tell the truth from when Mr Roa's vehicle was burned to when my property was destroyed, resulting in the death.

Next day, I went with Cr Yapi Pasul to Chief Sir Paul's wife's village at Wakumale in Wabag. We saw some very large pigs lined up along the fence. I thought that maybe he wanted me to select one of them.

But no, he gave us all of them – five large pigs and K4,000 cash. This, he said, was his contribution towards the compensation payment. He was happy my tribe had set the precedent to choose peace instead of payback.

He said he would also be fair with Kenneth Andrew and his Imma people and give them something when they were ready to pay their compensation.

"I am happy to hear that the relatives of the deceased have agreed to receive compensation instead of resorting to violence," Chief Sir Paul Kurai said. "That's why I'm giving you these pigs. God created us special and for a reason. People must forgive each other, respect our laws, respect other people's lives, their properties and their own lives.

"We must all try to maintain peace in our communities at all times and help develop our beautiful country. Our province needs peace to prosper," he said.

Grand Chief Sir Paul Kurai is an iconic figure, recognised for his tireless efforts to stop tribal warfare. He was also a major benefactor of the Catholic Church in Enga province.

He has been recognised by Pope Francis, King Charles III and the State for his efforts to bring peace to the province. A veteran councillor from Kaiap village in Wabag district, he was a popular leader and businessman, who shared his immense wealth generously with the needy.

I immediately loaded the pigs in my other daughter Laura's family truck and took them home to publicise the fact that an important person had assisted my tribe to pay compensation.

The next important person to help us was Provincial Administrator, Sanso Tsaka. He came to Kandep on Saturday 24 June with a large pig, K2,000 cash and 20 cartoons of coke. He presented them to me in front of a large crowd at Imali village. We had prepared ourselves well to receive him.

He said he would also help Kenneth Andrew and his Imma people to take responsibility and pay compensation for the deceased.

He was happy to see me take the lead in handling the potentially dangerous situation in a peaceful manner. He encouraged every educated elite in the province to intervene at the first instance before problems escalated.

Some people who had accompanied the Administrator also contributed to the cause. Porgera Law and Order officer Joseph Nana, Director Provincial Works, Charles Bannah, Laiagam Police Station In-Charge Sergeant Sam Begofa and Mobile Squad Commander, Steven Wally also searched their pockets and contributed K2,000 cash on the spot.

Later, our local priest Fr Sapius Peter Pii helped us with a large pig. He presented it to Jacinta Roa at Kimbalam village. It looked exactly like the pig given by Provincial Administrator, Sanso Tsaka at Imali village.

Frank Tokai, one of Kandep's top businessman sent K2,000 from Port Moresby. Mr Tokai's contribution added to more cash and 13 pigs we received from his people at Mugaip village right on the edge of Kandep town. And that's where my wife, Julie had escaped to when the thugs came and started destroying our property, followed there by Monica my sister and her children.

The other significant contribution was a cow from Hon Don Polye, our local member of parliament. He is a Kambrip tribesman from Gin village. The student killed was one of his own people whose family had supported Alfred Manase.

A member of parliament, two businessmen, a priest, the provincial administrator, policemen and senior public servants helped me to publicly denounce tribal war and promote peace, not only in Kandep but every part of Enga province.

I thanked them for their contributions to give to a good people – the Kambrip Yanagin tribesmen. Peace was possible only because they had accepted our peace offer. If they hadn't, there could have been tribal war resulting in more deaths.

The Yanagin people had come to Imali village that day to witness the presentation from the Provincial Administrator and public servants. I thanked them for choosing peace. Then gave them K500 and some cartoons of coke for refreshments before they returned home.

Chief Sir Paul Kurai, Provincial Administrator Sanso Tasaka, Frank Tokai and Fr Sapius Pii set into motion the compensation payment process. My Aimbarep tribesman started receiving food and cash from the Kambrip people. As was tradition, the recipients would give something equal to or more on the day we paid the actual compensation.

We received contributions from as far as Goroka in the Eastern Highlands, Mt Hagen, Wapenamanda, Laiagam, Wabag and many locations in Kandep – Lakis, Mugaip, Wasa, Imali, Tumbil, Kombolos, Pindak, Kimbalam, Lagalap, Winja and several other locations.

When we saw that we had enough, we sent word to the Kambrip Yanagin to bring us a pig called a tokait in the Enga language as was customary. They brought two pigs.

We told them that Saturday August 19 2023 would be the day the actual compensation would be paid. After that we would steam-cook our two tokait pigs in a mumu pit for a feast to conclude everything.

The Compensation Payment

On Tuesday 15 August, I went home with a substantial amount of cash to pay the compensation. I noticed that a man who had brought me a whole roasted pig had come to my brother's house to over-night.

I gave him a K50 note to make him feel welcome and to ensure that he wouldn't go home empty-handed when the actual compensation was paid.

Paying compensation is not a simple matter. It takes time to plan, budget – and skill to ensure the intricacies of payment were in order. The pigs to be given away would have to be healthy and sizable and in good number – two or more lots of twenty-four pigs or Yaki Mendai to compensate a death. The recipients would have to go home satisfied. That way, a conflict would never re-surface, but buried forever.

Soon after arriving home, I asked that all the pigs belonging to me and Jacinta Roa's family be taken to where my private forest was. They would be lined up, from the largest to the smallest. My three brothers and all our sons and daughters would also bring their contributions and fit into position on the line of pigs.

Our own family contributions included pigs given to me by Chief Sir Paul Kurai, Provincial Administrator, Sanso Tsaka, local priest, Fr. Peter Pii and the pigs we'd collected at Pindak, Mungaip and Lakis – my wives' villages. I was satisfied with our line-up of pigs.

I then went from house to house of all the family units that made up my Nauk hausman or sub clan. I wanted to know who had contributed which pig – and which married girl, nephew or cousin had come to contribute. That way I would know who to help when they were in trouble. I saw that at least everybody who was able, had contributed a pig.

Then we sent word to our three other sub-clans and major clans – Pipial, Marus, Tambol and Tumbil to present their contributions at the village square on Thursday 17 August, 2023.

Cr Yapi Pasul had contributed a cow and a pig. Cr Bus Pyaso had contributed a very large pig and some smaller ones. They had to, because they were the focus – the two leaders whom police had attempted to arrest. Many of our tribesman had contributed and presented them to me with a short speech.

If we had seen that the number of pigs was short or lacked large ones in the line-up, we could have postponed the payment to a later date and buy some more. But we didn't lack pigs. I was happy, but not really sure if I would ever be able to help those who contributed all these pigs in the future.

The Kambrip Yanagin tribesman and the relatives were there to witness all the transactions taking place. I selected the large pig Cr Bus Pyaso had contributed, some cash and bags of sweet potatoes and presented them to the Kambrip Yanagin for their dinner.

Next day we lined up all the pigs contributed towards the payment away from the main square. We took aside some pigs that we would use to pay those who had been injured. Then, when we saw that everything was in order, we invited a select group of the Kunias brothers to come view it.

We told them our distribution plan, to give a sizeable pig each to certain 'haus man' of the Kambrip major clans and to certain individuals. They accepted our plan but made just one change we had to follow. Then they left. They had accepted the payment. We were ready to make the payment next day- Saturday 19 August 2023.

But all the Kunias brothers were not present to receive the payment. While waiting, people gave speeches including Sgt Jim Panao the OIC police in Kandep, village court magistrates, councillors and village leaders – the type of rhetoric people often hear at such public gatherings.

I liked to hear people who applauded my tribe for reversing the established traditional system by paying the compensation first – something the Imma Kanda should have done. During compensation payments – the two opposing sides are referred to as Sagalis – the Imma Kanda side and Yourwaip – my side. We were paying more than the Sangalis side would normally be expected to pay.

This display of wealth, contributions from even important people in the province meant that we the Kambrip and Ambarep Pumbuti tribe were genuine in our efforts to retain peace among our people.

On that day, I made an important announcement. I said that I had a separate list of suspects including some leaders in relation to the destruction of my property. Some names on the list was the same as those who had burned Mr Roa's vehicle. I had lodged the complaint with police to make immediate arrests.

But my tribal leaders did not want me to pursue the case through the courts. They wanted us to pay compensation for the deceased and that's what we were doing now.

I said there was too much killing everywhere in the province. Police were understaffed, under resourced and poorly equipped. They were ineffective – unlike during colonial times. Arresting suspects would cause more problems and be a costly exercise on the part of the complainant. The government was weak. It did not fund the police force. Arresting suspects was not the answer.

I said the Imma must take ownership, pay compensation for the student killed and compensate Mr Cleopas Roa and me for completely destroying our properties. Compensation ended every conflict in Enga province. Nothing else.

"The complaint I lodged at the police station can be torn up and burned. But the paper on which the complaint was typed on will never rot," I said.

I told the crowd that Paul Kunias and Piso Nawe did not go to jail because of the charges against them in the arson case but because they had escaped from the court house. Nobody, not even Jacinta Roa had testified against them. People heard these sober words in silence. Nobody made any comments.

We kept talking about other relevant issues that affected Kandep on the occasion. Finally, we all realised that it was getting late. The Kunias Brothers had still not made an appearance to receive the payment.

So, I gave the Kambrip Yanagin K800 to buy food and sleep for a second night in my village. We all knew that the brothers were not against us but that grudges among themselves had caused the delay.

The next day was Sunday. But everybody waited for the brothers yet again. The poor pigs were restless. They were underfed and very thirsty. They had slept outside in the cold, tied to the stakes for four consecutive days and nights. The women and boys who tended them were equally tired. There was no more food to feed them.

Today, Sunday was a sacred day. I felt guilt. It was God Almighty who had made this peace process possible. All of us should have been inside a church praising Him.

'I regret that we have to pay the compensation today – Sunday. The two main men, Jonaip and Lak are not here. They are delaying everything,' I wrote in my diary. 'But in the end, I see that they are honest men."

They were honest indeed when they finally came to accept the payment. But clearly, their political differences had caused all the confusion and delays. When the select group came to view the line of pigs, Lak and

Stanley were not included. Among the Kunias brothers, supporters of Don Polye and Alfred Manase were suspicious of each other.

Prior to the payment, when we were collecting pigs, they had sent me text messages to do this or that in their favour. But I had ignored all their requests. I had treated them all equally and fairly. They all had to go home happy from my tee kam or compensation ground.

If I took sides, I knew what the consequences would be. As a journalist, I had reported on enough killings over who should get which pig. These nasty confrontations often led to more tribal conflicts.

But unbeknown to the Kunias brothers, I only hid, one large pig for Paul Kunias, their brother who was in prison. I believed he would reveal why or who initiated the move to destroy Roa's vehicle. Paul's mother was from my village, Kondo. She grew up here. If she was born a male, she could have been standing there amongst us – her brothers.

She had come to Kondo village days earlier to lobby for a pig for her son. But how could we, her brothers forget Paul? He didn't go to jail because of the arson case but because he had escaped from the court house.

When the Kunias brothers finally agreed to receive the payment, Stanley and Lak were now in the select group. We went to a secluded location and I revealed what I had done with all the pigs that came in for the payment. I revealed in front of all of them, how much cash I had given each of them in secret. It was the same amount. They were all satisfied.

I observed that the Kunias brothers had inherited the good qualities of their father. It was only political differences that separated them. It did not rain when we finally made the payment in the village square for all to see. The government officials, police and village court officials were witnesses.

Before they distributed them, we brought out, in a neat line, the pigs set aside for distribution to certain Kambrip clans or Akalyanda. After we had given them away, the brothers distributed the main line of pigs. I noticed that the mother of the student killed was given one of the biggest pigs that Chief Sir Paul Kurai had contributed. I added some cash on top. The mother ran towards me, shook my hands and received the cash.

After that my people paid back the Saintes' or credits, they'd received from the Kambrip people. I distributed more cash to councillors, village court magistrates, local leaders and people I knew. While everybody was busy, I separately led individuals recommended by Jonaip, Alex and Lak to where we had hidden a large pig for each of them. We showed them secret paths to take them away. This practice was customary. One or two immediate relatives had to be satisfied. They had to get something extra in secret.

I knew I would be busy. So, the day before I had asked the man who had brought me the cooked pork to come to one of my brother's houses. There I had left a pig for him. I also gave him K250. He carefully put the money in a wallet he carried in his string bag. Took the rope tied to one of the forelegs and led the pig away. He was happy. I had repaid his 'Sainte' – the cooked pork well.

I was sure everybody else who had given 'Saintes' had been repaid in full. I did not hear any complaints. But a little later, I heard noise and gunfire from the people who had been injured. But they saw the compensation was paid into the dark night. Did they expect me to continue in the night? Had they ever seen their fathers or anybody distribute cash or pigs in the night? Common sense was not present in the minds of these people.

I left word with Cr Bus Pyaso that I would return and pay them later. And the people who had been entrusted to look after the pigs intended for that purpose would continue looking after them. I would pay them something. For now, I was tired and left for Wabag in the night. I desperately needed a hot shower, a decent meal and a good rest.

The main compensation had been paid well. The Kambrip Yanagin clan had gone home without any fuss. And in fine weather. No single drop of rain had disturbed the proceedings. We had retained our traditional friendship.

When I returned later to pay the injured, I was again glad the night had separated me from the mob who were firing guns demanding to be paid in the night.

Four of the pigs intended to pay them were either stolen, went wild or died. Our luck held. We were able to replace those lost with pigs we received from two compensations paid simultaneously to my Naku subclan. The payments were not large, but a type called 'Laita' given to the mother's people after a person died.

In our case, a cousin John Anjo Poro and nephew Robin Mup Mapita had died under different circumstances. We were paid enough pigs to pay those injured.

Only one person had received serious injuries. His leg had been broken, a cast was made and he was hospitalised at Mendi General Hospital. In olden times, if people from the same clan received injuries, they were never compensated unless they died from the injury much later.

Everybody took ownership of the fight in the past. But nowadays, young people wanted something for an injury they sustained. This person whose leg was broken is from my village. I gave him four large pigs. The other injuries were minor. We still paid them something accordingly.

But we had to treat gun owners differently. We gave a large pig and some cash to the two Kambrips from Gin and Yanagin – the two who had sided with my people in the initial stages of the conflict and a third man, a Kambrip Kakale who had also taken his gun to my village and joined my people.

We would have paid them much more if we had used them in actual warfare. Nowadays, gunmen are given cash on the spot if they make a kill. That was the trend of tribal warfare, a very destructive, time-consuming, expensive, deadly exercise. The gunman chose at will young girls and married women from the tribe involved in the war.

The records of how much cash and pigs we gave away were kept by the village court officials who were present throughout the proceedings.

I do not wish to reveal how many pigs or how much cash we used to make the two lots of compensation payments. That would be to boast.

I do not equate pigs and cash with human life. A person's life is something more precious than gold or silver, let alone squealing, grunting pigs.

I am content, my tribe did right to pay compensation first to prevent more deaths. I can rebuild my property. But lives cannot be brought back.

If my own life was that important for my father to offer a pig sacrifice, as we shall find out later – how could I allow a fight that would result in death on both sides? I didn't want all that blood to be on my hands.

A few days later, a baby boy was born to my son, Jr. I named my grandson Freeman Kumbon. He and his brothers and sisters and their sons and daughters of the Kondo Taunde clan and Aimbarep tribe should always try and live free lives.

I know, that was the right choice we made to pay compensation first. The fine details of why Mr Cleopas Roa's vehicle was burned, who organised it and why my property was destroyed will gradually surface one day.

A Death Unites Us: Reconciliation & Peace on The Horizon

The two lots of compensations had been paid. Peace had returned. The Imma tribe, Kambrip tribe and my Aimbarep Pumbuti tribe were beginning to exchange greetings freely. Even two of the suspects surrendered to me. They came to my house drunk.

They came on the afternoon of Sunday 8 October 2023. Their names were on the list of suspects regarding the destruction of my property. The duo from Nagulam village belong to the Imma Kanda major clan. They said I could do anything I wished with them. Then they fell asleep on a bed in the living room.

What do you do in a situation like that? Do you chase them away? Forgive them? Harm them or report them to police?

No, we couldn't do any of that. What my family did was to cook them a good meal, make beds for them to sleep on through the night and allowed them to go on their way next morning.

I shared on Facebook a photo of the two young men sitting with me and Jacinta Roa. It attracted many favourable comments. Later, I appeared on Facebook with Imma Kanda Councillor, Alumail Ambone. We were with former member for Kandep, Jimson Sauk and Chief Sir Paul Kurai.

Then I met prominent Imma lawyer, Justine Issack at the Ribito Hotel. We spoke of peace and unity. Again, I posted a photo of us on Facebook. I intended to show people that at least small steps were taken to re-establish contact with the Imma people. We had paid the compensation to retain peace.

Then on Saturday 9 December 2023 one of my nephews, David Yalao died at the Wabag general hospital from liver complications. He had been taking medication from my house. We held a funeral at my house before we took his body home.

Although Kenneth Andrews's house is very close and Priscilla, his wife was David's sister, she never came to visit him in hospital or to the funeral. She still did not come to the main funeral in the village. It was the same people who nursed him who took late David's body home for burial.

They were Roslyn's husband, a pastor from nearby Pawas village, Jacinta Roa's family, my family and our neighbours who contributed enough money to buy the coffin, hold a small funeral feast at my house before we took the body home for burial at Kondo village.

However, Priscilla's mindset changed when her blood-brother, Jeffery Nathan died in Port Moresby on Wednesday night 5 June 2024. We all came together during the funeral at home. We all buried him properly in our village.

We had to unite. Life is meant for living, sharing in each other's sorrow, reconciling and moving forward. The death of Jeffery Nathan was a devastating blow.

He was the only top educated person from our Nauk sub-clan and from Kondo village. He had held an important senior position in the National Works Department Headquarters in Port Moresby.

Kenneth Andrew's Imma people came to the funeral in a big way. They brought pigs, bags of food and firewood. Their attendance at the funeral was normal. It's true, not every member of the Imma tribe had been involved in burning Mr Roa's truck or destroying my property.

For the funeral, I was assisted yet again by my long-time friend Grand Chief Sir Paul Kurai with 54 cartons of coke and bottled water. National Works Wabag branch gave us a large pig and 30 cartons of coke.

I gave 25 of those cartons to late Jeffery Nathan's two sons and their mother to take to Nipa district in Southern Highlands to hold a small funeral feast there, in their mum's village before they went back to school. The main funeral was held that Christmas.

Priscilla Andrew was present during the presentation. I said the death of Jeffery had united us and thanked her Imma people for coming in a big way. I told her that Jacinta Roa, Cr Yapi Pasul, the Ambarep Pumbuti tribe including me, her dad was not involved in burning down her Guest House. Her husband's people were wrong to accuse us.

This sort of dialogue, when the opportunity presents itself is how peace is restored, maintained, truth revealed, sorrow shared and assist one another. This was the path towards peace and reconciliation between the Imma people, Mr Roa's family and my people.

But my personal feeling regarding the sudden death of Jeffery Nathan in the prime of his life was the same type of loss I felt when my property was destroyed suddenly, without warning. Jeffery was a healthy young man. He was not sick but was found dead in his office.

We Lost Jeffery Nathan Like I Lost My Property

I maintain that human life cannot be compared with pigs, cash or other material possessions. I vowed to rebuild my property. But I still felt the loss, especially the 2000 or so different species of trees, shrubs and flowers, most of which I myself had planted over a fourteen-year period. That's how long it will take for new trees and plants to grow again on the property. It takes time and effort – just as an infant develops to adulthood.

I watered my trees and flowers, cleared the weeds around them and checked them every week, admiring every new leaf, limb and branch until the trees grew big. I watched the flowers blossom, giving off a sweet fragrance, attracting butterflies, birds and bees – and adding a variety of colours to the greenery. Even the logs I had milled to build my two permanent houses and the posts around the property were harvested from my private forest in the village. I had planted them when I was a student and when I began working with Enga Provincial Government in the mid-80s.

All children are looked after in like manner: cared for every step of the way, educating them, grooming them to adulthood until they marry and raise children of their own.

Jeffery's death broke our hearts so suddenly when he was found dead in his office in the morning. The night before, everybody else had been glued to their TV sets watching the State of Origin rugby league match, cheering on their favourite team – Blues or Maroons.

Jeffery grew up in Mt Hagen in a settlement at Newtown among Jika tribesmen. His dad, Nathan worked for a company named Namasu. My other cousin brother, Samuel Opop worked there too. I also worked in Mt Hagen with Radio Western Highlands as a broadcast officer. I often visited them at Newtown in the afternoons or weekends. I saw Jeffery grow up and go to school every day with his sisters – Alice and Priscilla. They grew up in a happy family.

After two years, I resigned from the National Broadcasting Commission and joined the Enga Provincial Government as press officer. Danley Tindiwi from Wage in Kandep had just been elected Premier of Enga province.

The next time I saw Jeffery Nathan was at my house in Wabag. His mother, Besi came with him to tell me he had been selected to study mechanical engineering at the University of Technology.

He needed money. But I couldn't help. I had children going to school too. But, more so, I was upset with Samuel and Nathan for allowing Besi to bring him to me. Weren't they working too? Besides, they didn't come to our village to help pay three compensations our Naku sub-clan was required to pay – deaths which occurred during one of two tribal wars our tribe had been involved in.

I was so upset with Nathan and Samuel to think of giving even a small amount to Jeffery. I regretted it much later when Besi and Nathan had separated for good. Nathan had married a new wife from Laiagam. And Besi, being one of my maternal cousins, had come independently hoping I would take pity. Understandably so, Jeffery never made contact with me again until he was married and had children. He rang me and explained his intention to come home and build a permanent house in our village. But asked me to talk with one of his brothers who wanted some money from him before he built his house.

I relayed the message home and the particular person came to Wabag. Jeffery sent him K300 to build a shelter. But it seemed that the person wanted more money from Jeffery. At the time, Jeffery had already built a permanent house in his wife's village at Nipa. And now he wanted to come and build one in his own village. One time, he showed me a property, a big house he was developing at Hohola in Port Moresby.

Jeffery had followed our footsteps to university and completed that which we, his fathers, never did. Samuel Opop had studied Surveying and I Communications Engineering in 1976. Samuel dropped out in his second year. Then found employment with Namasu Ltd in Mt Hagen.

I spent three years at Unitech, did not finish, became a broadcast officer and was posted to Radio Western Highlands. That's how I ended up working in Mt Hagen. Later, I attended the University of Papua New Guinea to study journalism while in the employ of the Enga Provincial Government. I became a journalist and author.

When Jeffery died, Samuel went to Port Moresby to bring his body home for burial. I paid airline tickets for my son and Mathew, a nephew, to go with him. I stayed back to prepare the funeral arrangements in the village.

When Jeffery's father, Nathan had died years earlier, Pastor Samuel Opop, Paki Pupukai and myself were left as father figures or elders in my Naku sub-clan. After we buried Jeffery and his tomb was not yet completed, Paki Pupukai died too. His death was a blow for me. We stood side by side to pay the recent compensation. Samuel Opop was of no help because pastors don't take part in such earthly, time consuming, wasteful activities. Such activities were slowing down the progress of Enga province in the modern era.

The future looks gloomy with the death of Jeffery Nathan. He should have been taking our place. But we lost him. He was full of promise. He was that sort of man who got things done, without much talk.

Unlike Samuel and me, he graduated with flying colours. We watched him advance, earning himself a Masters degree and then moving on to senior positions with major companies in the private sector before joining the national Department of Works and Highways.

When Jeffery's parents separated, he was looked after by a kind Christian family from Nyungu village in Laiagam, who treated him as one of their own children.

His sudden death left all of us in shock, a grief which is hard to describe. I admired my son Jeffery. He was the only person with a Master's degree in my Nauk hausman- sub clan – and the only person from my village to hold a senior position at national level.

My only hope now is in Jeffery's three children. I am glad that he prioritised education for them. Trevor, the eldest boy, came up from Australia to attend his dad's funeral joining his brother and sister at Kondo village.

I observed that he was an exact copy of his dad – quiet, observant and smart. I had high hopes that he would complete his studies and take his father's place.

While the late Jeffery's children went to school and with my brother Paki Pupukai's funeral complete, I began to cut down posts to rebuild my property.

We had heaped up some logs by the road waiting for a dump truck to transport them over when rumours began to spread that Paul Kunias and Piso Nawe had escaped from Baisu Prison in Mt Hagen.

Two Escape Baisu Prison, Roam Free

Somebody rang me from an unknown number on Tuesday 16 January 2024. When I did not answer, a text message, directed me to answer the phone when it rang again. It was Paul Kunias. By then, he and his mate had served nearly a year of their terms.

He told me once again to ask Jacinta Roa to withdraw the charge against him. Again, I repeated I had nothing to do with the case. He was in jail, not for the arson case, but for escaping from the Wabag court house. It would be impossible to ask the court to release him. Paul Kunias persisted.

I left it to Jacinta to explain it to him. It was her family car. She was visibly upset after the conversation with Paul. He had said that she should 'tie me with a strong rope' or else withdraw the charges. That was a bold statement to make from a prisoner already serving time in prison. He still had the arson charge hovering above his head. He did not seem to understand the law processes of this country. He would still stand trial after he completed his two-year prison sentence.

During this period, Enga was in total chaos. There was widespread tribal warfare in three districts resulting in too much chaos – death and destruction everywhere.

As long as your people are not involved, you think you are safe. But it's an illusion. You will be drawn involuntarily into a conflict whether you like it or not. Your life is not your own any more. You can't live a normal life in modern Enga. I have witnessed everything that was happening, working all my life as a journalist in my province. But this one post shared on social media, I will never forget. I never saw anything like it. It was so heartbreaking and disturbing.

On Saturday 24 February 2024, I saw this young boy beg for his life in a video posted on social media. It was so cruel, so brutal, so inhuman, so heartless. The boy realised he was cornered. He couldn't escape. He turned around and pleaded for his life, begging the attacker to spare his life. It was shocking to imagine a person take the life of an innocent child crying to you, looking at you, beg for his life with tears in his eyes.

This was the sort of situation that causes more hate, fear and anxiety in the province. This sort of situation must be avoided at all times and problems resolved from the start.

Two months later, I met Imma lawyer, Justine Issack at Ribito Hotel again. He was having breakfast with his family. His mother is from my tribe and we've been friends for a long time. We greeted as usual.

He said he was a neutral person in the conflict. I knew he was. In fact, his father, Cr Issack Luai had admitted Imma tribesman had burned Mr Cleopas Roa's truck. But he was shouted down by everybody else. That was a year ago at the top of the Kandep airstrip after Paul Kunias was arrested.

The Kambrip Yanagin people had summoned my tribe to discuss the release of Paul Kunias. They claimed he was wrongly arrested. But witnesses saw him with the mob when Mr Roa's vehicle was set on fire. He would have to defend himself in a court of law.

The Imma resolved that they would send Raymond, Cleopas Roa's son to go see his dad to release Paul Kunias. I interpreted that to mean they would compensate his truck in exchange for his release. I saw Raymond come to Wabag with one of his uncles. But nothing happened. Paul ended up going to Baisu prison.

Justine Issack and myself talked on, exchanged phone numbers and took a selfie, then published it on social media. Many people were happy to see us together, stating that this was how to promote peace by educated elites on both sides of any conflict in the province. With the traditional leadership structure breaking down, it was educated elites to whom people of Enga province looked up to.

There was only one negative comment by a person named George Kikil. Not sure if that was his real name but he swore insults. I didn't mind. The majority had spoken.

About this time, we started hearing rumours that Paul Kunias and Piso Nawe had escaped from prison. And they'd been spotted in Mt Hagen town.

Yes, Paul Kunias and his friend had indeed escaped. I was having breakfast with my bubu Rex Yapi Pasul at Ribito Hotel when an unknown number called. When I didn't answer, the person texted me. It was Paul Kunias.

That was on Sunday 14 July 2024. Paul spoke in a different tone of voice. He said he went to jail because we put him there. Now he was out and wanted to be free. He implied that he wanted something from us. But he forgot that I was the owner of a property that had been destroyed.

Another time, he rang from Kandep and said we – Jacinta Roa, my son Jr and myself had to go to Kandep when he called us there. He was putting his arrest and imprisonment in the forefront. I heard he was consistently under the influence of liquor and living with Piso Nawe at Nagulam village. He was demanding that my family pay him something. The Imma Kanda were entertaining him.

One Prison Escapee Attempts to Take an Imma Man's Life

It is Enga tradition that, after a compensation has been paid for a death, nobody from the same family makes demands like that. The two prison escapees seemed to be taking advantage of the fact that there was no police presence in Kandep.

District staff stayed away when the 2022 election win of Don Polye was challenged in court by runner-up Alfred Manase. Local village people were living in every vacant government house in the small township. People were dismantling the empty two-story Kandep district office and carried away doors, window louvers, furniture and even the veranda flooring. Only the roofing and brick wall remained.

Paul and Piso, the two prison escapees were free to roam Kandep and intimidate my people. Paul Kunias demanded my family pay him something. Each time my Kondo Taonde clansmen demanded from us to reveal if we had promised to pay a second compensation when he was in prison.

But how could I possibly do that when a vehicle and my property were destroyed. And when we had been the first people to pay compensation for the deceased when Imma Kanda should have been the ones to do so. I showed them the text messages Paul Kunias and I had exchanged when he was in prison.

However, we finally decided to set a date for the village court magistrates to hear Paul Kunias reveal why he was making his demands.

On the set date, before the village sitting convened, lightning flashed across a dark skyline followed by a thunderous roar. A fierce thunderstorm accompanied by strong winds followed. It lasted for some time. We took shelter at Pindak village and waited patiently for the storm to pass. When it was finally over, we walked over to Imali where the magistrates were waiting.

Paul Kunias was there with his mother, Jonaip his brother and some youths. Also with him was Jim Yariakali, the person with whom we had spoken when Paul Kunias was in the police holding cells in Wabag.

Almost all the other Kambrip Yanagin clansman who came to my village to receive the compensation payment were not with him. Paul told the village court magistrates things which did not make sense. And he repeated what he had told Jacinta from Baisu prison 'to tie me with a strong rope'. All along, he implied that he be given 'coke' because he was the wrong person.

I stopped the proceedings stating that the weather conditions did not permit proceedings to continue. The heavy rain, thunder and lightning was nature's way of intervention. The demand for 'coke' first when a vehicle and a property were completely destroyed was not right.

But some of my people said giving 'coke' was no problem. It was better to have peace in the community than 'coke' after we had already given a very large pig to Paul Kunias at the compensation. We dispersed, agreeing generally, to give him what he wanted. But he would first have to reveal who planned the destruction of Roa's family truck and why my property was destroyed.

A couple of weeks later, I heard from Wabag that Paul Kunias had nearly beheaded a man from Nagulam village after he had an argument with Piso Nawe, his fellow prison escapee after they had had some beers.

Paul Kunias had also burned down one or two houses in the night and escaped to Yanagin village. The Kandep Health centre vehicle took the injured person to Wabag general hospital.

The reason?

Paul Kunias allegedly said he had gone to prison when the person in hospital should have been the one. The Imma Kanda did not respond to the attempted murder or the accusation. Not even the person in hospital said anything, even after he went back to his village after he was discharged.

After this incident, Paul Kunias was reportedly involved in another drunken confrontation with an Imma tribesman at Pindak village. This time, the Imma Kanda retaliated by burning some property including a trade store operated by the Kunias family on the edge of Kandep township. It seemed there was no tribal leader among the Imma Kanda clan or the bigger Imma tribe. They said or did nothing to resolve the problem.

Meanwhile, in a Department of Enga Administration staff recruitment exercise, the Kandep District Law and Order officer, an Imma tribesman won back his position. Kenneth Andrew took over from Mr Cleopas Roa as Deputy Administrator, District Administration and Local Level Government. Cleopas Roa from Kimbe in West New Britain province had reached his public service retirement age. He had served the people of Enga all his life.

On top of that, the Imma Kanda Councillor, Cr Alumail Ambon was sworn in as acting President of Lai Local Level Government. The Kandep council executive officer, a Imma Kanda tribesman had won back his position. All these men are working with the Enga Provincial Government. So far, no attempt had ever been made to hand over the escapees or have they tried to resolve the issue concerning Mr Cleopas Roa's truck or my destroyed property.

The only time anybody from the Imma tribe who said anything was former councillor, Issack Luai from Kapaon village. The time he was shouted down when he admitted at the top of the Kandep airstrip that the Imma had burned Roa's truck. Up to now, it seems nobody will try to take ownership or explain why or who burned Mr Cleopas Roa's truck or destroyed my property.

Despite Issack Luai's admission, Mr Kenneth Andrew had said he would see Governor Grand Chief Sir Peter Ipatas, Provincial Administrator, late Dr Samson Amean and former member for Kandep Alfred Manase. But I had opposed his idea to take the matter to the top. Indecisiveness, inability to think and weigh the consequences, complete disregard for human life, an inability to take responsibility and ignorance of the laws of this country or inaction by police the instant a crime was committed seem to be some of the contributing factors as to why tribal rivalries still persist in Enga province.

I am glad my two councillors, and that my local leaders devised that brilliant peace plan and presented it to the Kambrip Yanagin people who accepted it from the start. Mostly people with inbred leadership qualities will always have the people at heart in difficult times. And most other people will think only of their own selfish interests.

My tribal leaders reasoned that pigs and cash – items used in compensation payments do not bring back a person's life. If it was pigs and cash that were used to end conflicts, then why not pay the damn compensation first before more lives were lost?

Cr Yapi Pasul is a nephew of late Nenk Pasul MBE, the first elected member for Kandep, and first Kandep Local Government Council President. He had also been appointed a Luluwai by Australian colonial Kiaps or patrol officers to help them in their efforts to bring change and development to the district. Now, Cr Yapi Pasul was acting President of the newly gazetted Mariant Local Level Government.

My other councillor, Cr Bus Pyaso, is the nephew of the late Inspector Peter Pyaso. One of my uncles, late Cr Saup Aiyop of the Nauk hausman was one of the first councillors working alongside Nenk Pasul during the colonial era.

And I, a senior public servant and a journalist who deeply understood the consequences of tribal war had to choose peace and harmony among our people.

I didn't want to forsake Jim Fenton, the first Kiap in Kandep or the first missionary to my area, Fr Jerry Theis SVD and other Kiaps and missionaries who came to Kandep with a message of hope and freedom.

I am still in contact with Jim Fenton and Fr Jerry Theis SVD, both aged 92. I didn't want to disappoint all those teachers who taught me from elementary to university. They did so well to groom and educate me to find employment, see places, meet new friends and enjoy and not destroy life.

Jim Fenton is the one who planted the first yar trees, some of which we still see today on the Kandep government station. I saw them grow up when I attended Kandep Primary 'T' School in the '60s until 1971.

I planted more yar trees to grow alongside those historic trees and developed an area that had remained vacant since Jim Fenton's departure. I can rebuild the property.

I had to collaborate with my two councillors and my local leaders to negotiate peace and harmony as early government officials and missionaries had intended.

It must be revealed that I have a special connection with the Imma and Alitip tribesmen, former landowners of the area in which Kandep township sits. I went to school there with some of the children from those two tribes. I spent some nights at Lunguteges and Paruli villages to avoid getting wet walking home on days when it rained in the afternoon.

The majority of the Imma people were innocent. Not everybody was involved in burning Mr Cleopas Roa's family truck or my property. I didn't want to see innocent people on both sides get killed or suffer unnecessarily.

If my own life was that important for my dad to kill a pig as a sacrifice to appease a dead relative when I fell ill, as we shall read later, why should other people die over property which can be redeveloped?

Peace was what Enga province needed. It was the foundation on which the people must firmly stand on to move forward.

Peace was what the Australian colonial government, influential local leaders and their people, early missionaries, policemen and public servants of that era had worked really hard to establish in the province.

The current generation of young people must respect and honour those people and learn to live in peace and harmony with each other. Especially from now on, after celebrating 50 years of nationhood.

2

COLONISATION: 'KIAPS' END TRIBAL WARFARE

"I would like to comment on our RPNG police detachments and their part in the march towards independence, which has never been acknowledged by the Australian and PNG governments. Perhaps in this 50th year of PNG independence it should be."

Jim Fenton 92
Brisbane
February 2025

Working For The 'Gavaman Kiap'

'Did he know me?' Jim Fenton asked me recently after seeing my dad standing beside mum in an old picture on my Facebook wall.

I took the picture in December 1975 during Christmas holidays after I had attended my country's independence celebrations in Port Moresby. I had also completed my Form Four national examinations.

"Of course, he did. He was afraid of you and your policemen," I replied.

My parents were both dead. But Jim Fenton, 92 still lives with his wife Rita 86, his second wife. His first wife, the mother of his children had died of cancer in 1983 at the young age of 51.

But when they lived in Kandep, I saw people crowd around the young mother and infant daughter, Tiana. She is now 63. They were the first expatriate mother and child; the local people had ever seen. My mother and I were part of the crowd of inquisitive onlookers. I think Tiana used to be pushed around in a pram. She looked like a doll when I saw her from the distance.

I used to accompany my mother to the new government station to barter sweet potatoes for salt. That was the first time I ever tasted processed salt. Before that, our source of sodium came along traditional trade routes, many miles away from the salt ponds at Yokond in neighbouring Laiagam district. I remember my father going there twice. Each time, he came back with several round parcels tied to poles on either end as men carry whole pandanus nut bunches.

Jim Fenton was the first Kiap or patrol officer to settle among my people in 1960. He had transferred there from Telefomin in what is now West Sepik Province. He patrolled the entire district making contact with all of the people and establishing rest houses.

"The base camp at the subsequent Kandep Patrol Post site was initially established by Kiaps from Wabag – Bob Bell and D. Permazel. I knew Bob Bell but never met Permazel. They located the airstrip site and subsequently commenced work on the construction of the airstrip and station buildings. They also conducted an initial census of the Lai/Mariant area but not the Wage," said Jim Fenton.

When he walked in from Laiagam and took over, Jim Fenton continued the completion of the airstrip and station buildings including the office, store, police and station workers accommodation and commencement of road works.

Tribal fighting had virtually ceased by this time – other than a few skirmishes which were investigated and settled. On the whole, under the leadership of headmen like Nenk and Liu, the people welcomed the advent of the administration and worked constructively throughout the area.

Jim Fenton undertook extensive patrolling to consolidate administration influence, to update the previous Lai/Mariant Census Division and carry out the initial census of the Wage Census Division.

Jim Fenton wondered if any of the village census books still exist having been handed down over time. I am sad to state that those priceless records no longer exist. My division, Media, Library and Archives had been the custodians of such old records but they had been destroyed by a contractor who had been asked to convert our offices at Keas to begin converting the facility into living quarters for health workers.

With the archives went our Ryobi printing presses, darkroom equipment, light tables and other equipment we had been using to publish the popular Enga Nius magazine. Luckily, computers and laptops began to appear on the market in the 80s. A British volunteer named Steward Hoggard encouraged me to learn to use it. The second Macintosh computer I used in the office is still in the living room of my house as a memory. Mobile phones, Facebook and the internet were introduced fairly recently.

Thanks to Steward Hoggard, I used desktop publishing software to continue producing Enga Nius after he was gone. But the archives were gone forever. The administration failed to allocate us adequate office space in the new state of the art Ipatas Centre provincial headquarters office building complete with a helipad on the roof.

Anyway, before Jim Fenton came to Kandep, I can remember the first census conducted from Wabag sub district in 1958. I walked some distance but most of the time I was riding on people's shoulders on narrow bush tracks.

My elder sister Clara remembers our people from Kondo going up to Kalimanga where the Kiaps or patrol officers were stationed and how I wanted to sit on people's shoulders to go there. Kalimanga was about 20 kilometres away.

"You were a bit demanding, you refused to walk to Kalimanga unless they carried you. Dad and other relatives did carry you to the census. However, you did walk some distances to give dad and other carriers some rest. You must have been around three or four years of age;" she said.

The first child my mum gave birth to had died soon after arrival. Then my sister, Clara came along followed by me. The child after me, a baby boy whose name I still remember – Nuamb had died in the string bag from suffocation. He was found dead on the way to the bush maternal hospital at Kandep Patrol post. He had developed an illness. I saw people holding him in the palm of their hands and cried. After that three more boys were added to our growing family – Paul, Michael and John.

Sometime after the census, I can remember walking to Kalimanga with my dad to get treatment at the aid-post for a large boil that appeared on my head. A man named Sik Manda, from Ipul village treated me.

"He is your tare or dad, don't be afraid," my father said as Sik Manda cut my hair before he cleaned and dressed it. He used an instrument that went 'snap, snap, snap' which did not cause pain unlike the bamboo knives that were used to cut my hair in the village. The instrument was scissors.

My father's great grandmother was from Ipul. That's why Sik Manda was my 'tare' a close relative. My paternal grandmother, whose name was Mokeamb was from the Yanjop subclan at Kalimanga village. Here, we stayed in one of my dad's cousin's house until my sore healed.

Kalimanga village was where Kiaps – Bob Bell and D. Permazel had established themselves. They had crossed the mountain ranges with our tribal leader, Nenk Pasul. That's where all our Korotep and Aimbarep tribesmen had gathered to have their names recorded. From there, the two Kiaps had completed the census for Lai/Mariant Census division. But they hadn't done census for the Wage division.

Two years later, on 17 May 1960 Jim Fenton did the census for the Wage Census Division for the first time. He also conducted the second census for Lai/Mariant census division. The whole exercise lasted for a month, ending on 16 June. Now, all the names of people in Kandep were recorded in the 'Yasa buk' or Census book. People were instructed to say 'Yes Sir' when their names were called. To the people, the two words sounded something like Yasa, thus the name of the census book.

For that second census, instead of all of us going to Kalimanga, Jim Fenton went from one Aimbarep village to another. I heard people discuss the progress of the census. I anticipated to see the patrol arrive at my village.

Finally, I remember Jim Fenton's patrol arriving in the afternoon from Andom village. I was old enough to remember everything. They had safely crossed the 'Wert Tok, the name of the vine bridge over the Lai River and had crossed it safely. We had a second vine bridge called Kondo Tok. It was the one I crossed every day to go to school four years later. Now, we have a permanent baily bridge across it.

Back to 1960, Jim Fenton camped at Wert Kamapu for the night. I watched people from my village help set up their sel anda or tents. People were warned not to go there in the night.

Next morning, my dad, mum, my sister Clara and I went to the table where the Kiap sat to record new births and deaths since the first census. Next day after census our Kondo Taonde sub-clan of the Aimbarep Pumbuti tribe was completed, so the patrol moved on to Lagalap village. They left behind a pungent soapy smell which still lingered in the air.

Before the 1960 census, my future father-in-law – Arnold Yauk Alo of Pindaka village had gone to Laiagam with other men from Kandep to move supplies from Laiagam up to Kepelam in Lagaip Headwaters before moving everything on their bare shoulders to Paruli to establish the patrol post there.

Arnold laughed aloud and paused for a moment in reflection. Then he related how he selected five crowbars, thinking they were small wooden poles. He thought he could easily carry them tied together in a neat little bundle all the way to Kandep. But when he lifted them onto his shoulders, they were so heavy that he couldn't go past Nyungu village. He had to rest ever now and then all the way to Kepelam. Next morning, he was sick. His whole body was aching from the previous day's heavy work.

But he had to carry the crowbars and follow the line of carriers to Kandep. He couldn't go far without constant rests along the bush track. Wantoks or fellow tribesmen helped him carry the crowbars over the Lian mountain range. But once they were inside Kandep district, poor Arnold was left struggling behind them. He didn't mind. He was inside Lai valley in Kandep. He would get to Paruli, no matter how long it took.

He and the long line of carriers couldn't complain. They were too fearful of a beating with the 'kanda' or cane the policeman and tanim toks (interpreters) carried.

The Kiap gave him one of the crowbars to keep when he finally arrived at Paruli, a day after they'd taken off from Kepelam. The crowbar is still at Pindak village to this day in one of his son's houses.

"I cannot remember the incident with the crowbars that your father-in-law relates. It could possibly have been me or more likely the previous Wabag Kiaps," said Jim Fenton.

The previous Kiaps had to be Bob Bell and D. Permazel. They were the ones who had established Kandep Patrol post before Jim Fenton settled there permanently.

Fearsome policemen ably assisted by influential local leaders ensured people came to work every day to clear land and build the new government station, the Kandep-Laiagam road and feeder roads in the new patrol post.

The people were warned that those who did not go to work would go to kalabus or jail. The 'haus kalabus' was a high structure, the fence built with thick strong posts and barbed wire. It was very high and difficult for prisoners to make an attempt to even think of escape. Inside the compound, was a Kuk haus or kitchen, the guard haus and one large building used to accommodate all the prisoners. I was afraid to go near it when I went to school in 1964.

The prisoners worked every day to maintain the Kandep station. But in the initial stages, local people from all over Kandep had gone to work on the station and roads in the new patrol post.

My father woke up early every morning to walk several kilometres to help build such other facilities – bush material houses for the patrol officer, his servants, policemen, teachers and health workers. These were later replaced with permanent houses, some of which still stand proudly today with their rusted roofs, wooden stove smoke-stacks, fibro walls, floors and stairs – reminders of a time when Kandep began to see change, a time when people worked really hard.

The government had ordered that work needed to be done and every man had to obey. Those who did not turn up for work were rounded up and beaten or put in jail.

But yet, I can still remember my father absconded from work one day. I think it was on a Friday, as did two or three other men from my village. The policeman came searching for them.

My father had warned me not to tell any stranger where he was – repairing a fence which needed urgent attention before pigs could break-in and destroy our sweet potato gardens.

The policeman couldn't find him. They left a word of warning that if they didn't show up on the following Monday, he would be jailed. I don't think my dad absconded from work from then onwards.

Nobody wanted to go to jail and spend each day at the Lungu Kana gravel pit, breaking the boulders into small stones, loading them onto a tractor or carrying them on their shoulders to place them on the new station roads.

Or collect the buckets of excrement every morning from the homes of the administration staff and empty them into the Yangip creek.

I reminded Jim Fenton that one of his kakabois or casual assistants was a mute, one of my own tribesmen from Kimbalam village. His name was 'Muma' the Enga word for mute. He used to plant vegetables for the Kiap.

"I remember the man you refer to as I had a large vegetable garden below my house alongside the top end of the airstrip. He could grow anything."

"Of all my postings in PNG, Kandep was my favourite. Residing and working in this beautiful highland valley was like living on top of the world," he said.

In 1972, I found Muma at Mukurumanda Coffee plantation, run by the Gutnius Lutheran Church. That was during a major frost which hit Kandep. The colonial government was able to provide enough food for every affected family. But Muma had somehow come and found work here.

At the time, I was in Form One at St Paul's Lutheran High School at Pausa. I met Muma there when I went to pick coffee cherries to earn a little pocket money during term break. I could not effectively communicate with him in sign language. When we met, he touched his teeth, made some flying motions as if to say, I am Nenk Pasul's brother who has flown over the mountain ranges to Port Moresby.

We also made signs to say we were all related to Nenk Pasul too. We smiled and hugged. Nenk Pasul had just won the 1972 national elections. And he had indeed flown over the mountain ranges to represent Kandep in the House of Assembly in Port Moresby. 'Nenk' means teeth in the Enga language.

Much later, in 2016, I and my wife Julie were able to meet both Jim and that infant girl in a pram, Tiana, in Brisbane. They looked very healthy and fit. Tiana must still have the bilum or string bag my wife presented to her. I gave Jim a highlands cap, the type I wear, all the time.

I was able to make contact because I went to a school Jim Fenton himself had begun to establish coupled with the hard work local people put in to actually build the classrooms and teacher's houses, level the playing field and dig a swimming pool – and the roads and bridges we walked on to go to school.

But above all, the administration needed strong influential local leaders to support them in their work. Jim Fenton makes special mention of three local leaders in some detail – Luluai Liu and his brother Liape in the Wage division and Luluai 'Nenke' Pasul of Lai/Mariant division.

They were all bigman and well established in their communities before the Kiaps appointed them luluais to assist the government in its work programs. However, there was jealousy between Liu and Liape as Jim Fenton soon discovered. And the Wage people had a tendency to dislike work.

The Brothers Liu & Liape of Wage

As in many parts of the Enga sub-district of the Western Highlands District, many local leaders rose to prominence by assisting the Australian colonial administration to bring the region under government control. Some like Nenk Pasul MBE of Kombolos village succeeded in politics and made it to the House of Assembly to represent the people of Kandep at national level.

But first we shall find out what Jim Fenton wrote about Luluai Liu of Karekare village and his brother Liape Omapu of Imaipaka village in the Wage area of Kandep.

He wrote a brief profile of both of the brothers on his first visit to the Wage area soon after being appointed as Officer-In-Charge at Kandep patrol post in 1960.

"Luluai Liu of Karekare is reported to be a 'big man' in the area and has a history of long association with the government. He was first taken out of the Wage pre-war by Jim Taylor and is reported to have performed good work during the war working for ANGAU. He has visited Rabaul and has associated himself closely with the administration in post war years.

He speaks pidgin as well as Huli, Enga and Ipili languages. He wields a considerable amount of influence throughout the whole of the Wage Valley, but handicapped in his efforts to arouse his people to some form of constructive work by a lack of support from the headwaters of the Wage River.

And as Liu is no longer a young man, he found it difficult to adequately canvas the whole of the area where the walking conditions are, to say the least, difficult. However, he is a vigorous supporter of the administration and earnestly wishes to see his area opened up."

On another patrol into the Wage River area Jim Fenton saw how Liu exercised his 'big man' status. He lined up 20 pigs, killed them all to host a huge feast for his people and shared the huge quantities of food with Jim Fenton's patrol.

Liu even asked Jim Fenton to shoot two of the largest pigs with a gun. After they cooked them all in mumu pits, they distributed the pork to all the people of Wage who were assembled at Karekare. This happened on a Sunday 3rd June as recorded in his diary.

"Large gathering of people from all areas of Wage Valley. Big pig killing during morning. Luluai Liu provided 20 pigs and huge quantities of native food for his guests. Requested writer to shoot two large pigs which could not be killed in the conventional manner with sticks.

"Those were two of the largest pigs I have ever seen and Liu stated that he purchased them from Mr Danny Leahy some years ago. Food and pig distribution to visiting groups. Singsing began in the early afternoon and continued on through the night until early Monday morning.

"Most impressive. Kandep carriers will have a story to tell when they get home. Food and pig issued to patrol members. Guard posted."

On yet another patrol into the Wage division, Jim Fenton had observed that Luluai Liu had used his influence to good effect by encouraging his people to build a road utilising his own ingenuity and foresight.

"Walking conditions throughout the area were not good, but the going was found to be considerably easier than the swampy areas in the Lai/

Mariant area. The tracks through the timbered area, between Longap, Karekare and Imapiaka had been cleared by the people upon instruction from Luluai Liu. The Wage River was crossed three times by the patrol by means of native bridges which were found to be in good order and apparently are in constant use.

Local leaders such as Liu and his brother Liape of Imapika, are keen to commence road works in the area, although the people do not appear to share their enthusiasm, having little liking for any form of work. It is intended to commence work on the construction of a vehicular road commencing at Longap and leading back."

Liape Omapu was the brother of Luluwai Liu of Karekare. Although Liu was recognised as a leader of the Wage people, he could not effectively cover all of the groups below Imaipaka and it was considered necessary to appoint another luluai to assist in the administration of this area.

Effective leaders were scarce in the Wage and although Liape's past history left much to be desired, he was the logical choice for such an appointment.

Liape was originally employed as an interpreter at Mendi. And spoke fluent pidgin. He later went to Wabag where he resided for some time with his wife's group. From Wabag he returned to Imapiaka and built a rest house and patrol quarters.

When the patrol post was being established at Kandep, Liape became involved in tribal disturbances in the Wapima area on the Lower Wage and was arrested. He was sentenced in 1960 to a total of 12 months for his misdeeds and subsequent escape from custody. He returned to Imaipaka in 1962 upon completion of his gaol term and since then, was of much assistance to the administration.

He was mainly responsible for organising the people to construct the Aid Post at Imaipaka and in bringing law breakers to the station at Kandep to be dealt with. Since his term of imprisonment, he has given no further trouble and has exhibited only a pro-administration attitude.

"During this patrol, enquiries were made to find out what the attitude of the local people would be to the appointment of Liape as Luluai. Nearly all the people stated that they would welcome such an appointment. But there was opposition from a few who had some grievances for or against Liape.

"Upon investigation it was found that the opposing minority were offenders whom Liape had brought before the court for minor offences and some who claimed that Liape's pigs had destroyed their gardens. This claim was found to be justified. But in most of the cases compensation had been paid by Liape, despite the fact that the gardens were not properly fenced.

"Luluai Liu was also unenthusiastic about the possible appointment of Liape as Luluai. However, it was later discovered that they were at loggerheads over the distribution of the proceeds of a compensation payment. Also, I think Liu is jealous of his position as undisputed leader of the Wage River area.

"In view of the above, I would suggest that Liape be provisionally appointed Luluai at some time in the near future. He could be kept under close supervision and quickly be set right if he tends to take too much upon himself," Jim Fenton wrote in his report.

After he left Kandep in 1963 some people of Wage killed a policeman at Bioko. Every male member of twelve tribes in the Lower Wage area was arrested and jailed for six months

Bioko Mass Arrests for Murder of Policeman: Home of Tundaka Ritual

Jim Fenton had been accurate in his observation that Luluai Liu was not able to cover the whole of the Wage area and that a second Luluai was needed to oversee the Lower Wage area.

He wanted Liape to be appointed, despite his previous jail term and the fact that he was Liu's brother because effective leaders were scarce in the Wage area.

Jim Fenton was also accurate in his observation that the Wage people were not generally ready to perform any form of work despite the enthusiasm of the Liu brothers. After he left, some of the people killed a policeman at Bioko village in the Lower Wage area.

Why?

Because it was claimed that the policeman had been persistently forcing them to work harder on the new road from Kandep station to

Margarima patrol post in the Southern Highlands district. It is not known if Luluai Liu was present when the incident occurred.

By then I was going to school and I can recall Kandep district office teeming with policemen brought in to arrest suspects involved in killing the policeman.

The new road to Margarima branched off at Imali village in the Lai/Mariant division. It crossed the Lai River through the swampy stretch to Wasa village. Then to Andakoe, on to Lumbipaka and on to Nerep. The policeman was killed when the new road reached Bioko. The concentration of policemen at Kandep moved in and arrested every male member from the twelve tribes in the area, tried and jailed them all for six months.

They had to build a second house in the prison compound at Kandep station to accommodate all the prisoners from the 12 tribes – Yamape, Yalipun, Kapin, Sakap, Kuniman, Waluni, Wao, Lanjap, Pakait, Angalain, Kunalun and Wao-Amang.

It was evident that nobody wanted to testify who the actual killer or killers were. Maybe, they all wanted to see him dead. But how could that be possible! It's plausible to think they all did not want to build the new road, abandoned it, spent time in prison, ate free rice and came out fat. They were so used to eating sweet potatoes all their lives.

But only if a true leader was among them, would he have singled out the perpetrators, punish them for their crime and spared all the others to continue on with the road construction and start other new projects.

As blind and stubborn as they were, they had failed miserably to realise they had killed a man who had come to save them and to get them to build a road that would bring immense benefit to them and their children.

Bioko was a central place of the Wage people. It is the home of the Tundaka Ritual. Bioko was the place where all the people of Wage came together to offer sacrifice to the Tundaka. Their lives revolved around the Tundaka Ritual.

Up to 150 or more pigs were offered as sacrifice by all the people of Wage. The biggest pigs, the best sweet potatoes, sugarcane, taro and best of everything else was reserved for the Tundaka Ritual and offered when it was time.

The people brought all the pigs and food to a place called Suama, left them there and then went back to their homes.

The ritual ceremony would be taken over by a select group who knew the secret ritual chants and the procedure to perform the actual sacrifice. This procedure cannot be revealed in public. And if members of the select group heard that their wife was having her monthly period, he would not participate. That's how sacred the Tundaka Ritual was.

In recent times, it is said a young man who described everything on paper and took it to Port Moresby with Don Polye on a chopper from Kokas in the Lai/Mariant area had died a mysterious death in the capital city. Stunned, Polye had to transport the body back home to Kandep for burial.

But back to the Tundaka Ritual. The pigs were killed and heaped up together with all the other foodstuff. Then in the blink of an eye, a thick fog would suddenly appear and cover the heaps of food on offer. The next instant all the pigs and food were gone – to where, nobody knew. It had all disappeared into thin air. And nobody knew how the select group of ritual performers returned home after every detail of the ritual was completed. Visitors and relatives would just find them in their homes smoking their big bamboo pipes.

In the Wage people's belief system, Bioko was a special place, a sacred place where everybody gathered to offer the huge sacrifice. Why the policeman was killed at Bioko remains a mystery.

Something else happened when all the prisoners in the murder case were serving their six months sentence in prison. One young man named Pomb Warao from the Anglaine tribe was among the other prisoners. He was in the work gang which built the Malai road from Kokas to the Lai River where speedboats were anchored. Some of the few expatriates in Kandep owned boats to travel around the waterways to shoot ducks, ski, fish or relax in the sun. The district administration had a speedboat too named Kandep Queen, and anchored.

After Pomb Warao had settled in to prison life, he met a young girl who was already serving time there in the Kandep Patrol Post prison.

She was put in prison together with her step-father whose name was Polye. He was a Kambrip tribesman from Gin village. He had married Ambor, a widow after her husband, Tek Kindun died leaving her behind with their daughter Akim, the girl serving time in prison. She had been enticed by Polye into having sex with him.

The Kokas community was not happy with Polye. He should have looked after the young girl as his own daughter. He knew, girls are a source of wealth in Enga province. The relatives were not happy with the girl too. She was old enough to speak out when the abuse started. Therefore, the administration put both Polye and Akim in prison for the shameful act.

Polye was a paralysed man. He walked around using a walking stick. He didn't do much but stayed in the prison compound most of the time while Akim joined the work gangs.

Pomb Warao was a strong well-built young man capable of doing anything. Whether Pomb knew why Polye, the paralysed prisoner was put in prison is hard to determine.

But he had a crush on Akim. They soon started an affair. Whether Polye suspected her of having the affair with the fellow prisoner, the young man from Wage is hard to say.

When his prison term was up, Pomb was released with the others. Polye also went home and took Akim as his wife. She was pregnant.

At Kokas village, Akim gave birth to a healthy baby boy. Polye named him Don. But the mother alone knew who the child's biological father really was.

At the time, the 1972 frost hit Kandep. The Colonial Administration provided enough food as well as support from many parts of the country. But Polye relocated his family to Avi Blocks in Mt Hagen. Don Polye the young boy, went to school there. That's where he learned to fluently speak the Melpha language.

Many years later when Don Polye stood for the Enga regional seat and later still, contested the Kandep Open seat, his mother knew, her son needed the votes to win the election. She revealed her secret of having had an affair with Angalain Pomb Warao while they were in prison. That's when Don's middle name 'Pomb' was added.

In 2002, Don Pomb Polye won the Kandep open seat defeating the incumbent, Jimson Sauk who was from Mambal village in the Wage area.

Jimson Sauk had kept the seat for three consecutive terms after winning it from John Yaka who in turn had defeated Nenk Pasul MBE back in 1977.

In the 50 years since the country gained independence, the Kandep seat was with the Wage people for 15 years under Jimson Sauk. The Lai Valley, in which John Yaka's Sawi Rest House stands, held the seat for two consecutive terms.

The Mariant census division has kept the seat for over 24 years between Nenk Pasul, Alfred Manase and Don Pomb Polye. It means that Mariant was the most politically unstable census division in the whole of Kandep.

Many of the politically induced tribal fights in Kandep were in Mariant. They held the whole district at ransom.

Back in the colonial era, Kiaps employed many people, irrespective of where they came from in Kandep, mostly as carriers, labourers and domestic servants. A few from Kandep were recruited as policemen, interpreters and correctional officers. They joined the Australian Colonial Government workforce and worked alongside officers from all over the country.

Kiap Jim Fenton 92, would like to see all the policemen and the other groups who served the colonial administration be recognised by the national government during PNG's independence celebrations.

Kiap Wants Recognition of Colonial Era Policemen, Workers & Carriers

The people of Lower Wage had killed that policeman in a matter of minutes and were imprisoned for only six months. But they didn't know how much he, as a policeman, had accomplished with his colleagues to help the Kiaps get work done towards the overall development of Papua New Guinea.

Jim Fenton laments the fact that both the Papua New Guinea and Australian governments have not acknowledged the work of policemen and other colonial era administration staff.

He hopes that they will be recognized when 50 years of independence is officially celebrated on 16 September, 2025.

I now allow Jim Fenton to express his feelings, in his own words:

> "I would like to comment on our RPNG police detachments and their part in the march towards independence – which has never been acknowledged by the Australian and PNG governments. Perhaps in this 50th year of PNG independence it should be.

> "The RPNGC members and their non-commissioned Officers or NCOs in those days were a different breed of men unlike those of today who appear more like an uncontrolled rabble. They were immensely proud of their uniform and service with their navy serge jumper and sulus with the red piping, polished bayonet scabbard and belt and their immaculately maintained rifles.

> "They were loyal, brave, resourceful and consummate bushmen. Without them, we, as Kiaps, could never have achieved whatever that was we did. It was a very foolish Kiap indeed, who did not heed the advice of his senior NCO when the going got tough.

> "It should also be remembered that many of these police men of my era fought valiantly alongside Australian troops during the war with great effectiveness and heroism. Again, this fact has never been adequately and truly recognised by successive Australian and PNG governments. This coming 50th independence celebration is an opportunity to recognise their great contribution to the development of their country.

> "It should also be remembered that it was not only Kiaps and police involved in the road to independence but also the invaluable work of missions, teachers, Didimen or Rural Development officers, medical personnel and a host of others whose contribution towards nation building was often far more important.

> "There are relatively few of us old Kiaps left now and when we die there will be a vast knowledge of the Australian colonial administration of PNG, warts and all, which will die unrecorded, with us. My family had the great pleasure last Christmas of having Hannah Dumu and her two beautiful children, Ryver and Ruby, stay with us. It is now a world of smart phones, computers and TV and sadly they will possibly never have any concept of how their country developed to what it is now or the part that their ancestors played in that long difficult road.

"Many think that we old Kiaps live in the past and we probably do. Like myself, we can never forget the years we spent living and working in that beautiful country of yours and the adventures we had that most men can only dream about.

"The carriers who signed on to undertake the patrols into the interior over extremely difficult mountainous terrain, inhabited by unknown tribes, were the unsung heroes of the early years prior to independence. They put their trust in the Kiap and police to take care of them and bring them safely home. They gave magnificent service in often dangerous and life-threatening circumstances.

"The development of the nation could never have been achieved without their strength and endurance which had to be experienced to believe.

"Consider that in the earlier days payment for their service carrying heavy loads of rations and equipment for up to a hundred patrol personnel, over some of the most difficult and mountainous terrain in the world, often for many weeks or months at a time, was a stick of twist tobacco or a shilling a day. For this they faced danger, hunger, illness and death.

"Many drowned while on patrol crossing or rafting dangerous rivers, suffered hunger when supplies of tinned fish, meat and rice ran out and the patrol had to rely on what little native food could be found along the way. Many were injured in clashes with unknown tribes and died of illness and exhaustion and were buried in the jungle in an unknown grave on the side of the track far from their home and loved ones.

"Patrolling in the high alpine mountain areas saw carriers performing feats of superhuman endurance at these altitudes where only moss forests existed with no water or firewood and extremely cold with icy rain. Man-handling their loads around and over deep limestone sink holes, where one slip could end in disaster, and with their feet cut and bleeding from the sharp limestone was a sight that most could only imagine. After 10 hours on the track members of the patrol could only huddle together for warmth, hungry and exhausted waiting for the morning to come.

"The carriers were truly the unsung heroes of the time and their valiant contribution to their nation should never be forgotten. The Kiaps and the police could never have achieved anything without their carriers. I would hope that the PNG government eventually acknowledges their extraordinary service to the nation in educating the younger generation on their past history."

Planning The Kandep Patrol Post Feeder Roads

Jim Fenton had planned the existing feeder road network in the three years he was stationed at Kandep patrol post. The only road that wasn't built was the Pindaka to the Lower Wage area.

A colonial era policeman was killed on the main Kandep to Margarima road at Bioko. Before reaching it, another road branches off at Kakaliak up toward Titip and Kanian on to Mambala and Porokale, then go over the Lai River joining up with the main road at Lakis village heading towards Laiagam.

Jim Fenton envisioned that the road from Longap could later be extended to Karekare and then go down the Wage valley to Imapiaka.

"A road will also be commenced at Pindaka below the Kandep station which will lead into the lower end of the Wage Valley where it will eventually cross the Wage River at a point opposite Paudaka and then swing up the valley to Imaipaka.'

"When that road was completed, it would give easy access to the entire population of this isolated area and will assist greatly in its economic advancement. Excellent stands of millable timber are situated around Imaipaka, Karekare and Longap which should provide means of introducing the beginning of a cash economy," Jim Fenton said.

I saw the administration begin construction of the particular road at Pindaka but it did not go far. A huge rock jutting out on the opposite bank of the Lai River prevented work from progressing. It could not be blown apart with dynamite, no matter how many times it was attempted.

I knew Ross Allen and Lloyd Warr were the Kiaps who attempted to build that road. Initially, I thought they were building the Pindaka road as an alternate route because of the swampy stretch of the road from Imali to Wasa as I had reported in one of my books, Victory Song Of Pingeta's Daughter. But now, new information from Jim Fenton shows that a road had been planned to reach the lower reaches of the Wage from Pindaka.

I knew Ross Allen who had taken over from Jim Fenton had been killed by pirates off the coast of Mexico, and his boat taken away. So, I wrote to Lloyd Warr who had been the assistant Patrol Officer at Kandep.

His wife, Moira who was my grade 5 teacher at Kandep Primary 'T' School in 1970 wrote to me on his behalf explaining how it was not possible in 1963 or 1964.

"Ross was setting some dynamite to shatter a rock face but he cannot recall exactly where the location was. However, he does remember that the dynamite, for some reason, did not ignite. Moving the unignited explosives was too dangerous and the only solution was to add further explosives.

"Because of having only, a short length of fuse left, Ross and Lloyd had to run like mad after lighting the fuse. It worked. Lloyd thinks this might have occurred in the area you mentioned but as he said cannot be certain," Moira wrote.

Lloyd was right. Although I was on the far side with other children, we were all warned to take cover as fragments might get into our eyes. But when nothing happened, I opened my eyes to see Ross and Llyod run like mad for cover.

The explosion did occur in a thunderous roar but did little damage to the rock wall. The Kiaps abandoned the project, baffled as to why the rock did not give into the powerful force of dynamite. But the local community had a reason why it didn't give way.

In olden times and up to that period, local women used to place the grass and leaves they'd used to clean themselves during their monthly periods in the small caves, nooks and crevices of the rock. The local people were certain that it was because of this reason that the rock face was not affected.

If it had been possible, the Lower end of the Wage Valley could have been opened up in the 60's. But it has remained isolated. And the whole of the Wage valley has been cut off for many years after the Imali to Wasa and Lakis to Porokale stretches of road had been submerged under water.

Only through a roundabout route from Yapum via Telytes to Longap down to Porokale, to Titip, up to Bioko and down to Magarima in what is now Hela province is it possible.

Dugout canoes were used, for a small fee, to ferry people and cargo from the Imali side of the Lai River to Wasa village. It's become a daily income generating venture for village youth on both sides of the river.

Why it was not possible to blow the rock face at Pindak, the sinking of the Imali to Wasa stretch of road and the Lakis to Porokali stretch of road is a mystery. Millions of kina were spent both by Don Pomb Polye and Alfred Manase to fix the Imali to Wasa stretch of the road – but did not succeed.

The millions went down into the depths to rest beside the logs and rocks that had been used by the colonial Kiaps to build the narrow stretch of road. The whole of the Lower Wage Valley has been cut off completely for many decades.

Some people wonder if the wilful murder of the policeman on sacred ground at Bioko and the inability of the people to co-operate with the government had cast a permanent generational curse over the whole of the Lower Wage area – like a dark cloud over-shadowing it from receiving sunlight – to ever advance into the modern era. It has remained so in the last fifty years.

How Nenk Pasul Went to Wabag in Search of Peace, Happiness

Nenk Pasul was not picked up like Luluai Liu who was taken away by Jim Taylor to expose him to another way of life – a peaceful one that called for all people to live side by side in peace and unity.

Instead Nenk Pasul went searching for the source of that peace – red-skinned people or Koneakali establishing themselves not far from Teremanda village in Wabag sub – district. His mother, Yano was from the Maralain major clan of the Kambrip tribe in the Mariant area of Kandep. Remnants of the Maralain clan lived at Teremanda. Their Hausman or sub-clan name was Paiyak of the major Kii tribe.

He told himself that he had a place to stay in Wabag. He heard one of his cousins, Erepan had been taken by the Koneakali or the Gavaman to work as a warder to look after the kalabus prisoners.

While his cousins were experiencing a new way of life, he was tied down at Kombolos village involved in iee or gardening using kamambu and yairr or digging sticks, tee or compensation, enda mok or bride price paying mena or pigs and mamaok or kina shells. And experiencing the occasional pipa or frost and yanda or tribal warfare.

Nenk Pasul was a member of the Aimarep Pumbuti major clan, the other being Aimbarep Kone together making up the major Aimbarep tribe consisting of fourteen council areas stretching from Kondo Kana all the way to Wert at the headwaters of the Mariant River.

Nenk Pasul was believed to have been born sometime in the 1920s, the first born of his father – Pasul Wii's first wife, Yano. Pasul had many more wives – up to 22.

He soon grew up a fine specimen of a man, well groomed, well-built, tall and strong. And handsome too, able to attract many a beautiful woman from many parts of Mariant in Kandep and later from Laiagam, Wabag and Wapenamanda. He married 12 wives in all, not counting other women who left him.

He loved his first wife very much. When she somehow died, he tore one of his ear lobes in two using a bamboo knife and cut off one of his fingers at Moeipaka. She was from the Laumbane clan of the Aimbarep Kone tribe. After that, he married his numerous other wives.

About the time his first wife died, a tribal war raged between the Pao and Kambrip tribe. The Aimbarep Pumbuti tribesmen were drawn into it, siding with the Pao who were a part of the major Aimbarep tribe.

Nenk Pasul received an arrow in his head. He had to be operated on by villagers using a bamboo knife to successfully remove splinters of the arrow-head still lodged in his head. The wound healed but left a big scar on the left side of his forehead.

His brother from his father's third wife was not so lucky. He was shot dead instantly. While nursing his own wounds, Nenk Pasul buried his brother and fulfilled the traditional obligations – paying compensation to the mama lain or maternal uncles and cousins of the deceased.

As a youth, he had seen his uncle Aae Wii shot dead too in another tribal war. This fight was between the Mamb and Akulya major clans of the Kupurup tribe. The Aimbarep Pumbuti sided with the Mamb. One of my own uncles, Kapae Mainu from the Naku sub-clan of Taonde major clan from Kondo village had been killed too when he went on a raid in Akulya territory to avenge Aae Wii of Kombolos village.

My mother was staying with her uncle, Akulya Talip at Kasu village when the war broke out between the Mamb over a pig named Lyarawan. When people spoke of the fight, they referred to it as the Lyarawan Yanda or Lyarawan War.

My mother's father whose name was Kush was a Mamb tribesman from Alawaip. The fight was between tribes where my mum's parents came from. She was trapped at Kasu. One of her aunts named Aii, married to a man named Tomba from Kondo village, rescued her as the fight raged on.

My mother grew up at Kondo. When she was of marriageable age, Tomba married her off to my dad, Kumbon Samai. In one sense, she was some sort of a war prize for my Aimbarep Pumbuti tribe. Not only had my father married her, Pasul Wii, Nenk's father, married two sisters from my mum's Alawaip village too. Their names were Tepo and Wambu.

The Aimbarep Pumbuti lost more men in the fight. They had to take revenge for men like Aae Pasul, Kapai Mainu and others killed in the fight over the pig named Lyarwan. There was one influential Akulya warrior the Aimbarep Pumbuti aimed for – Akulya Lale. They tracked him to a place called Supime where he had gone to reside after the fight ended.

Soon a handful of Aimbarep Pumbuti warriors went to Supime, cornered Akulya Lale in front of the gate or lome and ended his life. They had taken a big man's life in revenge for their men killed in his fight over that wretched pig.

There was tribal war everywhere in Kandep. Nenk Pasul saw death and destruction everywhere. He himself could have been killed too and a target now that Akulya Lale had been killed.

Nenk Pasul realised that tribal war was wasteful, time consuming and caused much death and destruction. He was fed up with what he saw and participating in the ancient practice of 'An eye for an eye, a tooth for a tooth' syndrome. There had to be a better way.

He decided to set off for Wabag and look for the Koneakali who were reported to be the source of peace and happiness.

Early one morning he set off along the Moe Duu bush track and into the thick jungle along rarely used bush tracks till he reached the pinnacle of Yambu Mandak or Mt Yambu. He built a shelter there, started a huge fire, cooked some sweet potatoes and slept on the wayside.

Next morning, he started walking again through the bush tracks until he reached Yopo Pauo, a big area covered in grass, a fern-like plant called papame and low-growing tree-like plants called poro. He quenched his thirst from the abundance of fresh streams and kept walking till he reached the tree line of the next mountain rage. He knew Wabag was on the other side and decided to overnight there on the foothills.

On the third day of his adventure, he reached Teremanda village. His cousins, Herepan, Toko and Tangui received him warmly. Soon, he went with Herepan the warder to Wabag and got to know some of the policeman, tanim toks or interpreters and local big men like Kurai Tapus, Yakale Wainge and others who were appointed luluais and tultuls to work for the Kiaps, the patrol officers.

After several months in Wabag, Nenk Pasul went back to Kandep following the same bush tracks. But he didn't go back alone. He returned with three white men of whom one he could still remember his name as Master Leon. The other two were of course Bob Bell and D. Permazel. In the party were also policemen, interpreters, cooks and carriers. Among them were Kii Kamberan from Teremanda village and Yakale Wainge of Keas village near Wabag town.

They established camp at Kalimanga where an aid post and rest houses for the Kiap and his patrol members had been built. It was from here that Bob Bell and D. Permazel conducted that first census in 1958.

The Kiaps appointed Nenk Pasul as a Luluai. There was no shortage of local leaders who volunteered to help Nenk Pasul bring the Lai/Mariant area under government control.

Stories circulated that the Aimbarep tribe opposed the establishment of the Kandep Patrol Post at Paruli. They wanted it established at Kalimanga. But the early Kiaps chose Paruli because an airstrip could easily be built there.

Unlike his counterpart, Luluai Liu, Nenk Pasul did not have much exposure. He had only gone to Wabag sub-district and saw the changes there before Kandep patrol post was established. While he spoke little tok pisin, he was a fiery public orator in the local Enga language. People both respected and feared Nenk Pasul. When he spoke with one eye closed, eye-brows raised, the other eye wide open piercing deeply into the crowds, he drew the attention of the people enabling him to drive his message across.

His grandfather, Wii was an influential leader among our Aimbarep Pumbuti tribe followed by his father Pasul. Then Nenk himself took over the leadership role. He had easily convinced the Kiaps to cross the mountain and establish camp at Kalimanga village.

Here is what Jim Fenton wrote about Nenk Pasul and what his people told him before work commenced on the roads in the Mariant area.

"The people seem to be keen to commence road building and Luluai Nenke, a most influential man in the Lai/Mariant area is the main advocate., urging his people to follow his advice and work hard during the forthcoming road construction program. The people were informed that the administration would do it's best to assist with the provision of spades etc for this work but I clearly stressed that funds for payment of workers would not be forthcoming at the present or in the near future.

"The people assured me that it was a matter of no concern but that they would like spades with which to work. If the administration found difficulty in providing sufficient spades, then they would continue the road with their hands and digging sticks. However, this I will have to see to believe."

Jim Fenton believed that these road networks in the Mariant area were possible. People who lived there would need a good road network. But another Kiap had reported that there was no likelihood of any road system being constructed through the Mariant Valley.

"I intend to commence construction of such a network as soon as a suitable number of spades became available,' he wrote in his diary.

"I am of the opinion that with the work force available, the roads should be constructed 20' – 24' wide, with proper side drains, bridges and culverting thus forming a vehicular road capable of taking land rovers, tractors etc from the outset,"

When I went to school, a tractor arrived first. I saw it at Sawi Apostolic mission. It was parked on the side of the road with its engine still running.

I both saw and touched a motor vehicle for the first time. The arrival of the tractor meant that the road which Jim Fenton had proposed starting at Kandep Patrol post to Laiagam sub-district had been completed. The 9,400[4] feet Lian mountain pass had been overcome.

When PNG gained independence there was an exceptional road network in Kandep. When I began work in Wabag, I was able to drive to Karekare, Laguni, Wert, to Mendi both from Kandep via Winja and Kambia down to Pingirip and Bela several times.

But soon grass grew back due to a lack of interest, lack of funds to maintain the roads, mismanagement and corruption in government. The committed Kiaps had left and unassertive locals had taken over.

The Kandep – Mendi Road via Winja continues to be in operation, since it is a national government responsibility. The road is sealed and people travel on it in comfort – in 25-seater buses. Only if the feeder roads in Kandep were in operation would it be a fair story. The whole of the Wage division is cut off as well as places like Yuripaka, Wert, Pura and other such outlying areas in Kandep.

People like Luluai Liu and Luluai Nenk had supported the Australian colonial government to help develop Kandep and bring total peace to the area. We, their offspring, the current generation ought to take responsibility and secure the future of our children.

While Luluwai Liu and Luluai Nenk have long died, Jim Fenton still lives. I and my wife Julie were able to meet him and that girl Tiana in Brisbane in 2016.

This was possible only because I went to school. But I could have died, or at least that is what my relatives believed if a particular pig was not sacrificed to appease the spirit of a dead uncle who they thought was causing my illness. That uncle had been killed in tribal warfare.

Sacrificing Pregnant Sow to Save My Life

Pigs were prized animals in Enga society. You have no status if you have no pigs. It was currency, an important trade item used in exchange for food in times of famine or for traditional salt. Pigs were the main item

---

4 - 2,865 metres, or nearly 3 kilometres high

used during compensation payments. Kina shells had also been used but have now been replaced with hard cash.

As such, pigs were not killed unnecessarily. They were hard to get and took time to grow. But my dad had to kill the only sow we had in the house at the time. It was pregnant, about to add more pigs to our household. But it had to be offered as a sacrifice to save my life.

Women breast-fed pigs, and the pigs were given names too. The unfortunate pregnant sow was called 'Pis'. It would grunt if you called its name. But Pis the sow ran to my mum at the sound of her voice or smelt her scent. She was the one who fed her and took extra care of her in the early stages of her pregnancy.

Mum shed some tears when the cruel village magician, Yambau Piui said my uncle was causing the illness. And poor Pis had to be sacrificed. Not any other pig, but Pis.

I developed the illness just before I could attend school. My parents, and relatives who came to see the progress of my illness, were alarmed when my condition worsened. I could hardly move and my breathing became difficult. Eating was impossible.

My relatives agreed this was no ordinary illness and they were fearful I might die. The village magician, Yambauo Piui, was summoned to determine the cause.

First, he had me sit up. Then he spat and breathed into some special leaves called kapaon yoko that he had brought with him.

This was followed by the chanting of some magical words. After a few seconds, he yawned hard and seemed to be in a trance.

Sometime later, the magician came to his senses and delivered the diagnosis. He said the cause of my illness was an uncle named Peruwa, who had been killed in tribal warfare between Apupi and Laubane clansman. He, along with other Aimbarep tribesman had helped their clansman, the Laubane. Uncle Peruwa lies buried at Wert Kamapus, the village square where our names were recorded during that second census patrol in 1960.

The magician said my uncle wanted my father to sacrifice our pregnant sow. The pig was to be killed at the mouth of a small spring that had been discovered in the middle of a new garden my father was clearing.

"If the pig is not offered by the spring as Peruwa wants, then the child will surely die," the magician said grimly.

Terror gripped me when I heard those cold words. I felt already paralysed.

"Okay, we will kill the pig my brother wants," my father said. "I just hope Peruwa stops making my son ill."

His words relieved me and a sudden peace descended on me. My mother had miscarried a child before me and my father was understandably worried, he might lose me as well.

Meanwhile the pig was untied and brought from the pen into the living room. The final part of the magician's ceremony was to begin.

The magician cut some hair off the pig with a bamboo knife and tied it into a bundle. Then he burned one end of the bundle. It gave off a terrible smell. The magician looked me in the eye and gave me the bundle of smouldering stinking hair. I took it in my hands.

"There, that's it. That's the signal. Peruwa is satisfied," the magician said. "The child will be all right if the pig is killed now."

The pig was immediately led to the new garden, where the spring had sprouted from the ground. Stones, ferns called tambo and vegetables were hastily collected on the way.

When the ingredients were ready, the poor animal was slaughtered. The blood oozing from its nose was allowed to drip into the mouth of the spring. This was the offering to the spirit.

The head and organs like the liver of the pig were cooked in a mumu at the mouth of the spring to further appease my late uncle. The rest of the pork was cooked in a bigger mumu nearby.

When the two mumu pits were uncovered, I was encouraged to eat some of the pork. This I did, to the obvious delight of my father. This was an indication that the spirit had let go of me and that I would recover in the next few days.

I had fully recovered when I began school. I enrolled in Preparatory class at Kandep Primary 'T' School in 1964. (The 'T' stood for Territory).

The Trust Territory of New Guinea refers to the north eastern part of the island of New Guinea. Before WWI, the territory was under German control, and after WW1 it became a League of Nations mandate. After WW2 it was administered by Australia as a UN trust territory.

In 1949, the Trust Territory of New Guinea was administratively united with the Territory of Papua, forming the 'Territory of Papua and New Guinea.'

In 1975, the combined territory gained independence as the nation of Papua New Guinea. After that there was no need for a school to be referred to as a 'T' school.

I Begin My Long Walk to School

I was born at the right moment when Australia was still in charge of the Territory of Papua and New Guinea. I was free to go to school at a time when the Australian colonial government enforced the rule of law with an iron fist. There was peace among a people who had been constantly fighting each other for generations.

They were soon brought under control and told it was against the law to fight. Those who did not obey the government were severely punished. A man who had killed both his wives in Wabag had been hanged for all to see. The Kiaps went about their duties with serious intent.

They attended to every complaint that was brought to their attention. At one time, I saw a woman flogged 20 times with the 'kanda' (kane) in an open court at one of our other Kondo village squares – Tambulipaka Kamapu after the Kiap found her guilty of cheating on her husband.

The Kiaps patrolled every area in Kandep, making contact with the people and their local leaders to ensure they were okay. This paved the way for dramatic change in the district. People began to enjoy freedom of movement.

The missionaries also came and supported the administration in its efforts to bring change and development among my people. Apart from preaching the word of God, they introduced mission schools and medical services. I remember nurses from Kokas Lutheran mission coming regularly to my village at Kondo to conduct regular children's clinics. When they ate lunch, I often saw them eat something red and throw away the middle part. I later discovered that the nurses had been eating apples.

After the airstrip, the school, hospital and other establishments were completed, the people were organised into labour gangs to build new roads and bridges into the Mariant, Lai and Wage areas. I drove as far as

Laguni in Wage and Wert in the headwaters of the Mariant River when I began work in Wabag. But sadly, these roads and other feeder roads like the Karekare road deteriorated from lack of maintenance.

The three groups – Wage, Lai and Mariant people were distinctly different from each other in terms of certain cultural practices. Wage people spoke the Huli language and dressed in the same attire as people of the current Hela province. The people of Mariant spoke the Enga language but had deep cultural connections with the people of Western Highlands and Southern Highlands provinces. People in the Lai area spoke only the Enga language and dressed the same way as people of the Laiagam district.

The Kiaps brought all these people together to work on the new Kandep patrol post. I saw my father go to work there every morning at the order of the government Kiap. The first Kiap to settle there was Jim Fenton. He told me much later that he had transferred from Telefomin in what is now West Sepik province.

When I went to school in 1964, my father boiled water every morning in a billy can. He washed me to attend school at the new Kandep Primary 'T' School. It had opened in 1963 after Jim Fenton had left. He still lives in Brisbane Australia in a retirement village.

Imagine Jim Fenton still writing to me at age 92 when almost all of the local people whose help he needed to develop Kandep are gone. People like Menan, Nenk Pasul, Liu and his brother Liape Omapu – some names I saw in some of Jim's early patrol reports.

"There was no school at Kandep when I was there. I started to build a house for the teacher but was transferred before it was finished. I believe the first primary school teacher arrived in 1963," Jim said.

When I started school, Jim Fenton was gone. The headmaster's name sounded something like McRae, McGray or McRay. His young wife was my first teacher. She taught me in preparatory class. They had a baby girl whose name sounded something like Lawani. I can still remember my teacher's beautiful voice teaching us the song 'We are all walking, walk, walk, walking…'

In 1965 her husband, the headmaster, taught me in grade one. The following year, my grade 2 teacher was from Manus Island. But I did not last long in his class, I absconded to Mariant Catholic Mission School. I was tempted to do so because it was very close to my village.

Kandep Primary T school was far from my village. Every morning, my father walked with me on the bush tracks until I was familiar with landmarks and became used to it. A proper road was being built and gradually reached my village and down to Winja towards Murumbu, present day Mendi town. Thankfully, this road is now sealed. And it takes just about seven minutes to reach my village from Kandep station.

Now, the effects of climate change have altered the climatic conditions to warm days and nights. But back then, it was freezing cold in the mornings. I had no clothes except a green laplap the headmaster issued to us. It was only in 1971 that I wore a pullover to school. It had been sent to me by Clara, my sister who was at Rabiamul Catholic Mission with Holy Spirit Sisters.

When it rained, my father took me to his cousin Yaok's house at Lungutenges village to overnight. Next morning, he would leave me at the school and go home. I would follow later after class ended.

Dad took me to two other houses to show me where to go and overnight if it rained heavily in the afternoons. The first house was my maternal cousin Kipam's house at Imali village. The other house belonged to Alitip Nepape from Patuli village. Nepape was my uncle Pupukai's maternal cousin.

If these families cooked sweet potatoes early enough, they would give me something for breakfast. But sometimes I went to school without food. No child from those homes went to school. So they were not used to cooking very early in the morning as my father did. In the afternoons, I often felt weak from hunger.

About this time a young Australian girl came to Kandep. I don't know if she was a tourist or a relative of the teaching couple.

The visitor wanted to see how local people lived so we took her to Patuli village after school. The tracks were very muddy but she did not seem to mind. In the excitement, I had failed to see that it was too late to go home. I went to spend the night at Lungutenges village.

When the primary school was established by Fr Gerald Jerry Theis SVD at Mariant Catholic Mission, I enrolled there to repeat grade 1 in 1966 when I should have been doing grade 2. I did not tell my parents of this arrangement but they didn't seem to mind so long as I was attending a school. My long walks to the school at Kandep had ended. But two years later, my long walks started again.

But first let me relate how some students were flogged for stealing loose cigarettes by a policeman as Ross Allen, the headmaster, a teacher, mission staff and the student assembly watched.

Flogging Students Caught Stealing Kiap Ross Allen's Cigarettes

One day at Mariant mission school, our teacher, Mark Reimb from Sari village in Wabag, told us to dress smartly the following morning. He said a Radio Man from Radio Western Highlands would be coming to record our songs.

I was at the front and singing with much enthusiasm into the microphone. I watched the Radio Man's every move as he turned knobs and flicked switches, changed batteries, tape reels and signalled us when to sing and when to stop.

It was awesome to watch the two tape spools spinning round and round. With a primitive background, I could not possibly comprehend the operations of the portable recording machine.

Before he departed, the Radio Man told us to listen to our songs in a special children's program transmitted over Radio Western Highlands. I did not hear the songs because there was no radio in my village in those days.

Another occurrence at the school so vivid in my mind was when one of the students was flogged in front of the assembly one morning for stealing two cigarettes from Ross Allen, the government Kiap who had relieved Jim Fenton in 1963 who had gone on leave.

Ross Allan had come to visit Fr Jerry Theis at the mission one day and had run out of cigarettes. He had asked either Fr Theis or the headmaster, Mr Carmichael to send one of us students to run over to the Kandep government station to buy him a new packet from one of three stores operated by Andy Flower, Waso Ltd and a man named Brian Heagney.

Waip Kisambu from Pindak village was selected to go. It was quite a distance, but Waip came back with the packet before school was over.

I saw Mr Carmichael hurry over to the residence he shared with Fr Theis and come out again a while later. He called us together and asked us to dress well and come early next morning. I noticed that he was tensed up and seemed concerned.

As we stood in assembly, the Kiap, Ross Allen appeared as if on cue. He took over from the headmaster and spoke to us using an interpreter.

The Kiap's face was red when he spoke in an angry, raised voice. He ordered Waip Kisambu to come to the front. And told him to identify the boys he had shared the loose cigarettes with.

After telling us that it was wrong to steal, and holding up the packet of Rothmans cigarettes he explained how Waip had removed the seal and pulled out two loose cigarettes before giving him the packet.

He had noticed the theft and showed it to Fr Theis and our Headmaster, Mr Carmichael. They had planned to confront Waip Kisambu in front of the whole school assembly.

Waip had gone home thinking Mr Ross Allan had not noticed the missing rolls and had come to school next day. After talking to us, he directed Waip Kisambu to look at him and said: "You have committed a major crime. Do you want to go to jail? I can do it easily. But I cannot because you are in school. I must warn you never to steal again."

How could pupils steal from the Gavaman Kiap, a man respected and feared in the whole of Kandep, he who represented government power surrounded by his policeman, dogs, interpreters, warders and teachers. Waip had done the unthinkable.

After our headmaster, Mr Carmichael left Mariant Catholic Mission School, nobody came to take his place. So, my class was transferred to Kandep Primary T School in 1968 to do grade 3. Our headmaster was a Frenchman named Mr Marquart. He taught me in Standard Three. His wife also took some classes. I can still remember them walking side by side coming down from their hill top residence. A permanent house had replaced the bush material house that my first headmaster and his wife and small daughter had used. Mrs Lloyd Warr taught me in standard 5.

Two other headmasters who taught me later were my standard 4 teacher, Mr Wilberg, an American and Mr Glen Warwick from Australia. I remember Mr Warwick telling us that he could have been fighting in the

Vietnam War. But recruiters had missed his name in the family records. Many young men were drafted into the Australian army to fight in the war.

I can still remember him distributing our school certificates to us, sitting on a bench in front of his office. The photographs we took earlier had arrived. He was gluing our passport-sized photos on the top right-hand corner of our Standard 6 certificates.

Mr Warwick taught us how to play softball which I enjoyed so much – especially when it was my turn to bat. I liked to hit the ball hard to make a home run.

But I learned to play soccer myself and nearly broke my right foot at lunch-break during a game. An elder boy named Salepen from Kam village kicked my foot together with the ball causing me to fly into the air and to land on my injured foot. This caused so much pain, I could not stand any more.

I walked into the classroom pretending I was OK. But in the afternoon, I hobbled along slowly using a walking stick. But I could not go all the way home. I had to take shelter at my aunt Alumail's house at Pindak village. Next morning, I forced myself to school relying on a walking stick for support.

I stayed permanently at my aunt's house and completed standard six successfully in 1971, topping my class. I went on to do Form One at St Paul's Lutheran High School at Pausa in Wapenamanda, the following year.

From there I applied to attend Lae Technical School in 1974. But there was a shortage of electrical instructors at the school so we had to be transferred to Port Moresby Technical School. I was fortunate to have been transferred there because 1975 was the year my country gained independence – the year I sat for my Form Four national examinations. And I passed with flying colours.

And during Christmas holidays of that year, I began meeting people who had worked with the Australian Colonial administration and the missionaries.

Christmas Message from My 92-Year-Old Teacher, Fr Jerry Theis, SVD

I absconded to Mariant Catholic Mission School when Fr Jerry Gerald Thies, SVD started a school there. When I should have been doing Standard 2 at Kandep Primary 'T' School I went and completed Standard One again at Mariant.

I was forced to do so because Mariant Primary School was very close to my village – Kondo. I didn't like walking to Kandep every morning in the cold with barely any clothing covering my bare skin. Fr Theis was my teacher at Mariant for a while. He was assisted by the local teacher, Mark Reib from Sari in Wabag. His son is currently the Provincial Police Commander in Kerema, Gulf province.

Fr Theis and Jim Fenton are the first two people to actually live among my people to bring change and development to us. I had often seen the two men having dinner at each other's houses. Jim sent me some pictures of them and his late wife in Kandep.

I was privileged to meet Jim Fenton and his first-born daughter, Tiana in Brisbane in 2016 while attending the Brisbane Writers Festival[5].

In 2013, at age 81, Fr Theis came to Mariant from Mt Hagen where he lived to celebrate his Golden Jubilee with my people – 50 years of spreading the Word of God. I missed that special occasion. But my family was there to participate in the festivities which lasted three days.

Fr Theis's Message…

> *"We are a bit early in exchanging our greetings.*
> *"Thank you for news from my 'home' in Kandep. How have you been keeping? I hope that many people are clinging to the world view of Jesus Christ and not that of tribalism and politics.*
> *"Our USA culture 'stinks' these days and so I am still preaching Christ crucified, died, buried and risen. The mention of your sibling, Clara, brought back many memories.*
> *"How is she? How is her life today? Of course, I still remember Agnes Maiapu and the 'boys'.*

---

5 - Brisbane, Queensland, Australia

> *"Give my greetings to all your family and all the members of Kondo and surrounding tribes. Ask them to be forgiving of any harm I may have unknowingly caused in my youth and inexperience; pray for me a sinner.*
>
> **Fr Jerry Theis SVD** *(the 'J' in my formal name stands for Joseph. 'Jerry' is what my family and friends call me."*

I replied to his short message on behalf of my family, wishing him a Happy Easter.

He had come to Enga province a young man.

I thanked him for starting the new mission school near my village. I don't know what I would be doing today if Fr Theis and the headmaster's wife at Kandep Primary T School hadn't guided me along the path when I took those first uncertain steps to receive an education. Me, a boy straight from the village, or straight from the stone age, should I say. A boy who didn't know one word of English or tok pisin.

"No, Father, nobody holds any grudges against you. You opened their eyes and ears to the outside world. You showed my people a new way of life. Your good name still lives among us," I said "Of seven students you taught, one became school headmaster, one a Didiman Officer, another trained to be a surveyor but instead became a church pastor.

The seven people I referred to are Simili Alonk who became a lawyer but sadly died in the prime of his life. The High School Headmaster is Simon Yanz who still teaches at Kopen Secondary School, the primary school headmaster, is Elijah Erapae Yauk. While Simon Yanz retired and went back to teach again at Kopen Secondary, Elijah lives in the village.

Philip Yangao Lopar is the Didiman Officer who lives in his retirement at his wife's village at Amanab in West Sepik province. And the person who still works as a pastor is Samuel Komb Opop. I became a radio broadcaster, journalist, and writer. The only girl, Agnes Alemaumb Amben is a retired primary school teacher, currently living in Australia with her daughter Angela Maiapu.

In 1971, of the nine students who were selected to continue onto St Paul's Lutheran High School at Pausa in Wapenamanda, six of us had transferred over to Kandep from Mariant mission school in 1968.

Late Philip Kai Morre said from Kundiawa in Simbu that he knew Fr Jerry Theis and such an emotional Easter message made him feel like crying because Philip was a product of SVD Missionaries.

Thank you, Fr Theis. God will continue to bless you and keep you in good health to celebrate more Easters. Sadly, Philip died recently but Fr Theis has lived on to celebrate many more easters.

Fr Theis has now reached the unbelievable age of 92 years in PNG terms. People in developed countries even live over the age of 100 because they eat good food, keep active and live in peaceful environments. In Papua New Guinea, most people tend to throw their lives away. We are not mindful of our health. We eat anything, chew buai, drink beer, all in the one mouth. Other people, particularly the youth, take marijuana which is so plentiful in the country.

Apart from Fr Theis and Jim Fenton, I am still in contact with another expatriate, a kiap who came to my bush material family home in my village at Kondo in Kandep, Enga province.

In Contact With 'Kiap Wantoks' Who Served PNG Till Independence

It was in the afternoon, the time of day when you expect people of the house to disengage themselves from the chores of the day and begin coming home.

My father was expected to bring firewood and my mother to bring food from the garden for the evening meal, next day's breakfast and sweet potatoes for the pigs too. And children would usher in the pigs or bring containers of fresh water, firewood or edibles like strings of insects, frogs, grubs or even fish to cook and eat.

The Lai River teemed with fish which the Didimen or agricultural officers at Kandep introduced in the 60s. I saw planes fly over the many lakes and waterways releasing fingerlings into the water when I attended Kandep Primary 'T' school.

I had just come home for the Christmas break after completing Form Four in Port Moresby. I was not expected to do any chores just yet. They hadn't seen me for a whole year and my parents wanted me to remain free until I went to school again. They were happy to hear that I had done well in my Form Four national examinations and received offers to attend the University of Technology in Lae the following year.

Nobody had yet come home that afternoon when I sat alone by the fireplace doing nothing. All of a sudden, a strange koneakali, a 'whiteman' appeared on the horizon. Was it real? I focused my eyes to see him clearly.

There was no road extension at the back of the house so he was definitely coming to my house. So, I went outside to greet him. Rain was about to fall so we went inside my family home through the low door.

The strange koneakali was John Gordon Kirkby, a Kiap working in Wabag. Somebody had directed him to come to my house because I was the only person who could converse with him in English.

They probably didn't know that John was fluent in tok pisin and could have been cracking jokes with them. But the sad fact is, nobody knew how to speak tok pisin in my village at the time. When they saw a storm brewing on Mt Kondo, they felt the right place for the stranger to seek shelter was at my house.

He was comfortably seated on the floor covered with lepe leaves, a sort of swamp grass and sugarcane stalks. John cared little about the house flies, cockroaches, fleas, dust and smoke in the house. And we talked on for as long as the rain continued to fall.

But there was nothing available I could offer John, not even sugarcane at the back of the house. I could not go fetch water for him either, leaving him on his own. And there were no sweet potatoes at the males, the space where food stuff is kept to cook for the visitor. Even if there was, the fire would have produced smoke.

When the rain subsided, my mother came from the gardens. I notified her in the Enga language that a visitor was in the house and she must avoid creating dust with her feet when she came inside or to start the fire as the smoke might get into his eyes.

So, mum just sat there on the woman's side of the house without making any noise. Finally, I think John Gordon Kirkby sensed the situation and excused himself to leave. I gave him my address at the University of Technology in Lae where I had been accepted to study communications engineering.

He wrote some very long letters to which I promptly replied, the best I could. By mid-1976, I did not hear from John any more. I knew he had gone back home down south. But I didn't know where he had gone to in Australia.

Much later, we made contact following an article I published in the popular blog, PNG Attitude. I was glad to see his name but did he notice mine? I quickly asked Keith Jackson, the publisher for my long-lost friend's email address. We again met online.

"This correspondence fills me with nostalgic joy," he wrote. "I once corresponded by post with many PNG people whom I had met or sponsored. This continued to a lesser degree when email took over. However, with the passing of time, they all dropped out.

"Thank you for having made me welcome in your humble home. We must not lose contact again. I am now 83 years old but I enjoy good health and lead an active life."

We have continued to keep in touch since. Towards the end of December, 2024, he emailed me a photo of himself stating that was how he was at that precise moment. He looked really fit and sharp.

'If this is how you are now, I am sure we will meet in Townsville,' I said. I had just been invited to attend the First Nations Writers Festival after voting me as a 'Living Treasure' – scheduled to take place in mid-2025.

"This is how I was a few minutes ago," he wrote back immediately. "I am sure we will meet at the end of May, 2025. But I will still be 88, not 89 till August, 2025. Doreen will be with me and she will be 84. We both keep well and active."

So, we looked forward to meeting in person exactly 50 years later. But our dream was shattered. My visa had been refused by Australian Immigration. I had applied for the wrong visa when it should have been under Cultural Exchange. My mistake. I intended to break the bad news from Wabag but on 17 March, John wrote to me wishing to know if I got my visa yet. I had to respond: "Sad story Wantok, I wanted to break the news to you from Wabag but now that you've contacted me, I will tell you that my Visa application has been refused.

I did not apply for a Cultural Exchange Visa. Nothing can be done. Maybe next year. But my heart breaks, I can't meet you and Doreen. Sorry tru – Daniel Kumbon, Port Moresby. PS, I will be going to Wabag tomorrow"

"Dear Daniel,
Hope you have a safe trip back home to Wabag today. Your news is indeed disappointing to us too! Can you try again, and do it yourself and get backing from FNWF in Townsville or ask them to initiate it.
Best of luck
Fondly
Chip"

The suggestions John made were not possible. Our bodies might be aging but, as they say, the mind was still young. Doreen and John were nearing 90. But they wanted to fly to Townsville to meet me. I had another reason to meet them. As Jim Fenton says in the Foreword, the surviving Kiaps were the last links to the Australian colonial era. They had brought peace to my area and I was educated by them. As a journalist, I wanted to record and preserve what would have been a memorable moment, our second and last meeting in person. I hope, they will still be there for me to see them if there ever is a chance in the future.

It would have been a privilege to meet Doreen for the first time. They live in a small house in Mornington, Victoria, 50km south of Melbourne. Previously, they lived in a large home on 5 acres near Bendigo.

John and his first wife left PNG in 1978 and went to New Zealand to settle on a farm. They separated in 1983 but remained friends until she died in 2018. She was a nurse working in Southern Highlands district when they first met.

John married his current wife, Doreen, also a nurse. They, too, were unsuccessful in having children. But they've lived a fulfilling life together and continue to do so.

It was worth noting that both John Gordon-Kirkby and Jim Fenton married their second wives only when their first wives died or when properly separated.

Engans seemed always ready to kill and destroy each other when the very people who first came and worked really hard to develop the province were still living. I really did not want to fight with the Kambrip and Imma people when my property was destroyed.

Both these tribes had been our traditional allies. Our people had never fought each other except that fight in which Nenk Pasul had received an arrow in his head. But that fight did not involve my Aimbarep Pumbuti major clan. He had just gone to help the Pao clan of our major Aimbarep tribe.

Do we ever sit down and consider how they feel reading in the papers or seeing on television all the mess we created in this province – and throughout PNG for that matter?

People like Fr Theis, Jim Fenton, John Gordon-Kirkby and Ed Brumby who edited the School Papers – supplementary reading materials and stories for school children throughout PNG in the 60s and 70s. I had even met the men who had inspected the Kandep airstrip to give the okay for planes to land. They still loved Enga province and PNG. They still watch everything that happens here in this country.

It was better to make them proud of their immense contribution to the development of the country rather than force them to ignore us with all the negativity. We should be continuing on with work with the same intensity from where they left. The right time to make amends with our enemies, get our lives back in order and serve the country with honesty, was the year 2025 when we celebrated our country's 50 years Independence anniversary.

When I asked John Gordon-Kirkby in January, 2025 if PNG gained independence too early, he responded by questioning where all the money went when PNG was supposed to be well off from the proceeds of its rich natural resources.

"You have set me thinking again about your country. I still have several PNG coins and notes. At independence the Kina had parity with the Australian dollar. Now, the Kina is only worth A39c. That seems to speak volumes about the mismanagement of your economy. PNG has an educated minority, but just why is a mystery to me. There was widespread primary and secondary education in much of PNG when I left.

"You are living proof of the status of education in 1975. Where are all your contemporary High School and University graduates today? What are they doing?

"PNG has a wealth of natural and mineral resources, so where is the money?"

Then in a separate email the former veteran Kiap sent me old pictures of tultuls, luluais and policemen. He said nothing about the pictures.

These were the very people the Kiaps depended on to pacify the untamed country. They did a lot of tremendous work to develop Papua New Guinea in a very short time leading to independence.

John's message was crystal clear. If these people in the pictures had gotten the work done without resources, then we the present generation can change the face of the country with income generated from our gold, oil, gas, copper, timber, fish, copra, cocoa and a host of other such rich resources. If independence had been rushed; it cannot be reversed. At the time, Bougainville Copper was the only mine in operation. The benefits from this one mine were shared equitably throughout the country.

Now, there was OK Tedi, Lihir, Porgera, Papua LNG, Southern Highlands oil and gas fields operating in the country. It still has enough natural resources in reserve to sustain the country and change the skyline of Port Moresby, Mendi, Tari, Lae, Goroka, Wabag – the headquarters of resource rich provinces – as seen in middle eastern capital cities. An example of change and prosperity is Dubai capital of the United Arab Emirates where oil is their only natural resource.

Maybe PNG got independence too early before the mindsets of people changed to understand what nationhood meant and its leaders serving their people with honesty and transparency towards a common goal to develop their country on par with the rest of the world.

But first let me take you to Sir Hubert Murray Stadium, the epicentre of PNG's independence celebrations where I saw everything happen – but couldn't really comprehend what it all meant.

3

INDEPENENCE & DEATH OF FOUNDING FATHERS

SOMARE, CHAN

Leadership is about making others better as a result of your presence and making sure that impact lasts in your absence
– Sheryl Sandberg, COO Facebook.

I Was There in September 1975, Not Sure What Independence Meant

I was fortunate to attend school in the capital city to witness my country's independence celebrations on 16 September, 1975. But yet, I did not fully understand what it really meant. People can excuse me for harboring that sort of thought on an important day which gave birth to a new nation.

But you see, I was born into a primitive society. And within only eleven years of completing my secondary education, my country gained independence.

I didn't know how to spell the word independence or what it meant. And my teachers never prepared me for self-rule. I don't think that the great man, Grand Chief, Sir Michael Thomas Somare's father had any clue either. He was like many other young village men who were recruited to help the Australian colonial administration to pacify the country inhabited by backward people living in some of the most isolated terrain in the world.

Sir Michael's father could have been like any of those policemen whom I saw come to Kalimanga village in Kandep for the first time in 1958 to conduct the first census. And policemen I saw building new roads with village people timidly glancing at them on my way to school.

Michael Somare himself must have been like the sons and daughters of policeman who lived at the new Kandep patrol post. I don't think he worked with expatriates or was exposed to politics long enough before he took control of the country. But he was a capable man, who peacefully led the country to independence. He held it together delicately until his death.

The people have been resilient to survive the test of time, to cling to our country without losing hope in the last fifty years, so as to celebrate our golden jubilee celebrations.

Only tribal warfare, election violence, sorcery-related killings and deep-rooted corruption was on the verge of strangling the country to death if we were not careful.

My teachers at Idubada Technical College told us what independence meant when they prepared us for the celebrations. Yet, I couldn't comprehend anything.

Our principal R Alterskye, a British national expressed his thoughts in our college yearbook. I have kept a copy to this very day. I realise that he had chosen his words carefully to a student population whose background was like mine. It was a time when there were hardly any local university graduates working alongside expatriates in the public service machinery. Or not many studying in overseas colleges or universities for that matter.

The first students to graduate from the University of Papua New Guinea – which included future prime minister, Sir Rabbie Namaliu was five years previously in 1970.

In that situation, our Port Moresby Technical College Principal, – Mr. R. Alterskyee, addressed us in our 1975 Yearbook. It brings nostalgic memories flooding back. That address and short pieces by our college captain and president remain vivid in my memory.

The College Principal's message:

1975 is the year for Independence for Papua New Guinea and the students of this college show every indication of facing and overcoming such problems as it may present, if their attitude and potential as judged by their efforts this year are a true sign of their performance. Management of teams and classrooms has generally been entrusted to students and standards have been kept high. Prefects, the SRC, and Captains have played an especially important part in maintaining this level.

Complete self-reliance is not our aim this year, but the increase in reliability and responsibility is very evident and promises well for the future. This is especially gratifying when we remember the college represents a mixture of students from all over Papua New Guinea studying in a variety of technical subjects, living and working close together for almost two years.

Founded on trust, cemented in mutual respect, the efforts of staff and students are well on the way to establishing new heights in achievement. Despite changes in Educational and Career possibilities, Idubadans who finish this year have the chance of a wonderful future, and shall carry the name of Idubada – and their memories – with grace, dignity and pride. Their worthy endeavors will be rewarded, and their contributions and triumphs will be as great a success for the College as they will be valuable to the country.

Our third-year students are nearly half way, and have the Christmas vacation for recreation, remembering that this time is for re-creation, for replenishing their minds and bodies ready to prove their worth in 1976. To all staff and students who have worked so altruistically I express the gratitude of the Governing Council, and declare our confidence in the continuing success of our college, whatever its changed goals next year.

Every kind wish for Christmas and 1976,

Sincerely – R. Alterskyee.

When I recently opened the pages of my copy to retrieve these fine words, the smiling faces of our Deputy Principal, Mr J Durnan, the register & Staff, our Librarian Mr. Foo Miva, a most kind man who always helped me locate a particular book I wanted to read, our College President Asi Tauaru and our SRC President Tore Arua. I don't know where they are now but they still smile from the pages. Also greeting me with smiling faces are staff and students of each class at Idubada 50 years ago. I wish them and their offspring best wishes during our country's golden jubilee celebrations.

My own 4A, 4B, 4C, 4D classes who took up Electrical are not in my priceless 1975 yearbook. It had peeled off due to old age because it was the center spread. Only 4E and 4F Electrical are still there. I am not in either of these two pictures. I notice that some of the pages had been scribbled on by my children long ago. They did not understand the significance of the book and the words it contained.

I wish to also reproduce the words of our two student leaders of that day and age, Asi Tauaru, the college captain and SRC president, Tore Arua for the benefit of all our off-spring where ever they may be in our country.

On behalf of my fellow students, I would like to thank the Principal, Mr Alterskye, the Deputy, Mr Durnan and staff for their cooperation with students during work parade, in classes and in sports.

I would also like to wish good luck to our former deputy Principal, Mr Huges, who was a great help to many students.

This year is very significant to many of us because of Independence: Our country's and our own. When many of us leave at the end of this year our training will be of great value to our country.

As I look back over my two years at the 'Home of Bachelors', as an SRC Member and the College Captain, I realise these were the happiest and most joyful years in my life.

Finally, to my fellow Form Fours, I wish you good luck and best wishes in your exam. I also wish the Form Threes good luck for the next year

— Asi Tauaru, College Captain.

And this message from our SRC president.

> *At the end of last year, I was appointed SRC President for 1975. The Vice-President and other members were also appointed by the body of students. At the beginning of this year, sixteen members were elected by their classes. Two months later, Asi Tauaru, College Captain, and Bora Moea, Vice-Captain, were elected by the students.*
>
> *Half way through the year, two of my executive members, Sports Officer and Social Officer, resigned from their positions. They were soon replaced by Ivali Gini, Sports Officer, and Kopie Ainaha, Social Officer.*
>
> *This year has not been a successful year for the SRC because the prefects and SRC members as well as the continuous students did not co-operate with each other to run the College properly.*
>
> *I was very unhappy with the way the college was run through the year. So, I am advising you future leaders of the college and you fellow students to co-operate with each other to make the SRC a strong body so that you and your fellow students will be happy.*
>
> Tore Arua 4B – SRC President

Note that none of the students from the Highlands region competed for student leadership positions. I think that was because we did not have the exposure or fully understood the significance of taking responsibility or maybe we felt it was time consuming and might affect our studies.

When official celebrations for independence commenced on September 15, the whole staff and student body walked over to the Sir Hubert Murray Stadium to witness the official program and see important people like Prince Charles, now King who represented his late mother, Her Majesty Queen Elizabeth II who was our head of state. She was represented by Sir John Guise, the first Governor General. Then there was the Australian Prime Minister Gough Whitlam whose Labor government granted us independence and other dignitaries.

I heard some of them speaking over the public address system.

As a journalist, I play around with a lot of words today. But back then I did not comprehend or fully understood the messages delivered by Michael Somare, Sir John Guise and our important guests.

It was a very passionate period of time and people wept openly at Sir Hubert Murry Stadium. But my attention was focused on the 100-gun salute and the army, navy, police, and correctional services accompanied by the police and army bands and singsing groups. Everything was new to me, having come from a remote patrol post of the then Western Highlands District.

The next day, I and Eric Kombeakali of Lungutenges village in Kandep walked over to the residence of our Member of the House of Assembly, Nenk Pasul at Tougaba Hill. He had invited all the people from Kandep living in Port Moresby to celebrate the important occasion.

He arranged his people, mainly rubber plantation laborers and casual employees in the city – according to their tribal groups and distributed the food and cartoons of beer to them. Groups that had more people got more food and drinks.

There were only a few of us from our major Aimbarep tribe – Kaeyao Watali a trainee policeman at Bomana Police College, myself a student, Yange Pasul, John Londokai and Nenk Pasul himself. Eric Kombeakali joined his own Imma and Alitip tribal groups. I opened the stubbles and served the drinks to people in my group. After a while Nenk Pasul looked at me strongly and asked me to help them finish the beer. There was so much. People kept buying more at the nearby Steamships outlet.

When I protested, reminding him that I was only a student, he said: "I know, I know. You are going to school and will work someday. But what will you do with all the money you get? You will surely spend some of it on beer. So, accept my offer now and experience how it tastes on this very important occasion. Try it."

Then he opened a stubby and handed it to me, his unblinking, glaring eyes penetrating deep into my own. I was confused. But yet it was hard to resist this offer from our big man. So, I took the plunge, drank two, three or more and passed out. I didn't know what happened next but woke up next day on a bed in Nenk Pasul's house.

Eric Kombeakali was nowhere to be seen. He had walked back to Idubada Technical College. He had seen me holding a bottle in my hands, consuming its contents, drowning out my thoughts, confusing me more to realise that today was the second day when PNG was beginning to stand on its own two feet. Would I be able to walk to my college on steady legs or would I stumble and fall on the way?

Kiap Reveals How PNG Was Not Ready: Independence Came Too Early

The question as to whether Papua New Guinea was prepared for self-rule is best explained by Robert Forster, a former Kiap in his book *'The Northumbrian Kiap'*. The British national published the fascinating book in 2018 with skill and honesty about the conditions Papua New Guinea was in during the sixties.

This was the exact time when I started going to school. I could easily identify myself with much of what he wrote. The remote areas he worked in were no different to the situation as it was in Kandep patrol post in Enga sub-district.

It was a time when people did not know anything about self-government and independence, let alone their meanings. This book clarifies many questions and doubts of Papua New Guineans who were born and raised during that period, the sons and daughters of primitive tribesmen. They had just witnessed with awe these men known as *Kiaps* lead long lines of carriers with armed police escorts as they penetrated deep into the hinterland and its traditional tribal lands.

These strangers established encampments, built patrol posts, constructed roads, hospitals and schools as they demonstrated to the startled people that there was another – perhaps a better world far beyond the high mountain ranges and the raging rivers.

But life comes and goes. Just like ancient civilisations left behind monoliths, pyramids and relics, the Kiaps left a legacy. They left and much of what they accomplished was abandoned and left to decay. On top of that, people destroyed remaining infrastructure in never-ending tribal feuds.

Robert Forster, the British-born author of *'The Northumbrian Kiap'*, was a patrol officer for most of the seven years he lived in pre-independence PNG.

When he arrived in PNG in 1968 there were places still to be explored and mapped. In the most remote valleys, there were people who had had no contact with outsiders and for whom knowledge of a rapidly changing world was passed on by word of mouth from ridge to ridge and across rushing streams.

Forster became a journalist after he left the country. He put his journalistic skills to good effect. There is opinion as well as description and analysis. For example, he believes PNG gained independence too soon. And he documents his observations and experiences in an entertaining manner.

He provided fresh insight about that time when Kiaps were most active, they had taken government into the bush and, in a sense, they were a government unto themselves. The problems they faced, the solutions they sought to bring to feuding tribes, their interaction with local people, how they related to their children and wives, the long lonely nights their young wives spent alone when their husbands were on long patrols are all dealt with.

And so, he takes us to the story of independence.

"In May 1972 Michael Somare had given the white dominated civil service, and many of the people of his country, a collective heart attack when he announced that PNG would be self-governing from December 1st 1973," Forster wrote.

Until then it had been assumed self-government would not be introduced until after the 1976 elections, with full independence trailing sometime after that. However, this was not the plan of the fathers of PNG independence, nor, as it turned out, of the Australian government.

Forster was a restless young man who over 50 years ago left cold county Northumberland to operate a sawmill as a volunteer in the isolated outpost of Bundi in the foothills of PNG's tallest mountain, Mt Wilhelm[6].

At first, he didn't know where PNG was, mistaking it for Sumatra in Indonesia. But it didn't take long to find out that he was headed for a place recently discovered to be inhabited by stone-age cultures, undiscovered valleys and an exotic people; a place of regular earthquakes and active volcanoes where muddy brown rivers meandered crazily from the mountains often to lose themselves in a series of coastal lakes and swamps. A rugged and beautiful country accessible either by foot or small aircraft landing awkwardly on dangerous apron-sized landing strips.

---

6 - 4,509 metres (14,793 ft) or 4.5 kilometres high.

After a 14,000-mile trip he did not enjoy, Forster finally landed in Port Moresby where the oppressive heat, dust and dilapidated airport failed even further to impress him. He then flew for two more hours to Madang and waited for three days before boarding something slightly larger than a model plane to take him to Bundi – perched on a hill and home to a government patrol post and a Catholic mission.

Like so many before him, Forster quickly engaged with this new country. He enjoyed flying between soaring peaks and along the rich valleys' peaks, levelling out above massed cloud before surfing through small gaps in the layer to the small airstrips below.

Forster had been in Bundi a week when he saw his first mud-covered village woman, naked to the waist towing a small pig on a length of string.

"Never before had I seen anyone so strange and I could not prevent myself chasing her down, skidding to a stop and pressuring her to stand in front of my shiny new camera. She posed readily enough for the astonished young man fresh from Hexhamshire. But I flinch at my reaction now.

"She had covered herself with mud because she was mourning a family death and was almost naked because she did not think it necessary to hide her body." That woman was any highlands woman of the time.

As Forster settled among the Bundi people and began to learn *Tok Pisin*, I was in Standard 3 at Kandep Primary T School learning how to speak English under the watchful eyes of a Frenchman.

It was to this general area in the then Western Highlands that Forster, by now a Kiap, came to work. After 18 months as a volunteer for the Catholic Church, he had gone back to England, married and migrated to Australia with his young wife, Paula.

In November 1971, his training at Australian School of Pacific Administration (ASOPA) over, Robert Forster the new Kiap was posted to Minj.

He enjoyed his time among the tall handsome people of the Wahgi Valley, rolling cigarettes and telling stories in their smoke-filled huts as he tried to understand them and their culture and trying his best to stop their tribal wars.

But self-government was approaching and the people of the highlands were worried, very worried.

The government phrase for local revolt on self-government day was 'civil commotion' and the mood in the villages was erratic. Forster suspected that, if there was to be trouble in his region, it would begin at Banz. He knew there was nothing the few Kiaps or police could do if trouble escalated.

"I would have been happy to stay if I was single but a secure family life did not mix with complex intercession between volatile village people and the new government's shifting demands," he recalls.

"Kiaps depended on bluff, reinforced by the implicit authority and neutrality of their white skins to maintain control, and too much of what was happening undermined it."

He asked for a transfer from Minj to a position on the coast. When it came through in April,1973 he left the Wahgi for Bereina in the Central District of Papua.

While the sub district office at Minj had been busy and cheerful, Bereina was the opposite – a tired, dust-covered, backwater inhabited by people who chewed buai and considered themselves more than ready for self-government.

When self-government arrived on 1 December 1973, Forster witnessed Josephine Abaijah, the leader of separatist group Papua Besena, declare independence for Papua. She raised her red and blue flag at Bereina in front of a few mildly enthusiastic people and almost as many journalists.

Nearby, hiding behind a barricade of guns in the Forster home, was almost the entire expatriate population at Bereina including the Assistant District Commissioner who proclaimed he was ready to fight. But when Abaijah left, the small crowd soon dispersed.

After six months in Bereina, a bored Forster pleaded for a transfer. A sympathetic District Commissioner posted him to Tapini in the Goilala area where he was quickly inundated with work – attending to murders and cult- related ritual killings.

He found life at Tapini good. The sun was pleasant. There was a well-maintained tennis court, a deep swimming pool fed by a mountain stream and a fine hotel with a terraced bar. The trade store was comprehensively stocked and planes landed regularly to deliver newspapers and mail from Port Moresby as well as frozen meat.

"There were three other white families with young children so socialising with peers was not a strain. The hydro-electricity supply was constant, and there was work for wives in the Post Office too. In PNG terms it earned a four star, even five-star rating," he recalls.

This changed when Forster took over the patrol post at Guari. Paula didn't want to go. The radio and generator were broken and the house in poor repair. Both her babies had arrived early and her third was expected in four months. There was no hospital at Guari.

Forster said Paula should leave PNG for England in February 1975. He would follow them in August the same year.

It wasn't until 1990 that Forster met another Papua New Guinean – a man from Mt Hagen who hugged him tightly as the two spoke together in *Tok Pisin*.

This is a fascinating book, which should be read by anybody who cares about the history of pre-independence Papua New Guinea – a time when the Kiap was king but, when he left, the bush grew back.

Robert Forster himself referred me to a reviewer for OnlineBookClub. org in the United States, a person named Kwahu who agreed the book should be read by historians and documentarians. He felt the contents of the book may not be known to many Papua New Guineans and therefore serves as a reference to their hidden history.

However, I am also interested in your response to the observation that "Papua New Guineans should have been allowed to choose whether they wanted a change or not".

By this I think Kwahu means the Europeans who were the country's first visitors should have sought village opinion before they imposed their own cultural imperatives on people who had lived undisturbed by global turbulence since pre-historical times.

As you know my own view is that it is impossible for Papua New Guineans, or anyone else, to hold back the tide of globalisation and that colonialisation was not a singular phenomenon but merely a forerunner of the ongoing, and unstoppable, cultural and economic global tide that threatens to engulf us all – wherever we live and whatever our ancestry may be, says Robert Forster.

Let truth be told that when Michael Thomas Somare died at age 84, many people in remote parts of the country still lived in isolation, not even a road reaching them. Despite these conditions independence was declared fifty years ago.

From a remote area in Kandep in Enga province, I know it was too early for me personally and my people to gain independence. I had outside contact for as long as I was in school. Imagine, just 11 years. There was nobody else from my village in school – just me.

I didn't go to a hospital when I was sick. A pig was sacrificed, thinking the cause of my illness was a dead uncle who had been killed in tribal warfare. I could have died. But luckily, I had recovered – to the delight of my relatives. That was the situation my people were in.

And just when I was about to complete Form Four, I was attending the official independence celebrations with Michael Somare at the helm. Then, I got drunk for the first time in my life in Nenk Pasul's house at Togauba Hill.

Last 50 Years & Onwards

That morning, I walked from Nenk Pasul's house, past the now empty Sir Hubert Murry Stadium, went through Hanubada, the big village and back to my college. When I met Eric, the first thing he did was to laugh as if I had committed a mortal sin. In 1974, he had come to Port Moresby Technical College when I went over to Lae Technical College. I caught up with him here in early 1975 when I transferred over when we had no electrical instructors at Lae.

Eric and I had been classmates at Kandep Primary and selected together to attend St Paul's Lutheran High School at Pausa in Wapenamanda in 1972 to do Form One. Nine of us had been selected including one girl – Salimbu Koka.

Much later, after we had left Idubada, Eric and I drank regularly, after John Yaka defeated Nenk Pasul in the 1977 national elections. My mother was from the Mamb tribe and I was related to John Yaka through blood. When he was appointed Minister for Justice, Eric Kombeakali worked for him as his First Secretary. Prior to that, he had trained as a High School teacher at Goroka Teachers College. I was working with the National Broadcasting Commission at the time and we used to catch up on the weekends.

But from my school days, some sad memories still linger in my mind. At least three of my school mates died, shattering the dreams and hopes of their parents. It could have happened to any of us, living away from our parents and relatives far up in the highlands.

At St Paul's High School, a Form one student from Lenki village near Wabag died after developing an illness in his liver. Our headmaster, Daniel Kunert noticed his eyes had turned severely yellow. The student wasn't concentrating in class so he was sent to Mambisanda Lutheran Hospital. A few days later, the school received the sad news that he had died. When we went home for holidays, classmates showed me where he had been buried at Lenki village directly opposite the current spare parts store and workshop run by Asian businessmen.

When I was on the coast doing my Form Three and Form Four, I heard one of our students from Kandep had jumped over the Pausa Cliffs because his parents could not afford to pay his school fees. He had been reminded constantly by the school administration when asking him when he was going to pay his school fees. And when nobody could help him, he had decided to end his life by jumping over the Pausa Cliffs.

Then in 1975, the independence year at Idubada Technical College, one of my classmates from East Sepik died. His name was Martin Trei. The night before, he had been running around the big playing field several times. When he finally sat down to rest, he vomited blood.

Next morning, when he complained about a throbbing pain in his heart, he was rushed to the Port Moresby General Hospital where he died a couple of days later. Five of us from our class went up, wrapped his body in some cloth and placed it in the morgue. We then went back and contributed small amounts of money towards the funeral expenses. Our class gave our small contribution to Sepik Students at the college. The Education Department organised repatriation of the body home for burial. Martin Trei was a top student, a bright young man whose life was cut short.

Most of us students were far from home doing Form Three and Form Four on the coast. Food was served well in the school mess. But we sometimes needed money to buy a bar of soap, an ice cream or soft drinks. We could turn to no one for a little pocket money. We had no option but to collect bottles. The school canteen paid 10toea for three empty bottles. That was big money at the time.

In Port Moresby though, enough *wantoks* from Kandep worked as casual employees in the city and some gave me pocket money. I never approached Nenk Pasul my tribal brother because he was always busy at home. He only came to Port Moresby for meetings. I think he paid less attention to the educational needs of his children. Not one of them made it in life from what I learnt. Much later, some of his many nephews from his many brothers graduated from universities.

On the other hand, Luluai Liu Omapu had been sending his children to school. He understood the importance of education more because he was exposed to other parts of the country and had seen children going to school.

Luluai Liu's first son, Kem worked with Rothmans of Pall Mall at Goroka. Tau Liu rose to the top and held important positions in the country. He served as Provincial Administrator of Enga province, Kerema in the Gulf province and later as a Public Service Commissioner. His brother, Moses Liu rose to the top as Managing Director of the PNG Development Bank, the position first occupied by Masket Iangalio before he entered politics to win the Wapenamanda seat. James Liu became a lawyer but later died at a young age. Many others from the Liu family succeeded in life too.

While still at high school, I developed an interest in photography. I saved up enough money and bought myself a polaroid camera. It was with that camera that I took a photo of my parents during the Christmas holidays in 1975.

That picture is still with me as a memory of my parents and my country which gained independence that year. I immortalised my parents by placing their picture holding their first granddaughter in one of my books, *I Can See My Country Clearly Now* published in 2016.

In adult life, I gave up the amber liquid, cigarettes, *buai* and certain other habits harmful to my health and the wellbeing of my young family.

I sometimes wonder what would have happened if I received the bad news about the complete destruction of my property if I was in a state of drunkenness? I am sure the story would have turned out negative. I am glad I was sober and far from home, in Port Moresby. I absorbed the shock, reassuring myself that the property can be redeveloped. And life was more precious than anything else on this planet. I knew revenge killings amplified the situation by creating more enemies, deaths, suffering and destruction.

The country was celebrating fifty years of independence and certainly, there was nothing for me to be happy about. My lifetime investment was gone. But God gave me two hands and a mind to choose between right and wrong. Choosing peace was the best decision I ever made in my life on the eve of my country's 50 years of independence anniversary celebrations.

If the people responsible for destroying my property realise they had made a mistake and decide to compensate me, that will be fine. But if they do not own-up, nature has a way of dealing with the truth.

I believe people in Enga will not keep on fighting and destroying each other. They will eventually put down their weapons and openly declare that fighting was bad. And surely leaders cannot keep mismanaging the country and milking it dry, pretending that everything is in order.

In Enga, people continue to face hardship and suffering. They have no one to blame except themselves. It seemed it was hard for leaders to offer any solutions in a situation where everybody, leaders included, appeared to have an attitude problem. If they all changed their mindsets, the province would transform itself to new heights.

If not, the style of leadership provided may not be conducive to the people's tastes and needs. If leaders were honest, they should admit their failures and consider resigning. Maybe the people did not like their leadership style. Why was there continuous fighting and destruction in Enga province? Rational leaders from around the world have resigned when it looked like they couldn't handle a given situation anymore.

Take for instance New Zealand Prime Minister, Jacinda Ardern who resigned during the time of COVID-19 pandemic. She shocked many of her people and leaders from around the world.

"I am leaving because with such a privileged role comes responsibility. The responsibility to know when you are the right person to lead and also when you are not. I know what this job takes. And I know that I no longer have enough in the tank to do it justice. It's that simple," said Prime Minister Jacinda Ardern before she vacated office. She was only 42 years of age.

"There is something other global leaders should take from this moment of gracefully bowing out while keeping reputations largely intact," experts said.

Grand Chief Sir Michael Thomas Somare and, Sir Julius Chan have run the country in a more graceful manner. They had their shortcomings. But their people voted them in continuously simply because they were honest and transparent.

Somare and Chan were in that first cabinet as soon as independence was gained. They were the first two men to become prime ministers and the last two men to die in old age while still serving their people as elected leaders. They have both left with their reputations intact.

In 1975 during the official independence celebrations, I aimlessly wandered around, mingling with the crowds, observing all the activities taking place in the main arena. If anything, I was more interested in the 100-man gun-salute consisting of all the armed forces and the various colorful cultural dances from around the country.

Now after fifty years, I wish I knew if people really understood what independence really meant. We, as a people inherited a beautiful, bountiful country blessed with an abundance of rich natural resources left to us by our ancestors.

I am inclined to think that it does not seem to have sunk in well with some groups of people like Engans. Do they know that we are an integral part of a country called Papua New Guinea and that it was up to us to develop our own province and enjoy benefits from resource developments like the Porgera gold mine in a peaceful manner?

Enga people fail to see neighboring Western Highlands, Jiwaka, Simbu and Eastern Highlands provinces prosper in economic growth from their coffee, tea and vegetables grown on a massive scale which they supply to Lae, Madang, Port Moresby and even the Wabag town market.

What have Engans done to show that the Porgera gold mine, one of the richest deposits outside South Africa, is located in their province?

Completely nothing! But only ruins of homes, gardens, rusting frames of vehicles, shops and the graveyards of the fallen warriors due to continuous tribal warfare and revenge killings in almost every part of the province.

Yet sons and daughters of these warriors, who have yet to experience and understand what it means to live in peace and harmony celebrated PNG's 50 years of independence. While some of our people like the Hewa, Yengis, Yambaitok and Penale still dwelled on the peripheries very much as their ancestors had done – hunting and gathering.

Not a single road has reached them in all these 50 years. Do they have a reason to celebrate independence? Do our leaders eat and dream well when such people continue to struggle on the edges of modern civilisation?

We, those of us living in the urban areas of our country, must work hard to connect and expose these groups of people still living in isolation. We must not force them further into the jungle when we fight each other. Let these people reach out to us, learn from us and grow our country together. Maramuni, a part of Wabag district, has recently been reached with a good road that will eventually link with the Sepik region.

Papua New Guineans must be thankful Australia did not stay long enough to exploit our rich natural resources. Except for the Paguna Copper mine, which spilled into an unfortunate civil war, every other mineral deposit in the country – gold, oil, gas, copper was left untouched for us to make our own decisions, to negotiate the best deals and to manage the benefits by ourselves.

Such was the historic case with the Porgera gold mine when Porgera landowners, Enga provincial government and National government all participated in the negotiations for their share in a major resource project in the country.

Who but the soft-spoken humble Premier of Enga province, Ned Laina was at the helm to achieve the major milestone for his people.

Unfortunately, Ned Laina lost his seat to Danely Tindiwi in the elections. He never benefited in any way from Porgera Gold Mine nor from the Enga Provincial Government.

He died quietly, an ordinary man on 29th March, 2025. But the work he did to benefit the people of Enga in a major resource project will be his legacy.

Premier Ned Laina Set Precedent in Mining Law & Policy in PNG

I can still remember when Engan leaders were happy when Porgera gold mine paid the first dividends of K500,000 in November, 1990 – that's within the first three months of the Porgera Gold Mine operations.

It brought smiles on the faces of Premier, Danely Tindiwi, provincial member Kensary Lowaipa, Administrator Luke Kembol, provincial government members, senior public servants and the Legal Officer Harry Deckley.

The cheques were the fruit of their hard work, or rather Ned Laina after playing a major part in formulating the Porgera Agreements – the first of its kind in Papua New Guinea since independence.

Enga Provincial member for Porgera, Kensary Lowaipa picked up two cheques, one for K58,344.20 for the children of the landowners who had been relocated from the Special Mining Lease area. It was to be deposited into a trust account.

The second cheque was for K46,675.44, a royalty payment for the landowners. The reminder of the K500,000 dividend went to the Enga Provincial Government.

The Enga Provincial Government has received K335,035,785 in royalties from the Porgera Gold Mine since it began production in 1990. Since July 1996, the mine had paid royalties at a rate of 2.0% of the value of sales, less selling expenses.

Prior to that, the royalty rate was 1.25%. The Enga Provincial Government initially received 77% of these royalties, and since July 1995, had received 50%. Much of these funds were directed to the Ipatas Foundation at the request of the Enga Provincial Government.

The Porgera Joint Venture, in its annual financial information report in 2019 stated that the mine also provided voluntary financial and material support to a large number of events and institutions such as the Enga Show, the Enga Mioks, and the Ipatas Cup. Over the life of the mine, millions of kina had been provided to support these and other initiatives and important public facilities in Enga – often at the request of Enga Governor, Grand Chief Sir Peter Ipatas.

The Enga Provincial Government has also received hundreds of millions of kina in net revenue from its equity interest in the mine, through its joint ownership of 5% of the Porgera joint venture equity, held by Minerals Resources Enga, which is held equally by the Porgera Special Mining Lease Landowners and the Enga Provincial Government. This share of the Porgera Joint Venture has been held by the Enga Provincial Government for the entire operating life of the mine.

This is a lot of mining revenue for a backwater province like Enga. The credit should go to former Premier Ned Laina who did the hard work of achieving a major milestone in mining law and policy in Papua New Guinea.

A former Kiap, Ned Laina was elected into office at the precise moment the win of lucrative benefits from Porgera gold mine was about to start operations. He set Enga province on the right course for a bright future.

He was ably assisted by Harry Derkley, the Australian born Enga Provincial Government lawyer. He formulated the Porgera Agreements which, for the first time, involved the provincial government and landowners in formal negotiations over the development of a major mining project in the country.

Premier Ned Laina was so busy with the agreements in Port Moresby that he was not able to attend his mother, Sakame Limbait's funeral. After the job was completed, he was only able to visit his mum's grave at Kaindan village, a couple of kilometers from Kompiam government station.

Ned Laina knew he was fulfilling his mum's vision that, one day, he would be recognised and she made sure he attended school each day even when his father opposed her. He wanted his son to stay in the village.

The historic agreements were the Mining Development Contract between the National Government and the Porgera Joint Venture partners, between the National Government and the Enga Provincial Government and Porgera Landowners and between the Enga Provincial Government and Porgera landowners.

When the mining agreements were finally signed on 12th May at Parliament House in Port Moresby, Ned Laina's name was exalted province-wide. He was enjoying much publicity.

Apart from involving landowners and provincial governments in formal negotiations, Ned Laina had also secured contracts to ensure proceeds would be utilised for the benefit of his people in the billion-kina gold project, one of the ten top gold producing mines in the world.

In addition to normal royalty payments amounting to more than K400million, the national government had agreed to a special support grant of about K35 million over the next 20 years, and would also help the provincial government and landowners acquire share equity worth a further K50 million.

Premier Ned Laina's achievements caused major repercussions within the mining industry and created important precedents in mining law and policy in Papua New Guinea.

Previously, in the case of Bougainville, OK Tedi and Misima, the only formal negotiations had been between the national government and the multi-national mining companies.

This resulted in the national government setting up a 'Mining Development Forum' in each major mining project to enable landowners and provincial governments to participate in negotiations.

Ned Laina was not known in the country until the signing of the historic agreements. If provincial elections were held immediately after the agreements were signed, he would have easily won with an overwhelming majority.

After the agreements were signed, Premier Ned Laina asked me to accompany his team on a tour of the province to explain to the people what the agreements meant. He also wanted to formally announce the setting up of the new Enga Corp Pty Ltd which would win contracts at the new mine on their behalf. He also told the people not to involve themselves in continuous tribal warfare.

Ned Laina's touring party included Deputy Premier, Frank Taso, Education Minister Theo Yange, Law and Order Minister Don Anjo and Councilor Peter Ipatas who had just been appointed an interim director of the new Enga Corp Pty Ltd. The Enga provincial government was given K500,000 by the national government as seed money – when Paul Pora was Finance Minister, to start the business entity.

Enga Corp Pty Ltd teamed up with Curtain Brothers (PNG) Pty Ltd to sign into existence a major joint venture agreement. The joint venture would obtain many of Porgera gold mine's earth moving and engineering contracts and the financial benefits that would come with it.

Put simply, Curtain Brothers had the technical expertise and Enga Development Corporation had the political muscle.

A day before the joint venture was signed into existence, the joint venture was awarded contracts that were worth over K100 million.

The new joint venture was tasked to construct the new Karik airstrip, construct the new town site, develop the mine's limestone pit, and build new haul roads. The new venture also expected more contracts during the life of the mine based on the experience and track record of Curtain Brothers.

Enga Corp Pty Ltd was incorporated for the expressed purpose of getting contracts from Porgera gold mine. Chairman, Ned Laina said the joint venture could remain for the entire life of the mine and beyond.

Premier Ned Laina knew the Enga Provincial government would secure a significant amount of revenue for its annual budget from the lucrative contracts. And with separate royalty benefits, he knew that the provincial government would have enough money to develop the whole province and lift the living standards of its people. When he addressed the people, he spoke to them with confidence.

At Mapumanda, a pyrethrum grower told the premier: 'We are happy to see you here. If we were dogs all our tails would be wagging and you would be covered in dust. We see that you are an honest man and have achieved much for us and generations to come.'

This kind of recognition was uniform throughout the areas he visited – Wapenamanda, Wabag, Laiagam, Kandep Maramuni and Yengis. He was telling people that his government would have enough money to bring unapparelled change never before experienced in Enga province. He told the people to first stop their 'silly game of death'- tribal warfare – which was impeding smooth progress.

"I have done this for the future, for our children. Their future will be determined by what we do today. Fighting is a sickness in this province. Open your eyes to what is happening around you. Stop fighting and do something worthwhile for yourselves."

Ned Laina was a member of the Seventh Day Adventist church. He believed God had blessed Enga with rich gold deposits in the province.

It was anticipated that, after the Porgera gold project started production, Mt Kare would follow suit if there was enough extractable gold there.

At the time, several Prospecting Authority (PA) licenses had been granted to mining companies to conduct feasibility studies in the province.

"Enga was last, a disadvantaged province, but now we are up there somewhere. God has blessed us. God blessed other provinces with copra, coffee, tea and other natural resources. But He blessed Enga with gold."

Premier Ned Laina was a man of few words. But he listened to people and made decisions without influence. He wanted his 200,000 people to listen, and believe that he would bring equal benefits to all the districts.

He was the last born in a family of four children, two boys and two girls. His mother Sakame was from Yokora village in Wabag.

Following in his father's footsteps, he married Julie Pakau also from Teremanda in Wabag district. He also fathered four children – two boys and two girls.

Premier Laina completed his primary education in 1968 and went to Tusbab High School in Madang. He spent the next three years at Mt Hagen High School. After he completed Form Four, he was accepted at the Administrative College to train as a Kiap. That was in 1972, three years before independence.

His first posting was to Laiagam as the patrol officer where he remained till 1979. The following year, he went back to the Administrative College to complete a two-year diploma course in public administration.

After he completed the course, he was posted to Kandep as District Manager. Based on his work performance, the Kandep Local Level Government passed a resolution to keep him there. But, to everybody's surprise, Ned Laina was transferred to the Sepik.

The Kandep people were dismayed. They protested, resulting in 300 of them marching into Wabag to complain to the authorities demanding that Ned Laina remain in Kandep.

Ned Laina did not go to the Sepik but received a threatening letter ordering him to move to Laiagam. He had no option but to move but did not stay in Laiagam for long. In September of 1983, he resigned to contest the premiership race in the provincial elections.

But there was no election because Premier Danely Tindiwi had been suspended for misappropriation of public funds and was later found guilty and jailed for seven years.

While Tindiwi was serving his sentence, and the provincial government suspension was lifted, the elections were conducted in 1986. Ned Laina was declared winner. He received 14,979 votes, nearly 3000 votes more than Malipu Tindiwi, brother of Danely Tindiwi.

Ned Laina admitted that his father was not a big man in the Tangaip tribe of Kompiam. Nor had he ever dreamed of becoming a politician. So, what was it that prompted him to stand for election?

"It's a long story', he told me. 'First, I was pressured by Kandep and Laiagam people to contest the elections based on my work performance. They also saw that I was going to be transferred to the Sepik not because I had committed any crimes, but for petty reasons initiated by Premier Danely Tindiwi."

Laina said he was forced to move out of Kandep because he had refused to allow Premier Danely Tindiwi to use a government house on the Kandep government station.

"I pointed out to him that a well-equipped rest house was available. But the premier refused to stay there."

As a result, Ned Laina was told to pack up and go to Laiagam – which he did. While there, he didn't intend to resign to contest the provincial election against Danely Tindiwi. But people from Laiagam and Kandep pressured him to nominate.

"I resigned because of pressure from the people of Kandep and Laiagam. They saw I was a hard worker and pressured me to resign and stand for election."

He finally gave in, resigned and won.

One of his main priorities was to see an end to tribal warfare. But he admitted, he was powerless to wipe it out completely. It seemed to him that both the provincial and national governments had to apply a significant amount of force on the people to give up killing and destroying each other.

He suggested one option. He wanted to approach the national government to seek authorisation to raise and maintain his own police force to counter tribal warfare in the province

"I could change Enga province overnight, if I was given authority to have my own police force. There are many killings and the police are ineffective in dealing with serious crime. This means there is no control over law & order issues. They are not making arrests,' he said.

He could not give direct orders because politicians have no jurisdiction over police operations. But he would fight to have his own police force, just as, in Australia, each state has its own.

"In Australia, they have state and federal police which work very well. I can't see why the National government will not allow my government to establish our own police force in the province?"

It wasn't a surprise that he was successful. He had already achieved a lot of 'firsts' under his name. He established the first University Center, the first Tokples Preschool program, the first community school agriculture program and established the Enga Vegetable Marketing Depot, all of which did not exist anywhere else in the Highlands region.

He had even ordered the Department of Personnel Management to withdraw all the appointments in a Department of Enga restructure exercise because he believed nepotism had been involved. He wanted to see the best qualified officers recruited to serve the people with efficiency.

Now he had involved a provincial government and landowners in a major resource project, the giant world class Porgera gold mine.

Premier Ned Laina had reason to be worried about the law-and-order situation in Enga because he knew significant revenue from the mine would enable the provincial government to undertake many major projects that would require police protection.

But before he could approach the national government to establish a police force based on the Australian arrangement, the provincial elections were on again.

By then, former premier, Danely Tindiwi had been released from prison earlier than expected. He nominated and soundly defeated Ned Laina.

It was Danely Tindiwi who welcomed Prime Minister Rabbie Namaliu at the official opening of the multi-million- kina Porgera gold mine on 20th October, 1990.

It was Tindiwi who received K500,000 dividends from the gold project in only three months of operations at Porgera.

It was Tindiwi who would budget the royalty payments the provincial government would receive. And income generated from the lucrative contracts won by the Enga Corp Pty Ltd partnership with Curtain Brothers.

But Tindiwi did not last long to continue enjoying the benefits with the people. Three years later, on 12th April, 1993, he was suspended a second time.

Ned Laina, who had worked so hard, disappeared in the background. The people had put him down. But he left with something more respectable – he exited public office with his good name intact.

Tindiwi's government was suspended and he was jailed for seven years, Governor Jeffery Balakau had been dismissed from office and Governor Peter Ipatas was found guilty on 16 counts and charged K1000 each. He was lucky to escape dismissal.

Now, Governor Sir Peter Ipatas who Ned Laina had appointed as interim director of the Enga Corp Pty Ltd gradually took over reins of the Enga Provincial Government and has held onto power since, winning consecutive elections.

Sir Peter Ipatas & The New Porgera Gold Mine Deal

In 2023, the Porgera gold mine restarted operations after being closed for three years. It had cost PNG up to a staggering K26billion for as long as the mine remained closed.

Meanwhile, in negotiations that went on to restart the mine, Enga Governor, Sir Peter had worked really hard to involve the landowners and the Enga Provincial Government with the national government to own 51 per cent stake in a new deal when the mine reopened.

It represents a lot of money for Enga province. And the life of the gold mine was expected to last for the next 20 years.

Governor Sir Peter Ipatas was a fearless orator who spoke his mind—and to the point as he tried to drive his message across to the people. There appeared to be nobody in the province who could topple him at election times.

Hundreds of people at Wapenamanda Airport swarmed an Airlines PNG chartered aircraft, packing it up like sardines in a tin while crew members looked on helplessly in August 2004.

Ipatas apologised to Airlines PNG management saying the incident was unfortunate pointing out that the behavior of the people was not criminal, but opportunistic — just trying their luck for a free lift to Port Moresby knowing it was a chartered aircraft.

Ipatas had flown in on that aircraft after narrowly escaping dismissal from public office when a Leadership Tribunal found him guilty on 16 counts of misconduct in office charges. Over thirty-two thousand Kina (K32,000) was raised by supporters within minutes of the Leadership Tribunal handing down its decision to fine Ipatas K16,000—one thousand kina each for 16 counts he was found guilty.

That was a big win – a major political victory for Governor Ipatas because many expected him to be dismissed from holding public office.

Ipatas had said previously that he was "a hard man to put down" – a man who had proven over and over again that he was capable of surviving when all odds were against him.

But how did he rise to power?

Soon after withdrawing from studies from the University of Papua New Guinea in the mid-1970s, he came home to his Irelya village in Wabag and started small businesses, which included a village tavern.

Ipatas was, at the same time, elected by his people to be their councilor in the Wabag Local Level Government Council and served consistently to gradually become its President.

He was very vocal on many issues that affected the people and kept the provincial government under Danley Tindiwi and later Ned Laina on their toes.

At the time, the provincial government system did not favor the National Government when numerous provincial governments were suspended and their premiers jailed one after the other for misappropriation of public funds.

The Enga Provincial Government under Danely Tindiwi was suspended twice—the first on 9th February, 1984 which led to him being jailed for seven years.

The second suspension, again under Tindiwi, occurred on 12th April, 1993.

During that period, extending into 1995, the government reforms were being introduced and one member in the Constitutional Review Committee that introduced the new system was none other than Wabag Local Level Government President, Cr Peter Ipatas.

The reforms paved the way for council presidents to become members of provincial assemblies and regional members became automatic governors – performing dual roles as governors and members of parliament.

The title 'premier' was done away with and no more elections were held to elect provincial members of constituencies.

So, on 8th August, 1995 the Interim Enga Provincial Government members were sworn in. Hon Jeffery Balakau who was the Regional Member was sworn in as Governor and Tindiwi who was the Premier became his deputy.

The rest of the assembly members consisted of the five Open Members and Council Presidents among whom was, of course, Cr Peter Ipatas.

But by late 1995, the Enga Provincial Government was suspended for a record third time, now under the new reforms, which led to the dismissal of Governor Jeffery Balakau.

Once again Danely Tindiwi rose to his former top seat as acting Governor—but did not last long. Peter Ipatas, whom he had appointed as his deputy, knocked him down through a successful court action.

And so Ipatas became acting Governor leading up to the 1997 national elections which he won very easily. But three years later, in 2001 the Enga Provincial Government was suspended for a record fourth time – which Ipatas fought vigorously to successfully get it reinstated.

When the people saw him win this court battle – where Tindiwi and Balakau had failed to fight for their rights – Ipatas returned to power for a second term in the 2002 national elections.

But the attempt to get his character and ability to run a government into disrepute continued when he was referred to the Leadership Tribunal in 2004 over allegations of misconduct in office charges.

Yet again the people saw him winning when he returned as their governor after being fined the K16,000. There was feasting and jubilation right across the province. However, an appeal from the Public Prosecutor for the decision to be reviewed was pending, a move viewed by supporters as a political maneuver to destroy him in the next national elections.

But true to his character, Ipatas did not waver to that impending threat but registered his own political party—the Peoples Party (PP) and put up his hand to become the next Prime Minister. He and his party executives were traveling extensively throughout the country to identify candidates to endorse under the PP banner.

"Somare is a policeman's son. I am a driver's son. Our fathers served the Kiaps" Ipatas said. "Somare has been PM for a long time and I respect him very much. But what mistake will I make to aim for the top job?"

On the home front, those likely to oppose Ipatas included former Enga Regional MP, Paul Paken Torato of Laiagam, Michael Yangao Pupu from Wapenamanda, Fr Paul Kanda from Wabag, Poko Kandapaki from Wabag and more candidates were expected to nominate against him. But he easily won back his seat and retained power.

But when everybody else was expecting to benefit from the rich development of the multi-billion Porgera gold mine, the landowners were overwhelmed with all the rapid change that was taking place as soon as the Special Mining Lease Agreements had been signed. A gold rush at Mt Kare drew thousands of people to the rich alluvial fields by foot and by helicopter.

Some people thought the world was going to end. But that did not happen. What happened was that the Porgera valley was transformed into a killing field. There was simply too much death and suffering in the valley and it was hard to document all the losses.

I won't indulge myself to talk about the prolonged conflict in the valley made worse with illegal miners and opportunists fighting security forces and burning company property.

But it must be mentioned that there was a serious leadership crisis in the Porgera/Paiela district soon after the gold mine was reopened. The situation was made worse when the newly elected member of Parliament Maso Karipe, died on 7th November, 2023.

It was interesting to note that the Porgera gold mine under new arrangements was reopened a month later on 22nd December, 2023.

No attempt was made by the national government to conduct an immediate by-election. Enga Governor, Grand Chief Sir Peter Ipatas and the other five elected members did not pressure the government to conduct a by-election knowing that Porgera is a volatile district.

The Porgera gold mine is far from the capital city, Port Moresby, and the government cannot depend solely on the security forces to keep the mine functioning. Local leadership was needed.

The Porgera people were in a vulnerable situation. With their duly elected leader dead, they could not take their problems to anybody.

Two illegal miners were shot dead by security forces inside the main pit area in early March, 2025. The relatives dug a huge ditch across the highway at Yonge village in Laiagam where the illegal miners were from.

With only one highway to move supplies to the Porgera gold mine, the task ahead was hard since everybody was dependent on the mine. Illegal mining had become the source of income for many people.

There was no leader the people could go to with their problems or to talk on their behalf on the floor of parliament. They appeared to be hopelessly lost.

Even when the mine started operations, the people were lost. But finally, after so much loss and hardship in the Porgera valley, writs were issued for a by-election for the Porgera-Paiela electorate.

On 24 April, 2025 nominations opened together with Local level Government elections in Enga province and throughout the country. The people were campaigning when this book was prepared for publication. Among the candidates was late Member's son, Gidron Maso Karipe.

I now draw attention to a local Porgeran tribal leader with whom I spoke when the mine started operations. His name was Philipolo Oko.

He might provide some clues as to why Porgera people and Engans in general behaved the way they did. They rushed to engage in tribal war or attack security forces as if there was no tomorrow, no family, no property or no possessions at all to worry about.

The Porgera Gold Mine was also a sitting duck which could be forced to shut down if genuine landowners were not relocated and the illegal miner issue resolved with a duly elected leader at the forefront. Otherwise, the mining township of Porgera may continue to see death and destruction – the sort of situation which people like Philipolo Oko thought may lead to the end of the world

Facing The End of The World

Philipolo Oko was born into a primitive society many years ago. He grew up at Painadak village in Porgera, Enga province.

He was the second-born in a family of three boys. Oko, his father was a happy man in the village because three sons meant added strength to the family and tribe. He had lots of land and proudly showed his sons the clan boundaries, giving each a portion of land that they would have to work when they grew up.

It didn't occur to him

When he was about 10, Philipolo encountered Kiaps coming to his area. He also saw prospectors searching for a shiny stone they called 'gol' in the Porgera and Kogai rivers not far from his village. This was in the period between 1938 when gold was first discovered in the Porgera valley.

Philipolo, like his father, was ignorant of these developments for he was very much a product of traditional teachings. So, he concentrated on learning skills like house building, gardening, rearing pigs and attending to village affairs with his father. At other times, he went into the nearby mountains to hunt for the marsupials and cassowaries so abundant in the area.

In adulthood, he married four wives- from Porgera, Paiela, Kandep and Tari, who bore him thirteen children, five girls and eight boys. Philipolo was content, for he was following in his father's footsteps. With many wives and much wealth, he soon became a 'big man' in the Pulumani tribe.

But he was rather late in realising that the life he knew was now on the verge of extinction.

The whole of the Porgera valley was to catapult into world headlines, all because of the shiny stone he had seen prospectors searching for as a youth. The impact on his life was immense.

Old tribal beliefs and customs became meaningless to him. Philipolo saw streams of people coming into Porgera on their way to the gold rush.

Every single day, he heard the deafening sounds of helicopters, as if the Vietnam War was being re-fought in Porgera. Prices of goods soared sky-high and simple 'kanakas' like himself were buying expensive vehicles.

He could not explain why all this was happening. Raised in a superstitious society, he had one possible answer – that this was a signal that the world would soon end.

So, he convinced himself that he should give up his land together with his house, gardens and the yar and pandanus nut trees, he had painstakingly planted in his lifetime. He decided he should enjoy himself as much as possible on the proceeds.

Philipolo gave up his land to Porgera Joint Venture (PJV), the Porgera gold developers. He was assured that the company would pay compensation for everything disrupted as a result of a gold mine on his land. He was also told that he would receive regular royalty payments throughout the life of the mine.

"I am sorry I gave up my land and property. I thought the world was going to end. I realised I was wrong but I cannot do anything now. The mine must therefore go ahead," he said firmly.

Philipolo wasn't the only one – lots of men from the Pulumani, Tieni, Angalaini and Timiropi tribes had also given up their land to the Porgera Joint Venture.

The venture was managed by Placer (PNG) Pty Ltd, a subsidiary of Placer Pacific Ltd. The other partners, Highlands Gold Properties Pty Ltd and PGC (Papua New Guinea) Pty Ltd, have invested more than K80 million in the billion-kina project.

When the special mining lease was granted by the national government, the company had plans to spend another K663 million to construct the required facilities which included an underground mine, an ore-processing plant and supporting infrastructure.

Construction had already begun and it was anticipated that the job would be completed within three years, during which time employment would peak at 1,200 people.

A significant package of community improvements and support was provided by the mine development. Community facilities such as the airport, police station and road system were upgraded.

In addition, company officials said K4million was to be set aside for possible future expenditure on community services and facilities.

PJV was to continue providing funds in a drive to educate as many Engans as possible, particularly Porgerans. The current business development program set up to provide management and guidance assistance to Porgera people involved in small scale business enterprise was to be contributed.

But the most significant aspect of the whole mine development was the relocation of the landowners whose land and property fell within the special Mining lease (SM) zone. More than 3000 people were relocated in the largest exodus of people in the history of mine development in PNG.

PJV built modern houses at a cost of K14,000 each for landowners whose homes and property had been destroyed to make way for construction of the main gold processing plant.

The houses had four bedrooms, a bathroom, an outside toilet, a 500-gallon water tank which led to a sink in the kitchen with a wood stove.

The company had plans to build 320 of these houses of which 140 had been completed with 120 of them occupied. And a further 100 houses were still under construction.

In addition, landowners had been paid K1,400 for land they had given up, K1000 for general disruption and payments for every yar or pandanus nut trees destroyed.

While more than K17million had already been spent, company officials declined to reveal the expected total cost of the re-location exercise. But they said that, on the whole, this was one of the best deals landowners had struck with the company.

Philipolo Oko secured three of these modern houses to accommodate his large family – one under his eldest son's name with his mother from Paiela, another for himself and three wives and children. The third house, Philipolo said, was for the eldest daughter and her husband. But still, he wanted another two houses to accommodate his other two wives and children.

The Philipolo family was among the first to be moved up to the Pulumani re-location site at Anawe in February that year. I found him sitting on the steps to one of his houses smoking a roll of *mutrus* (tabacco) with one of his wives.

I joined him on the steps and started a conversation. No sooner was I seated than all his children, wives and visitors surrounded us. I realised how large a number of people he had to look after.

Living with him was Mr Luke Yakema and his family of seven. Mr Yakema was a former Aid Post Orderly (APO) who had resigned to go to the gold rush at Mt Kare but had since returned when the gold ran out. He said he was now waiting on the company to get himself a new house.

Philipolo Oko complained that he felt embarrassed sending visitors away, particularly when it was bedtime because his house was always overcrowded.

He declared: "In Enga we do not send visitors away. To send them away is inhuman. So, I just tell them to sleep on the floor, which is much smoother than a wooden bed in the 'hausman' or houses for men only".

Almost all landowners in the relocation area put on radiant smiles when I asked them how they felt about living in modern houses.

PJV had recruited a welfare officer to help these people adjust to their new surroundings.

Susan Bonnel, a long-time resident of Papua New Guinea, had become familiar with the life-styles and culture of Enga people when she was involved in the pyrethrum project in Laiagam from 1966 – 1977. In a few weeks she had taught the relocated women basic housekeeping skills.

"The women are proud of their homes. They seem happy," Susan said. But we must tell them that you cannot pour pig-grease into a modern sink."

One of the major problems Philipolo encountered was the separation from his eldest brother and four other relatives who remained in their old village of Painadak. One of them, Mulu Munakap had come to see him.

Mr. Munukap said that he felt insecure with only four relatives because they would be easy targets in the event of a tribal fight.

"In former times, we felt safe. We were close to each other but now we feel afraid and our tribe seems fragmented," he said.

I asked Philipolo if any of the other tribes involved in the relocation exercise were enemies of the Pulumani tribe.

He answered almost immediately that one of the relocated tribes was in fact a traditional enemy and added: "We Pulumani are enemies of this tribe. If trouble comes than we will fight."

"That means your new houses will be burnt down," I said.

"Fighting does not care about women, pigs or whatever. We fight," he replied with a grin spread across his face.

Indeed, Philipolo was right. With an increase in people concentrated in the Porgera valley, the mine was plagued by violence between former enemies, warlords, illegal miners and landowners. Much death and destruction occurred.

But I do not wish to indulge in that but on the death of one of the greatest men, the country has seen – Grand Chief Sir Michael Thomas Somare.

He had envisioned that when he declared independence for the country fifty years ago, he hoped the people would live in peace and harmony with each other.

I sometimes wonder what went through the great man's mind when he heard about all of the problems in Porgera.

I knew Sir Michael personally. He came to Kombolos to endorse late Nenk Pasul under the PANGU Party banner in 1977 when Nenk lost to John Yaka.

He flew to Kandep in a chopper with Masket Iangalio to endorse me in the 1997 national elections under the National Alliance ticket. Jimson Sauk who was the incumbent MP, retained his seat.

Five years previously, I had been with Sir Mchael at the United Nations General Assembly meeting in New York in September, 1991 when he nominated to be elected 46th President of the United Nations General Assembly. But we lost and Mrs. Lohia Renagi, wife of the PNG Ambassador to the United Nations cried. The few of us men felt the emotion as well but did not show it.

Much later, I had to cry alongside with people from all over the country when the great man passed on. I formally went to the *haus krai* or funeral at the Sir John Guise Stadium with other Engans living in the city together with our leaders.

The Death of Sir Michael Thomas Somare: 'Father of the Nation'

I wiped away some tears when I saw two elderly men of the same height and age smile at each other and hug tightly as best friends do after missing each other for a long time.

One of the two men, Sir Michael Thomas Somare died on 26th February, 2021. The other gentleman Sir Julius Chan followed him five years later on 30th January, 2025 at Huris, New Ireland province.

Both men had attained independence together. Both were prime ministers and served the country all their lives.

I was in Port Moresby when Sir Michael Somare died. I was able to join mourners inside the Sir John Guise Stadium and watched a sorrowful video of the two great leaders farewelling each other at Kavieng airport.

I saw both these men proudly deliver speeches, meeting important dignitaries like Prince Charles, Gough Whitlam and many others who had come to witness Papua New Guinea gain independence from Australia.

Indeed, they were best friends – two of the country's founding fathers, Grand Chief Sir Michael Somare and Sir Julius Chan. They probably knew this was their last time to be together and wave farewell in Kavieng, New Ireland province.

The video was played as part of the funeral program, on the big screen, where hundreds of mourners from Enga filled to capacity the stadium at the haus krai or funeral home.

I am sure former Kandep MP, Jimson Sauk who sat with me wiped away some tears too. We knew these two men very well, tireless men of integrity who had been returned to parliament for a lifetime by their people.

We sat through to the end of the proceedings at the *haus krai* which lasted for over four hours. It was Enga's turn on Friday 5th March to mourn along with Manus and the Autonomous Region of Bougainville (AROB) in the two-week long national mourning period set aside for the death of the man who led PNG to independence.

A positive outcome of Sir Michael Somare's death was a display of unity among Enga's elected leaders, civil servants, business leaders and people living in the city. They had turned up in huge numbers painted in white clay to cry and pay their last respects.

Who would have expected to see Enga Governor Sir Peter Ipatas, Sir John Pundari, Don Polye, Rimbink Pato, Sam Abal, Dr Lino Tom would walk arm-in-arm to the funeral home?

Engans could be fierce rivals on the battle field or on the political front, but they know instinctively when to hold hands and come together. Today they demonstrated respect and humility and expressed deep sorrow for the passing of a great man whose departure was felt by the whole nation – like the tremor of an earth quake.

The Engans had come prepared to pour their heart out. But there was no member of the Somare family in sight to whom they could really express their emotions, deliver speeches and present gifts as is custom in Enga province.

Only East Sepik Governor Allan Bird and Aitape Lumi MP, Patrick Pruaitch were present to receive them.

Nevertheless, Sam Abal, Isaac Lupari, Sir Salamo Injia, Don Polye and Governor Sir Peter Ipatas reminisced their past experiences with the great leader. Some of the events, like the hijacking of his government, was so controversial but the great man had absorbed it all.

Each spoke highly of Sir Michael Thomas Somare and likened him to Nelson Mandela of South Africa, George Washington of America and Ben Gurion of Israel, visionary leaders who always had the people at heart.

Governor Sir Peter Ipatas then presented an undisclosed amount of cash contribution on behalf of Enga people to his counterpart Allan Bird to help the people of East Sepik people with their *haus krai* in Wewak.

If there was anything that could be deduced or predicted from the presentations, the Father of the Nation had united the Enga leaders and future prospects for their province looked promising.

Moderator of the Enga segment of the proceedings, Peter Mision Yaki nailed it when he said Grand Chief Sir Michael Thomas Somare had united PNG not only as a people from a thousand different tribes but also through blood.

He then introduced a confident young girl of eight years whose father is from Enga and mother from Manus and with grandparents of Enga and New Ireland heritage.

She is Pauline Wapen Mango, a 3rd grader at Lahara Avenue school in Boroko. She stood in front of a packed house and recited her poem from memory.

Grand Chief Sir Michael Thomas Somare had visited Enga frequently, starting in 1973 as chief minister. He was met at Wapenamanda airport by Pato Kakaraya. I remember following them towards the Waso stores.

Somare was wearing his familiar laplap, or sulu and wore on his feet a pair of leather thongs.

The year before, Sir Tei Abal had come to Pausa Lutheran High School where I completed Form One or grade 7. He said Michael Somare was trying to accomplish the impossible by trying to 'chew sugarcane and sweet potatoes' at the same time.

'Wanpela man ino inap kaikai kakau wantaim suka. Wanpela blo daunim na narapela bilong tromoi,' Sir Tei said figuratively in Tok Pisin meaning that PNG had to experience self-government for some time before independence could be considered. But Somare was rushing it when much of the country was not yet developed.

Two years later, on September 16, 1975 Michael Thomas Somare won through and successfully attained independence for the country.

At that time, Pauline the young poet's grandfather, Paul Mango was a student at Sogeri National High school.

He was one of many students who were dressed in traditional attire to escort visiting foreign dignitaries during the celebrations. Now, 46 years later, his grandchild was reciting a poem at Sir Michael Thomas Somare's funeral home.

Nenk Pasul MBE of Kandep and Sir Pato Kakaraya of Wapenamanda were staunch supporters of Somare and his PANGU Party.

A couple of days before Sir Michael passed on, my new book 'Victory Song of Pingeta's Daughter' was released. The great man is featured several times, together with all prime ministers except Sir Mekere Mourata who have all visited Enga at different stages of its development.

Australian prime minister Bob Hawk graces the pages too, meeting public servants and local leaders on a visit to the Porgera gold mine.

Cr Paul Kurai, was branch president when Sir Michael's National Alliance party won four of the six seats in Enga during the 2002 national elections.

Sir Michael Somare demonstrated what leadership was all about when he came with his full cabinet to conduct a National Executive Council meeting in Wabag as if to share power with the people.

The great leader chose to sleep at Pawas village in the humble home of late Sir Tei Abal who had been his ace political rival during PNG's formative years.

Later, Somare handed over the reins of the top executive post to Sir Tei's son Sam Abal before he left for Singapore to receive prolonged medical treatment.

I've had my share of personal contact with the great man too. I saw him come to endorse Nenk Pasul as a Pangu Party candidate in our village at Kombolos in 1977.

Twenty years later, he came to endorse me as a National Alliance party candidate in 1997. Jimson Sauk won back the seat to serve a third term before Don Polye defeated him in 2002.

If I had had the opportunity to speak at the funeral home, I could have talked about a time in New York when Mrs. Renagi Renagi Lohia, wife of the PNG Ambassador to the United Nations wept bitterly after Somare lost the race for the mainly ceremonial role as President of the 46th UN General Assembly.

Mrs. Lohia and her daughter were the only women in our small group as we stood at the gate of the UN building as Sir Michael Somare shook hands and calmly thanked foreign dignitaries who had supported him.

It could have been a perfect independence gift for us – the few Papua New Guineans if Somare had won, for it was September, 1991.

Then we walked across the street to a restaurant and sat together at two tables to have lunch and discussed how we had lost a race that we had all been certain to win.

Sir Michael was the hot favorite from the start but managed only 47 votes against Saudi Arabia's Samir Shihabi's 83.

"We lost out because of Europe or Africa,' Ambassador Lohia said bluntly. He believed many of the African leaders were bribed. "They were bought off."

Then Education Minister Utula Samana blamed the defeat on the Gulf War coalition partners and Western Europe.

"They voted for Saudi Arabia as a way of saying 'thank you' for the role it played in the Gulf War," he said.

Most of our votes came from Asian countries, other Pacific Island states, the Caribbean and Latin America. The only definite vote from the Middle East was from Israel.

"The Middle East is always in the news. We want somebody impartial to deal with issues affecting Israel," Minister Arie Tenne, Israel's permanent representative to the United Nations, had told me at a pre-election gathering the night before.

Sir Michael remained calm as the results were declared. He sat through to the end as president-elect Samir Shihabi read a very long prepared speech in Arabic.

I was proud of Sir Michael's great patience and diplomacy.

I did not want to read or see Sir Michael's defeat on television that evening or read it in the newspapers so I explored New York City. With me was Perai Manai from Tapini in Central province. He had come to America with Utula Samana.

First, we headed for the Empire State Building. From the 102nd floor, we could see the Twin Towers of the World Trade Centre shining white in the distance, the only building taller than any other on the New York landscape.

A decade later, the Twin Towers were blown-up reputedly by Osama Bin Laden's Islamic terrorist group al-Qaeda. They flew two hijacked passenger jets straight into the buildings on 11th September, 2001, now referred to as 9/11.

America immediately declared war on terrorism. Osama Bin Laden the master mind evaded capture for almost a decade before he was located in Pakistan by the U.S. military in May 2011 and shot dead.

Just like the memories of the Twin Towers keeps flashing in my mind, so too will the memory of Grand Chief Sir Michael Thomas Somare for not only among my generation but many more generations to come. His presence will remain with the people of Papua New Guinea. Generations will continue to appreciate his efforts to unite a country of a thousand different tribes.

I now present, Pauline Wapen Mango with her poem: titled:

'What it means to be a Papua New Guinean.'

Independent and free
You helped us to see
What life could be
Living together in unity
A thousand tribes and me
Thank you, Grand Chief Sir Michael Thomas Somare.
From the children of Enga (and Papua New Guinea)

- Pauline Wapen Mango

Pauline's 'Thank you' goes to both Sir Michael Somare and Sir Julius Chan. They both died happy men. Both worked hard to keep PNG, a very complex country with a thousand different tribes united for exactly 50 years. They had stood side by side to celebrate the attainment of independence on 16 September, 1975.

The great Michael Thomas Somare was a former journalist and radio broadcaster in the Sepik before he rose to prominence. I knew of Raphael Doa and Kindi Lawe winning elections after working for Radio Western Highlands – *Krai Bilong Tarangau* or Voice of the Eagle. They were my members of parliament when I lived and worked in the Western Highlands, of which Enga was still a part.

And if that radio man hadn't come to our school at Mariant Catholic mission school, I wouldn't have met the people I did or recorded the deaths, destruction and personal pain I have suffered as described in this book.

His coming had determined my future life working in the media industry as a radio broadcaster, journalist and author.

4

LOSING MY JOB, LIKE I LOST MY PROPERTY

"Mistakes are always forgivable, if one has the courage to admit them,"
Bruce Lee
– the Hong-Kong American martial artist

After 12 Years, I Meet the 'Radio Man', Then Lose my Job

One can easily draw parallels with raising children and rearing domesticated animals, growing vegetables or planting trees. We watch them grow to maturity. Likewise, every parent raises their children to succeed in life and then retires to enjoy the fruits of their hard work.

But I don't know if my parents were happy or not when they saw me lose my job due to human folly.

I went to school, established my career and raised a large family. But when I lost my job, we all suffered. I did not step on anybody's taro garden to deserve the harsh treatment. I have already revealed how we lost my property after spending so much of my resources and time to develop it, two years shy of my country celebrating 50 years of independence.

It was a double blow on my life really. I lost my job seventeen years previously. I remained an unattached officer until I reached retirement age. I didn't make any mistake to deserve such harsh treatment. The hard work I put in to serve my country came to an abrupt stop on 19th May 2008.

My journey to finally work with the Department of Enga Administration began when that 'Radio Man' came to our school to record our songs at the mission school. His visit had left an everlasting impression on my mind.

Four years after independence, I met the 'Radio Man' again in 1979 as a staff member of the National Broadcasting Commission. His name was Paul Lare. I came to know all the other staff members too – whose names I'd heard only on the radio.

Then, there was our station clerk, Joseph Aie Yangao. I was especially happy to meet him because he was from my major Aimbarep tribe. That made two of us working for the National Broadcasting Commission's Radio Western Highlands – Krai Bilong Taragau (Eagle). But Joseph never told me how he found employment with the national broadcaster.

Joseph was from Wert in the upper reaches of the Mariant River where Jim Fenton had been patrolling just 10 or so years previously. He was among the first lot of students to enrol at Kandep Primary 'T' School in 1963. He and all the other staff at Radio Western Highlands formed the core of public servants from the populous highlands region to work for the government at the time. I was probably among the next wave of workers to train in various fields to serve our new country.

I had never dreamt that, one day, I would be a broadcaster and a journalist. I grew up with the understanding that, when people left school, they would either go back to the village and join their relatives or be picked by somebody to work as policemen, aid post orderlies, interpreters, drivers or perhaps Kiaps. It never occurred to me that education was the key to open up possibilities beyond measure.

I could have been among the first few university graduates from our tribe but had just dropped out during my third year of study at the University of Technology in Lae.

In 1975, I had been selected to attend the University of Technology in Lae. I had been mistakenly selected to study chemical technology, electrical engineering and communications engineering all at once. No, the Education Department had definitely made a mistake and I would go and choose one of the three.

But I didn't have a clue about any of the courses. I had put further studies as my first choice on my school leaver application form. Maybe three different selectors had picked me to study the three courses.

There was nobody to turn to seek advice in those days. I was born into a primitive society, but fortunate to come into the world at the right moment to attend school. And here I was selected to study courses I didn't know anything about.

At Lae Unitech, I thought communications engineering involved people talking on the radio, so I chose to do that course in 1976. But never made it in the third year.

The course became more technical. I had the option to repeat the course at my own expense or leave. My parents were poor and could not afford the costs. They lived far away up in the highlands and didn't have a clue what was happening to me and my life.

Luckily, I had been sponsored by the National Broadcasting Commission and when I dropped out, I asked Sam Piniau, the Chairman of the National Broadcasting Commission if I could train as a broadcast officer, and maybe later I would return back to university to continue the engineering course with a fresh mind.

Mr Piniau kindly approved my request. My NBC principal of technical training at Wonga Estate, Ian Dunn, a British national encouraged me to make a career in broadcasting. That was the sort of encouragement I needed in those days. After two months of training, I was posted to Radio Western Highlands in Mt Hagen. Don Penias was one of my trainers at the time.

Mr William Kundin, a kind easy-going man was the station manager at Radio Western Highlands. Many years later, I met his son, a lawyer, in Wabag town.

Other radio personalities like Michael Namba, Paul Piel, Paul Ray, Jennifer Pahun, Anna Pundia, Paul Yane, Mathew Tena, Michael Mekela, Michael Mel, George Kagl and of course Paul Lare provided me with the right kind of atmosphere at the station. I enjoyed the work so much I never thought to go back to complete my studies.

Radio played a huge role in those days and impacted on the lives of everybody in post-independence Papua New Guineans. Radio was the only source of news, information and entertainment in the country. The Post Courier had started operating in June, 1969. But it reached only those few people who could read. But radio broadcasts could be heard by almost anybody, anywhere.

I enjoyed my work and stay in Mt Hagen, where fresh fruits and vegetables – paw paws, bananas, pineapples, sweet potatoes, sugarcane, taro were sold in abundance at the market. Even large pigs were sold there too.

After about three years, I went to Wabag in Enga province to join the staff of Danely Tindiwi from Wage census division in Kandep. He was the first person to be elected Premier of the new province. I worked as the press officer for the Enga Provincial Government.

But soon I realised I had no future working in a political environment. The politician could easily be voted out of office and employees vacated the building with him.

Luckily for me, I joined the World Bank-sponsored provincial development project, called Enga Yakaa Lasemana or EYL for short. I was recruited as an Information Officer in the newly created Media Unit in 1983.

Communication development was one of the project components. Of five staff recruited, I was understudy to a British VSO volunteer named Archie Markham.

Archie was a published poet and playwright. He was the man who got me interested in literature. I published suitable poems alongside his poems and satire in the pages of Enga Nius at the time.

Archie and I started the *Enga Newsletter* produced on several sheets of typewritten A4 paper folded together. We sat at a light table with glue, scissors, Letraset, rulers and rubber to prepare our news pages.

We were ably assisted by the printer, Watai Yakasa who had trained at the Goroka Technical college as a graphic artist. He was featured in a book called Shaping the Future compiled and edited by Friedrich Steinbauer. It was published by Kristen press in 1975. Sir Tei Abal and Anton Parao's brief profiles were also included in that book.

I still have copies of the book together with the Idubada Technical College Yearbook of 1975 and UPNG Enga Students Association Year Books published a decade later. I placed copies in the PNG section of the National Library. Other copies I have remaining together with copies of my books will be donated to the new Wabag Public Library in Wabag town, an initiative of local member, Dr Lino Tom, MP.

That was the beginning of the popular provincial news magazine, *Enga Nius*. But I had no proper training in journalism. So, I asked to be released to study Journalism and Media Studies at the University of Papua New Guinea.

One of Luluai Liu Omapu's sons, Tau Liu was Director of Staff Development in the Enga Department. He approved my release to go for further training on full pay. This was the beginning of my exciting career in journalism which took me to many parts of the world – the UK-based Thomson Foundation, the US-based Alfred Friendly Press Foundation and the National Press Foundation also based in Washinton DC and the inaugural McKinnon – Paga Hill Development Company Fellowship scheme. They offered me scholarships in 1989, 1991, 2008 and 2016 respectively in recognition of my efforts to remain in my province and publish a worthwhile provincial newspaper and to promote literature.

I contributed news and feature stories to the Post Courier, The National, Sunday Chronicle and Paradise, Air Niugini's Inflight Magazine.

Many years later, I was an active participant in the lively discussions in the popular Australia-based blog – *PNG Attitude*, published by Keith Jackson AM a former employee of the National Broadcasting Commission. He was, at one stage, the Station Manager at Radio North Solomons, now Autonomous Region of Bougainville, AROB.

I was proud that Papua New Guinea has a free press, much like in America, Great Britain and other free democracies. There was no government control over what was published or broadcast. But many people in PNG did not have the capacity to run their own media outlets.

For a while, it was only Port Moresby which had a fully functional press. Consequently, almost all journalists lived and worked in the city – which continued to be one of the few capitals in the world cut off from the rest of the country. It was only accessible by air or sea at huge cost to the traveller.

Our two dailies, two weeklies, two commercial TV stations, one commercial FM station and the National Broadcasting Commission were all Port Moresby based, almost all of them foreign owned.

Except for the NBC, few of these organisations had regional or provincial representation. Only recently had the *Post Courier* and *The National* begun establishing regional bureaus in Lae, Mt Hagen and Rabaul.

Given this scenario, I had been privileged to enjoy support from the Enga Provincial Government to publish Enga Nius a newspaper that was as free as any other operating in the country.

It was probably the only publication of its kind published at provincial or regional level. Of course, there had been other newsletters like Arawa Bulletin, Southern Highlands Kirap, Western Highlands News, Madang News and others. But they all ceased to operate a couple of years after independence. Soon, Facebook took over. Nobody seemed to want to read anymore. Nor were provincial governments prepared to fund such publications.

Enga Nius had a large supply of news stories like cold-blooded murders, pack rapes, violence against women, tribal warfare, corruption, nepotism, HIV/AIDS, drug and child abuse – the type of stories that make headline news anywhere.

With a handful of committed staff, we kept reporting on these issues, without fear or favour, in the hope that, one day, our province and country would struggle free from these social woes.

But I soon got into trouble for a story we published in the March, 2008 issue of Enga Nius. The article was about the position of Provincial Administrator which had just been advertised. Potential candidates had also been short-listed.

EMTV's John Eggins, on a job assignment to Wabag told me indirectly that the provincial government was not happy with that month's issue with a marijuana farmer and known drug addict arrested by police published on the front cover. But there was nothing wrong with it. I shrugged it off saying that wasn't possible.

But it was.

I got the suspension notice papers – not for police arresting the drug addict but for the article on the administrator's position. I should not have mentioned it. But didn't the people have a right to know?

I Win Public Service Commission Appeal, Not Reinstated to My Position

The last Enga Nius issue I published was on 31st March,2008. It was the issue that got me into trouble. It carried a commentary type news article about who might win the top administrator's position that had just been advertised.

It was a clear tussle between the incumbent, the late Dr Samson Amean whose contract had not been renewed and former Provincial Administrator Mr Kundapen Talyaga.

Enga province did not have a confirmed provincial administrator since Dr Samson Amean's contract had expired back in 2007.

There were rumours of certain people as having been appointed to the position by the National Executive Council, NEC but they were just that – rumours.

Late Dr Samson Amean and late Kundapen Talyaga were reportedly in Port Moresby seeking support including from the four Engan National Alliance members in government – Mick Kaiyok, Sam Abal, Philip Kikala and Don Pomb Polye.

Other names of possible candidates popped up too, like former Administrator Luke Kembol, former Wabag MP, late Daniel Kapi and former Kandep District Administrator late Naipet Keae.

But of all the rumoured names floating around, public opinion had it that the most likely candidates to be appointed were either late Dr Samson Amean or late Kundapen Talyaga. It was a tussle between the two. And that was the story I published for public consumption.

But somebody in the administrative system did not like the word 'tussle' and decided to suspend me. I was also demoted by two grades. This happened on 19th May, 2008. With my suspension went Enga Nius out the window. All the years of hard work put in since the World Bank sponsored project Enga Yakalaseman – EYL commenced had become like sand dunes along the seashore. Rough waves rolled in and levelled them out to nothingness.

But I kept writing, feeding the national press with newsworthy stories that kept happening in my beloved province. God gave me a gift that I had to utilise. I could not sit by and watch.

At the same time, I had appealed to the Public Service Commission, PSC arguing that the Department of Enga had erred in suspending me for a newsworthy article that the people had a right to know.

It took three years for my case to be finally heard and a decision was reached on 29th September, 2008. The good news finally came on 25th November, 2011. The Public Service Commission had ruled and ordered the Provincial Administrator to follow four decisions:

> *That the Commission annulled the decision of the Provincial Administrator dated 9th May, 2008, and the decision to demote me by two grades below my substantive grade 13.*
>
> *That the Provincial Administrator reinstate me to the substantive Grade 13 I occupied immediately prior to my demotion.*
>
> *That the Provincial Administrator immediately thereafter effect payment to me any salaries and service entitlements that I might have been deprived of in the course of the disciplinary action having been taken against me.*
>
> *That the Provincial Administrator effect the removal and destruction of all relevant disciplinary documents relating to my demotion, and that this be done in my presence.*

These lawful instructions were never actioned. Although I kept getting my pay, I never received my service entitlements like the annual gratuity payments and housing allowance.

The Department of Enga did not honour the Public Service Commission (PSC) decision to put me back in my substantive position. During two staff recruitment exercises in seventeen years, my application was never considered allowing me to remain unattached.

This made me wonder if the lawful PSC decision was intentionally ignored. When I wrote letters to the Provincial Administrator to reinstate me, I did not receive any feedback. But yet, the Provincial Administrator, late Dr Samson Amean and myself remained close friends. That was after he had easily won back his position in that 'tussle' for the post.

I detected that late Dr Samson Amean regretted the decision to suspend me. He involved me in various other activities at a personal level. Once he took me to Porgera Gold Mine on a tour. Another time he gave me spending money when I went to attend the Brisbane Writers

Festival in 2016. This enabled me to take my wife along to see the place from where all those Kiaps came from – and to breath some fresh southern air after we had suffered rejection after all the hard work, to keep Enga province afloat on a positive vibe. Enga Nius had kept the people informed with local news and information. It generated revenue for provincial government coffers too.

On another occasion, Dr Amean rang me in Port Moresby to go and stop a tribal war in my district of Kandep. I relate that story in Chapter 5. But here, he needed me and the people needed their newspaper – Enga Nius.

I was suspended. But the biggest accomplishment in my career had been to live and work among my own people opening their eyes and ears to the outside world and alerting them to dangers like HIV/AIDS, Sars, Covid 19, tribal warfare and other social concerns that threatened their very existence.

I highlighted important projects the provincial government was involved in, including the Enga Teachers College, Enga Nursing College, the multi-million Enga Provincial Hospital, The Enga Children's Fund properties, The Bank of South Pacific building in Wabag town, Tsak Secondary School and many other such impact projects.

Trainee journalists from the University of Papua New Guinea and Divine Word University came to work with me on field attachment. One of them was a niece of Paul Lare, the Radio Man. Her name was Alice Thomas. Later on, when I came across her and her husband in Port Moresby, they bought me lunch.

Another person I assisted was Sikin Rex Thomas, a high school student at Wabag Provincial High School. He wrote from Vanuatu in early March, 2016 to express how he felt about helping us produce Enga Nius during his term break.

Sikin Rex Thomas wrote: "In 1986, I was doing my year 9 at Wabag Provincial High School. I went to seek Christmas Holiday Job in the Media unit where Daniel Kumbon was running Enga Nius in Wabag. Without any hesitation, I recall him calling me "Kamio meaning brother"

"He engaged me to assist in processing Enga Nius – getting the articles glued to the pages after cutting the typed articles with scissors and rubbing the Letraset on to form the headlines etc then getting the actual printing done, before collating, folding and distributing them.

"That was my foremost job experience in my life as a student and well appreciated his assistance. Now, I enjoy working abroad in another foreign Land with the World Health Organisation (SSA) in Vanuatu. By reading his life story reminds me of my part-time job working with him. Thank you, Daniel."

I was born into primitive conditions and struggled my way up to receive an education. I worked hard putting to good use the skills acquired during training. I was ready to help others succeed in life and, at the same time, promote peace and unity in the province. I kept the people well informed and provided an avenue for them to exercise their democratic right to express themselves freely.

However, I had been unceremoniously dumped by the system. But the Lord is my Shepherd. He provides for me that which His Divine Mercey wishes me to have and comforted me in times of injustice.

Immediately after I was suspended, I received an email from the American-based National Press Foundation. They had approved my application requesting sponsorship to attend the 17th International AIDS conference in Mexico City. It was to begin on August 3rd 2008.

They had been impressed with my reports on the intentional spread of the dreaded AIDS virus to innocent women by rapists in Enga province.

My suspension seemed a scratch on my back, a flea bite really. My commitment to my professional career bore fruit. The sponsorship package from America overcame the pressure. Once again, I was taking the name of my province and country across the oceans to the world stage.

My staff and I had been doing something worthy. The system failed to notice or acknowledge the dedicated service we provided. Names of committed staff like Thomas Amean, Watai Yakasa and Rose Pakio – the reporter, the printer and the typist were committed staff who needed recognition.

If it was my decision to make, I would have asked Thomas, Watai and Rose to come with me to Mexico that great country in South America once inhabited by a fierce, well-organised ancient civilisation. Their contributions and total commitment had made my work much easier.

An International Scholarship Takes Me to The City of The Gods

I will never forget my visit to a place shrouded with mystery and intrigue – a place where human sacrifice was offered to the gods is etched forever in my memory.

Teotihuacan is an ancient ruin near Mexico City which I was privileged to visit during the 17th International AIDS Conference 17 years ago. I was dressed like always in my handwoven PNG Highlands cap and long beard.

We 60 international journalists met five people living with HIV and AIDS at the Clinica Condesa – an impressive government-funded health facility specialising in free treatment for 4,000 patients in the city.

They bravely told us how they had contracted the virus in different ways and warned against risky sexual behaviour. With broad smiles spreading across their faces, they wished us a safe stay in the city and a safe return to our countries.

A safe trip I did make home, but not without learning something about the Mexican people and their ancient past. I have always been inspired by books like Chariots of Fire, Montezuma Daughter and the Kon Tiki Expedition which talk about advanced Indian civilisations of South America.

I longed to see some of these ruins. Our first stop was Templo Mayor an important historical site within the city limits. Known as Tenochtitlan, it was the hub of the ancient Aztec empire.

The Indians who once lived here were gifted architects, mathematicians and artisans. Herman Cortes, the first of the conquistadores described Templo Mayor as a most beautiful city. But he destroyed it forever.

They killed the civil, military and religious leaders but often spared the women and married them off to the conquerors. Spanish landlords replaced Indian nobles as masters of the estates and reduced the people to nothing.

But many centuries before the Spanish destroyed Tenochtitlan, the pyramids and temples at Teotihuacan 30 miles north east of Mexico City – and the 125,000 people who once lived there had met a different fate. They had simply vanished without a trace. But the ruins are still there today.

The ancient metropolis is thought to have been established in 100 BC and kept on growing until AD 250 and lasted until sometime between the 7th and 8th centuries AD. It was listed as a Unesco World Heritage site in 1987.

The Pyramid of the Moon and Pyramid of the Sun are two imposing stone structures at the site. They loomed over us as we drove along an ancient narrow road paved with round grey stones and pebbles.

Gift shops dotted the route, full of hand-woven clothes, colourful blankets, stone carvings, silverware, necklaces, Mexican Hats and hot food flavoured with chilly. I bought a beautiful necklace made of beads with an image of the sun as a memento for my small daughter.

Teotihuacan guards' secrets that have yet to be unravelled. Human sacrifices were made here, often in correlation with astronomical events. When the site was excavated, many tombs were found, some with the remains of people sacrificed to the gods.

Many people today believe that Teotihuacan is a place of great energy from which they can draw strength. When I sweated up to the summit of the Pyramid of the Sun, I witnessed a group of Indians in white robes and red headbands meditating – all facing the sun.

From the summit, I marvelled at the same sights as had been seen by the ancient priests who ripped out the hearts of unfortunate souls for sacrifice to the gods. Even now, it drives fear in my heart when I watch Mel Gibson's, Apocalypse a terrifying film that seemed so real.

From the corner of my eyes, I saw a man carrying a bilum aim his camera and take a shot of me. He smiled and introduced himself as Fr Jan Jaloorski from Poland but now a medical doctor at Kundiawa General Hospital.

It was easy for us to meet because of the way we were dressed in our PNG attire. How proud we were to meet and share a moment at this eerie spot.

I bade farewell to Dr Jaloorski and walked the distance of the main avenue known as the Calzada de los Muertos or Avenue of the Dead. It connects the Pyramid of the Moon and the Pyramid of the Sun and other minor temples and courtyards.

It was awesome to imagine why the people had toiled so hard to build this elaborate city which had taken ages to complete only to vanish without a trace!

The answers could be found in the mythology of ancient Mexico – especially in legends of the Nahua People as recorded by a Franciscan friar Bernardino de Sahagun (1500 – 1590) and brought to light by Julie Black in 2000 in essays on Ancient Mexico.

One is the 'Legend of the Fifth Sun' which is a telling of the past before the existence of the world as we know it today.

After the gods created the earth, the heavens and the underworld, a chain of destruction and creation unfolded that caused the existence of five different worlds throughout time. Each world is an age dominated by a great burning disc in the sky, and therefore each age is called a sun.

The One World cem-a-nahuac has existed for many millenniums. But even before the world as we know it, there were four suns and four earths. Each sun ended in a catastrophe, a cataclysm, and each time the world was created again, fatally identical to that before it.

And a new circle began, and this cycle brought about an improved form of life. The four primordial forces presided over these suns – water, earth, fire and wind – until the age of the Fifth Sun of Movement, which is the sun we live in now. The first age was the sun of water, and the first humans were giants. These men and women, in spite of their great size, were, in reality, weak beings. When they fell, as in an accident, they fell forever.

In the second sun the people were nourished with maize water. But this sun too, was destroyed. The people were eaten by jaguars.

In the third age, the Sun of fire, men and women lived in the world and were nourished on cincocopi, an ancient form of maize. But they too met a tragic end. The sun rained fire, and all the people were transformed into turkeys.

Finally, the people who lived and dwelt in the fourth age, they ate maize as we know it, our substance, discovered by the god Quetzalcoatl. These humans, when they met their final doom, were converted neither into fish nor turkeys, but went to live among the mountains as monkey people. This was the sun of wind.

The fifth age in which we live, the sun of movement, had its origin in Teotihuacan long, long ago. This is why Teotihuacan is called the city of the Gods. It was there that the gods united to create the age of movement. Movement is Ollin. All that exists is in constant movement of the sun across the sky. This Ollin, the sun of movement, is the world we live in today.

Another legend tells of how the world began, not with a Genesis overseen by one almighty god, but with a creation from a group effort of many gods at Teotihuacan and the courageous efforts of two in particular.

One of the deities, a deformed god with a humble spirit, became the sun and the other the moon after they had thrown themselves into a great fire. It is for these two gods that the Pyramid of the Sun and the Pyramid of the moon were built and exist at Teotihuacan.

The power and might of ancient Indian Empires were evident in those ruins. I saw how the native Indians had dressed and looked like in ancient times in the Mexico City Museum.

But by sheer luck, I came across a cultural dance group performing live near the museum grounds. Three beautiful women and some men with elaborate headdresses – one in particular with a skull above his forehead danced to the haunting rhythmic beat of a three-legged stool-like drum.

They reminded me of a Mekeo Cultural dance group I saw in 1975 at the Moitaka Show grounds in Port Moresby. I came home convinced that as we learn to understand and appreciate other people's histories, cultures and traditions –we will soon learn to respect and be proud of our own rich cultural heritage passed on to us from generation to generation.

That's why I always took a piece of my cultural heritage with me whenever I travel – my hand-woven PNG highlands cap, a string bag and long beard. I have never shaved my beard in later life.

Because of the way I was dressed, I met another man. We smiled as soon as we saw each other. It was a pleasure meeting, in person, Hon Jamie Maxton-Graham, PNG's Health Minister at the time. He had led a group of health professionals from PNG to the international AIDS conference in Mexico City.

Sadly, he died 14 years later. But the health advice from across the table in a temporary restaurant on the conference grounds is still fresh in my mind.

He had persuaded me to look after myself, my life. In fact, everybody should change their life-styles – eat healthy, stay healthy, think healthy because there was only one life to live.

Jamie Maxton-Graham Imparts Healthy Words from Mexico City

When we met for the first time far from home, the late Jamie Maxton Graham encouraged me to give up Coca-Cola and other carbonated drinks.

It's not often you come across a national minister who talks on a personal level about health and other important life issues. Late Jamie Maxton-Graham was different.

He was Papua New Guinea's health minister, chairman of the parliamentary committee on HIV/AIDS and three-term member for Anglimp South Wahgi.

The global village where we met had an area of over 8,000 square meters and was the heart of the conference.

Here, more than 22,000 delegates from all over the world spent a week participating in conference sessions, special meetings, exhibitions and a wide cultural program.

Maxton Graham led a PNG team of doctors, activists and health professionals to interact, debate, share knowledge and skills, build coalitions and exchange ideas.

I was part of a group of international journalists at the conference. We joined hundreds of other journalists who shared a large media centre.

I met Maxton-Graham at one of the venues in the global village. Nearby, in a huge auditorium, official speeches were delivered by world leaders, scientists and company executives involved in research to find a cure for the virus.

After he and I visited many stalls, he suggested we pay a visit to the display of the host country before finding some refreshments. When we arrived at the stall, we found communication was a problem. They spoke Spanish and we did not.

At the restaurant table, Maxton-Graham did not talk about the things tourists usually talk about. He spoke about healthy living. I probably provoked him because I ordered Coke with my meal.

"Bro, we must look after ourselves," he said. "Many things we eat and drink are not good for our health.

"Our health is very important. There is no second life. This life we have is just one and our very own. We must nourish it with good food and drink."

I knew he was right but drank that damn can of coke anyway in that busy restaurant where the waiters all spoke Spanish.

But later, when I got home, I gradually gave up coke, and beer, cigarettes and *buai* as well. The nation's health minister had spoken to me in a faraway country. I had to listen to him.

I didn't have to wait for a miracle to happen or a giant from outer space to come and order me to stop these bad habits! I just had to quit.

It was shameful for me, an educated person to consume products that caused so many health issues and which definitely killed people prematurely.

There was still no cure for AIDS. But, despite millions of kina spent every year by the government and aid agencies, people were still involved in extra-marital affairs, prostitution and unsafe sex.

Three young men from my village – a trained teacher, a trainee teacher and a security guard died from AIDS complications soon after I returned from Mexico. They all had prior knowledge there was no cure. People were sometimes like that firefly that threw their lives into the flames of a burning fire.

I was thankful that a national government minister played a part in convincing me how important it was to change my lifestyle and look after my life.

Late Sir Julius Chan said in his tribute that Maxton-Graham had strived to make this country a better place, especially through his advocacy on health and a sustainable way of life.

"He has left his mark in this world. The good he left will never be forgotten but live on in every person he has impacted,' Sir Julius said. I totally agreed with him.

Jamie Maxton-Graham was born in Bargana village in Minj, Jiwaka Province to his mother Gol Milin and father Peter Maxton-Graham.

His early childhood was spent in Wasne, his mother's home village, where he had fond memories of being looked after by his maternal grandmother.

Much of his later childhood was spent in Madang where he and his mother had moved with her partner Posu Pouta after his father had died. Madang was where he went to school.

He completed Grade 6 at Tusbab Primary School in 1969 – the year Neil Armstrong landed on the moon.

Then he went to Tusbab High where he consistently topped the class. In 1977, he was accepted into the University of Technology in Lae to do a mechanical engineering course but withdrew after three years.

Later, he attended Port Moresby Technical College and worked for different companies around the country until the turning point came for him when he worked as advisor to former prime minister Paias Wingti from 1990–93.

It was in these years that his political aspirations blossomed, eventually propelling him to pursue a seat in parliament.

He won the Anglimp South Wahgi Open seat in 2002 and remained the MP for 15 years.

In 2008, when I met him in Mexico, he must have sensed that his own health was failing him when he told me to give up Coke and aim to live a healthy life.

According to his daughter Carmella, he had a health scare in 2009 that drove him to change his lifestyle.

"He was told by a doctor that he had blocked arteries and had to get bypass surgery. But he was determined to find another way."

His own journey motivated him to inspire others, which led to the opening of the Wellness Lodge in Port Moresby where he and Carmella also ran a health-conscious restaurant.

Most people's memories of Maxton-Graham are of his adventurous spirit and his intelligence. He was always reading and he had a broad range of topics on which he was knowledgeable.

"He was also a very simple person," Carmella said. "He loved to spend time with his grandchildren, playing sport with people much younger than him and engaging in outdoor activities like camping and eating fish cooked on a fire. Playing the guitar and singing – his memories of his childhood made him happy."

His healthy lifestyle kept Jamie Maxton-Graham going for another 10 years, and I will remember him as the man who, in a strange land far away from home, encouraged me to live a healthy life.

He has left us. But his words remain with us to follow if we care at all about our short life on earth. Fr Garry Roche, a priest who now lives in his country, Ireland knew Maxtone Graham when he lived at Kamunga, near Rebiamul in Mt Hagen. At one time Jamie played rugby league with a local Hagen team. Jamie was open-minded, had lived in different provinces in PNG and was an avid reader.

Many people in Papua New Guinea do care about their lives and look after them. But there was widespread fear and concern that young people, even university students, were misbehaving and involved themselves in drugs and homebrew.

Some were even rude enough to disrespect elders both in the village and at the work place. Michael Yahu a very senior public servant from Manus was one of those people who had come to Enga province with the tide of outsiders – Kiaps, missionaries and workers from other parts of PNG during the colonial administration period.

Some fool played a stupid prank on him on April Fool's Day. Late Michael Yahu was struggling to get his public service entitlements – his *'pinis pei'* for all the years he served the government in Enga province. The silly prank proved how cruel people had become.

April Fool's Day: Silly Prank on Senior Citizen Waiting For 'Pinis Pei'

Before I relate how poorly the government treated him and about the prank, allow me to begin with a lively discussion I had with an influential local leader from Kopen in November, 1994 during a council ward opening.

We exchanged views based on our observation that people's attitudes had changed. Respect for authority, other people's lives, their families, their own lives and property, both public and private was disappearing.

Walenate Pyalie, the man I spoke with, was the village court magistrate from Kopen and a member of the Joint Village Court in the district. He was popular and respected because he made fair decisions during weekly Joint Village Court sittings in Wabag town.

They dealt with all sorts of issues – domestic violence, robberies and serious crime like murders, tribal war issues and other such complaints. He always tried to deal with the issues with skill, wisdom and fairness so opposing groups would accept the village court decisions.

In his youth Mr Pyalie saw that village life was orderly and people were well behaved. They respected each other and it was every man's duty to maintain order in the community. A man and his wife never quarrelled in public as frequently as is evident today. Children used to respect and listen to their parents. Tribal wars were fought but not as intensely. Few men were killed with bows and arrows. Most often, men would easily recover from arrow wounds they sustained.

But now huge numbers of people were killed instantly involving sophisticated weaponry smuggled into the province.

"Now, the situation has changed dramatically. I can't even cope. Society has really changed for the worse," the village chief said.

"Yes, that appears to be happening all over the world," I said, citing media reports I had seen of small boys murdering other children, wives cutting their husbands penises off, parents murdering their own children and other such hideous crime.

Mr Pyalie looked at me strongly, intently and appeared to understand the situation in a broader sense. Then he told me something he had heard in the *hausman* from elders when he was growing up.

"They said that if you see Papame, a fern-like plant that grows in the high altitudes of mountain peaks, begin to grow in the lowlands, then that will signal that this earth will pass. I have seen it grow here in the lowlands. It was never like this before."

I added that coastal flowering plants and trees like coconut, betelnut, oil palm and mangoes were also doing well up here in the highlands. They were bearing fruit and there could well be plantations established in the future.

"This is attributed to something they call the 'Green House Effect', I said. "Pollution is playing a part in these environmental changes. All the smoke from big factories and car exhaust are playing a part in changing our environment."

He seemed to understand my explanation. He looked at me, took my hands and squeezed them.

"Certainly, there is a lot of change happening around Enga, PNG and the world. It was a really frightening situation. People have no option. But they can do only one thing," he said.

"What is that?" I asked and felt rather stupid when he gave the answer.

"That is, all of us must go to church and give our lives to Jesus. This way we will end up on the good side. Everybody must humble themselves, respect each other and live in peace until the end comes."

I just nodded my head.

Our conversation took place 30 years ago. Sad to say but now the situation hasn't improved. It has become worse.

Disrespectful behaviour is evident everywhere, even towards the elderly, even public servants who had served this country all their lives – people like late Michael Yahu.

Somebody foolishly announced on social media on April Fool's Day that Michael Yahu, a retired public servant from Manus had died. Michael had come to Enga in his youth. He was patiently waiting for his entitlements. He didn't need that kind of prank. How cruel some people had become!

For a while I did not realise that Good Friday was April Fool's Day and joined my family to cry when I received news that he had died on Manus Island.

Whoever fabricated the story was senseless to circulate such a joke on social media. He lacked all understanding of human relations and etiquette.

He did not think for a moment of what Covid-19 was doing to Papua New Guinea. People were dying, their families, relatives and friends lived through traumatic times, cried every day for people who so easily succumbed to the onslaught of a virus sweeping across the country like wildfire.

The perpetrator of this cruel hoax was not concerned that a number of senior public servants and community leaders around Wabag had died in the last few weeks. Others were reportedly fighting for their lives.

So, I wept when the sad news came that Michael Yahu died on Good Friday. When I was at school in the 1960s, I had seen him working at the Kandep district office.

How could I stop my tears, now that Covid-19 had killed him just as it had killed my former classmates, neighbours, friends and workmates?

Michael Yahu was about 75, in an age group susceptible to Covid-19. He worked in Enga Province as the provincial personnel officer. He was directed to retire at age 69 in 2015. I was very close to Michael and wife Susan. I still miss them when I looked across the street.

Senior public servants who died included Michael's former boss, Lucas Sikin, who was director of human resource development; former district administrator, Jeffery Dia; former deputy administrator Albert Macsaene; education officer Danny Titakai; director of assembly services Aino Neakson; and Demmy Yakapo Kandelyo, a senior audit officer.

There had been so many other deaths as well throughout the province. The official figure for Covid-19 victims in Enga was recorded at just over 50. But hundreds of people were believed to have died unnoticed in the villages.

The onslaught of the virus had forced hospitals and schools to shut down. Wabag General Hospital had reportedly run out of testing equipment.

As soon as the cruel prank was published on social media, my family rang me in Port Moresby to say they were crying around Michael Yahu's house across the street. They said he had died on Manus.

I immediately dialled Michael's phone number. When I dialled it many times and did not get an answer, I was certain he had died. I hoped his wife Susan, or James, his small son, or some relatives I had met on a recent trip to Manus would pick up the phone.

I thought that he might have died not from Covid-19 but from a heart attack. When I visited Manus, he complained that he was still waiting to get his 'pinis pei' and other public service entitlements.

He showed me the location where he had been planning for five years to build his retirement home. The timber was prepared, but had begun to rot.

He said he had brought his thick personnel file with his claims to Manus so he could travel to Port Moresby himself to lodge his claims when government finances improved.

Michael had complained to me that it was due to deep-rooted corruption that he and other retired public servants did not receive their entitlements on time.

They were forced to wait many years, some dying without knowing if their next of kin would receive an inheritance.

Who Told You, I died?

I was distressed to hear Michael had died without receiving his entitlements. Did the government not respect, appreciate or care about the welfare of these ageing people who patiently waited for their hard-earned savings?

It was not much of a consolation that Michael, a devout Catholic, had gone to join his Creator on the day Jesus himself died on Calvary to save the world from sin. Michael had grown tired of waiting for his pension money, so he asked Enga provincial administrator, Dr Samson Amean, to provide his family with tickets so he could take them to Manus. They planned to return later.

Later, Ted Taru and I met up with Michael, Susan and James in their village inland from Lorengau along the 32- kilometre Manus Highway.

Michael smiled when I told him I had featured him in one of my books because he was among a handful of senior public servants from outside Enga Province who had come to serve the people as a young man and still worked and lived in the province to the time he waited for his retirement.

As a 16-year-old in 1972 he had accompanied his uncle to cold Kundiawa in the Highlands, travelling over the vast expanse of water and rugged mountains.

But it was in Enga that he found permanent employment with the colonial Administration. He settled there to live among people he described as generous, friendly and innovative.

When he retired in 2015, he could not go back to Manus immediately because the government he had served faithfully had no money to pay him.

But why shouldn't Michael Yahu, the Personal officer who had been processing other public servant's entitlements not receive his own rightful retirement benefits?

"*Mi mekim wanem rong na ol mekim olsem, mi no save,*" Michael told me. "I don't know what mistake I made for them to do this to me."

A couple of hours after receiving the sad news about Michael Yahu, I received another sad text message advising that my cousin-brother, Tolao Pupukai, had died in our village at Kondo. My family told me they were making arrangements to travel home for the funeral. I told them to take precautions and wear masks at all times.

Shortly after, I received another call from a phone number I didn't recognise. I hesitated at first, but then answered.

It was Michael Yahu, ringing me from Manus.

"*Daniel, husait tok me dai? Mi no amamas long lukim stori olsem mi dai long Facebook.*"

"Daniel, who said I had died. I am not happy to read about my death on Facebook."

I told him the name of the person who it was that had made the announcement. "Ring him and find out. I am here in Port Moresby," I said.

OK, I'll do that. But I'm coming there to POM in three weeks to check if we retirees will be paid our dues."

"I hope they pay you this time," I said.

Then both of us burst out laughing for a full minute. But we were certainly not happy with the person who perpetrated that foolish prank.

When he finally died later, I never found out if he had got his leave entitlements. The nursing sister who lives in late Michael's house said, Michael was one of the few lucky ones who had received his entitlements. If he did, I am not sure if he completed his retirement home.

I am not sure also if Michael had made friends with older students at Kandep Primary 'T' School. One of them was Yapi Koka from the local Alitip Kewan sub clan of the Alitip tribe. Both of them have passed on. That made it harder for me to find out if they knew each other. Michael had only one child, a boy who, unfortunately, died in Wabag. We held the *haus krai* or funeral in his house. James the other son mentioned earlier was adopted.

Yapi Koka had many children. Unfortunately, he died when all his children were very young. One of them, Kolly Koka successfully completed his studies at the University of Papua New Guinea.

I sent Kolly Koka a photograph of his late father as a graduation gift expressing my thoughts as to how happy his dad would be to see him graduate, if he were still alive.

His dad had trained as a warder after Standard 6 to look after prisoners. Yapi was among the first students to attend Kandep Primary 'T' School. Almost all his classmates have died. Only three remained – Aino Yangala of Mambala village, Tondo Kiakange of Wasa village and Peter Tapolo of Malai village.

After Yapi Koka died, his children were left to fend for themselves. His orphaned son Kolly had been raised by his mum.

The photo I sent him was taken when the late Yapi Koka was presenting grade 10 school certificates in his capacity as chairman of the Kandep High School Board. Although I was married into the Kewan *hausman* I didn't know that Kolly had never seen his dad.

I Didn't Know My Dad, Then You Sent Me His Photograph

Kolly Koka graduated from the University of Papua New Guinea with academic excellence and a leadership award. Two proud uncles were beside him on behalf of the Alitip Kewan clan members. It had been a very long battle for the graduate.

When Yapi died in the 1980s, young Kolly desperately wanted to attend school but nobody could help him with school fees. At one stage he was chased from the classroom by a class teacher accompanied by a tirade of abuse.

When Kolly graduated from UPNG, by way of congratulating him I uploaded the 30-year-old photograph of his late father on my Facebook page.

As it happened, this was the first time Kolly had seen a picture of his dad. The experience had left him in tears all night. He was so upset he was unable to join the graduation party his friends and relatives hosted for him.

The following morning, he poured out his thoughts to me, recounting how he had struggled to finally graduate from university. This is what Kolly Koka wrote:

"I know the word 'thank you' is not enough to express the sort of feeling I have right now after reading your post and seeing my dad for the first time.

"You know, it's about 20 years since my dad left us to be cared for by our poor mum. I never even had a photo and I sometimes wondered who among my siblings actually resembled our dad.

"This is one of the thousands of unanswered questions I have always had. But you have just answered one. This picture and everything you said just had me filled with a shower of tears all night.

"Senior, once again I just thank you for the photo you have kept for decades to publish on the day I graduated. Today, I'm happy that it's been exposed with a new dawn.

"I am compelled to share a bit of my story. It starts from the life I started alone with my mum.

"The world completely crumpled around me when my dad died. There were moments when I wondered: Why do bad things happen to some people and not to others. Why is this life so unfair to us?'

"I never thought I would ever be awarded a degree and an award for academic excellence. Those things seemed to be for the brilliant ones who seemed to be the kids of rich people.

"I thought of myself as poor like many others in the village. I never thought a new day would dawn with a fine sunrise.

"I really wanted to go to school. But when I actually started the expedition, it wasn't a smooth flight. It never was. No one ever believed I could make it either. I even suffered the vengeance and verbal abuse of some people who knew my poor mother.

"One of them was a teacher who chased me out of the classroom accompanied by some cruel words which I can vividly recall: 'I can pay your fees and that's easy. The amount charged is nothing. But I cannot do it. You go home right now because your mother wants you to look after her pigs.'

"*The teacher even suggested it would be better if I went to my mother's village which I actually did and stayed there for a complete year without attending school.*

"*I still remember walking out of the classroom never holding back my tears. I wondered why the teacher was removing me from class when he was not the school board chairman or the headmaster for that matter.*

"*I couldn't argue with him. I was powerless. The only thing I could do was cry. I said to myself: 'This person who is supposed to teach me, give me knowledge and take me through the year is removing me from the class. So, I must go.*

"*I walked out of the classroom with tears flooding my cheeks. In those days, it was really hard for me to return to the school area. I stayed away to avoid being seen by my former school mates.*

"*I didn't want to see them go in and out of the classrooms either. I was that poor little village boy, a fatherless orphan who had to stay away from school. At the swamps, in the gardens, in the bush or wherever I went I could only shed tears.*

"*But somehow, my mum managed to enrol me back into school after I had spent one whole year in the village.*

"*The worst part of my continual endurance of pain was to see my elder siblings dropping out of the education system. This depression was much stronger than any other.*

"*I indeed thought of quitting studies too because I was literally told by some that I was wasting my time only to fail in the end like my siblings.*

"*They said I could never achieve anything through education. It was better for me to live in the village and help my poor mum. I sometimes wished I never existed. Those disheartening words were so harsh, painful and unbearable. But my mum had faith and kept me in school by working hard to earn money for my school fees.*

"*It is clear today that the Lord God Almighty made those people so stubborn to say negative things but which have kept me going. As I progressed up the education ladder, a lot of people began to help me with school fees, travel fares, clothes, food, accommodation and other necessities.*

"*My old perspectives shifted entirely. Through the continuous pessimisms and doubtful discernments, I heard a wonderful, charming voice which talked softly to me of excellence, fortune and success waiting ahead of me. It was as if a man was literally sitting next to me to speak like that in my ears.*

"*The voice impressed upon me that I was a completely different person, born at a different time, with a different purpose with a distinct destiny. I and my siblings may have been born from the same mother, in the same village into the same clan and tribe. But we are all completely different individuals.*

"*My life and my future were my own responsibility which can never be influenced by the actions of my other siblings. There is one more thing, the voice said vividly, which I will never forget, 'Failure only comes to people who are lazy and do other things when they are supposed to commit their time to studies.*

"*The voice continued to speak to me and seemed to be right there beside me to provide comfort. I never faced any problems. I was with someone who knew me perfectly, my background and visibly showed me my life 10 years ahead in time.*

"*I was aware of myself, who I am, what I was doing; where I was and for what reason; with whom I should be with, where and at what specific times I should be. Nothing was hidden anymore. I could see the glimpses of success from ten years back.*

"*Now I know, the God of Topaz (my grandmother) to whom I committed my life and whom I serve today was always with me. She is the one who guided me all along and prioritised my studies.*

"*But yet some people's inverse perceptions never changed despite me moving up to the higher levels of education.*

"*I would like to emphasise that the life I have experienced is coloured both by laughter and pain. Boldness in the midst of anguish is a secure foundation like a boulder on which to build a strong house, a house based on determination and an aim to succeed.*

"I have endured hardships and overcame them to prove there is always success in the end."

Dominica Are from Goroka reaffirmed that students who were forced to struggle to complete their studies after one or both their parents had died understood what life really meant and quickly learnt what they needed to do to succeed.

"My dad passed on when my siblings and I were still in school. But he invested so much in our education. We stood strong and managed to continue and complete our education from primary school to university," Dominica said.

It is hoped Kolly Yapi Koka, the son of a warder during the colonial administration period did not face any sort of unnecessary hardship like I did – losing my job and then losing my property both of which took me years to nurture. Or the problems that lawyer Justin Issack suffered at the hands of rogue police.

Justin Issack was able to counter his unjustified treatment because he was a lawyer. But I couldn't. Not even when Justin tried to help me with my case. The Department of Enga had wronged me and I did not feel like facing them again.

Justin Issack was from the major Imma tribe of Kanda clan but not from the two sub-clans Kul and Anep from Nagulam village. Most of the suspects involved in burning Cleopas Roa's family truck and my property were from these two sub-clans.

Justin Issack's mother was from my Aimbarep Pumbuti tribe and I am his uncle. He worked with Paraka Lawyers soon after completing his studies at the Legal Training Institute in 2001. The year before he had graduated from the University of Papua New Guinea with a Bachelors of Laws degree.

He resigned from Paraka Lawyers and joined Warner Shand Lawyers for a while before he won the Provincial Legal officer position with the Enga Provincial Administration. But like me, they dumped him after the 2012 National General Elections while he was in their employ.

Sad Start, Happy Ending for Justin Issack the Lawyer

On the eve of PNG's 50 years of Independence, the State is faced with a hefty K10 billion in lawsuits brought by its citizens.

Secretary for the Department of Justice and Attorney General, Dr Eric Kua made a public statement that the Solicitor General was defending the State and suggested many of the claims may be based on false claims. He called on his lawyers to be diligent in their work of processing the claims.

'We checked with the court registry and our records all show that the Solicitor General lawyers defend an estimate K10 billion in lawsuits,' Dr Kua said.

This meant that the State was constantly at risk of giving large payouts to a certain individual or group who alleges a crime against the State.

'At the moment we have lawyers carrying a workload of 500 files per lawyer and that was too much work. In normal legal practice, a lawyer could be carrying less than a hundred,' he said.

Within 10 years up to January, 2012, human rights abuses by police had cost Papua New Guinea more than K100million in compensation payments. That was the staggering amount that had already been paid out. Another 17,608 cases and court proceedings against the State were outstanding.

This grim fact was revealed by former Minister for Justice and Attorney General, Sir Arnold Amet at a Ministerial Forum in July, 2011.

Sir Arnold had blamed this on poor advice to the government from his department, lack of lawyers, poor funding and low employment conditions.

But now, Dr Kua was at least happy that the government had recently approved new conditions for State lawyers including housing and vehicle allowances.

'We are hoping for security and book allowances as well as medical insurance as the work load can cause lawyers to be ill,' he said.

The thousands of cases being handled by the Solicitor General could be for various reasons. For Lawyer Justine Issack, he lodged a claim for K15million in damages in 2012 for police brutality. Justine was arrested in front of his wife and three startled young children early in the morning at the Highlands Lutheran International School – HLIS where he and his family were residing in 2009. He was whisked away as if he was a common criminal like William Kapris.

He was refused bail, barred from speaking to his relatives, not fed properly for a total of fourteen days and lived in appalling conditions in various police detention cells in Wabag, Mt Hagen, Port Moresby and Kokopo.

The lawyer was taken to Kokopo to stand trial for criminal charges arising out of a civil suit he had won on behalf of a businessman who was acquitted of murder charges.

Justin Issack who was born in 1975, now 50, was the Provincial Legal Officer with the Enga Provincial Government. He was arrested and charged for allegedly fabricating evidence and conspiracy to defraud the State of K10million.

Mr Justin Issack who now runs his own private law firm is a senior litigation lawyer who had worked for ten years with reputable law firms in the country like Warner Shand Lawyers. He had grounds to sue for damages because criminal charges laid against him were thrown out by the Kokopo National Court on 8th July, 2011. State lawyers failed miserably to prosecute him after charging him.

It appeared that the roughhouse tactics employed to arrest and the subsequent treatment Mr Issack encountered on the trip to Kokopo had all been for nothing.

Motuwe Lawyers, on behalf of Mr Issack filed for damages at the Attorney General's office on 12th July, 2011. The total compensation damages claimed was for nearly K15million.

Some basis for this huge claim was that from day one, wide media coverage gave the impression to the general public, relatives, friends and colleagues in the profession that Mr Justin Issack was a criminal and he had committed the crimes.

As a direct result of the pending case Mr Issack was denied job opportunities with the Solicitor General's Office, the Ombudsman Commission – and his application for Unrestricted Practicing certificate with the PNG Law Society was refused.

More so, his Contract of Employment with the Enga Provincial Government was not signed in a staff selection process owing to the fact that he had a pending criminal charge.

Justin believes the Enga Provincial Government was wrong to deny him his former job. He strongly feels that he had been arrested by Port Moresby police because he had represented the Enga Provincial Government to incorporate all the DSIP funds of all Engan members of parliament in the provincial budget.

He won the case at the National Court and the Engan leaders, most of whom were National Alliance Party members, did not like that arrangement. Justin had reason to believe that the Enga NA members had conspired with Port Moresby police to arrest him and make him suffer the humiliation of spending time inside the police detention cells on his way to Kokopo to stand trial.

"Somebody just wanted to see me suffer and discredited in public," Justin Issack said.

All this put him under extreme pressure and he suffered mental distress – not to mention the suffering of his wife and three children aged 5, 7 and 9 at the time. All of them were attending international school.

The drama unfolded on 13 August, 2009 when an Ombudsman Commission lawyer and two Port Moresby-based policemen from the Internal Investigation Unit (IIU) based at Badili arrested him at his Amapyaka (Highlands Lutheran International School) home at 7 am as he was preparing to go to work.

But why did a lawyer and two policemen from Port Moresby travel all the way to Wabag to arrest Mr Issack?

To find out we must travel back in time to 6th November, 2004. On that day, two members of the Police Mobile Squad in Rabaul went to Kulon Plantation in East New Britain and apprehended three young men who were suspected of stealing cocoa.

The owner of the plantation, one Mr Bernard Uriap was also there on the spot. In the course of the arrest one of the suspects, the late Marum Uralia Junior was kicked, punched and belted severely which resulted in his death.

The medical report filed in court confirmed that he had died from a ruptured spleen as a result of the kicks and beatings he sustained.

Police arrested and charged Mr Bernard Uriap, the plantation owner and put him behind bars for the young man's death. He was granted bail of K1000 and for nearly three years he maintained his innocence.

Mr Uriap was a well-established businessman in East New Britain Province. He owned Kulon and Rainau plantations and eight other cocoa plantations known as the New Ireland group, two ships, a fleet of PMVs, a service station and workshop.

These were all affected during his lengthy court battle and anticipated loss of income was approximated at K8-K10million. He had also spent nearly K100,000 in legal costs and other expenses including contribution of K10,000 to cover funeral expenses of the person killed on his plantation.

Finally, luck turned Mr Uriap's way. On 14 August, 2007, he was cleared of the wilful murder charge by the National Court, an outcome that he anticipated would happen all along.

But what was surprising was that State lawyers utterly failed to offer any evidence at all in court. And the blame of the killing of the suspected cocoa thief was shifted to the police.

Mr Uriap then sued the State for unlawful arrest, malicious detention, malicious prosecution, defamation, loss of business and other heads of damages.

He engaged Warner Shand Lawyers based in Kokopo to represent him. Mr Justin Issack was assigned the task to handle the case.

He successfully executed it at the National Court which awarded damages to Mr Uriap. State lawyers had again failed in their duties to file a notice to defend against the decision within the required time.

In preparation for the assessment of damages, Mr Issack filed various affidavits. These were yet to be presented to court and the truth or otherwise of all of the statements were yet to be tested.

Mr Issack wondered why police had drawn the conclusion that he had fabricated evidence in a conspiracy to defraud the State of K10million – thus his subsequent arrest in Wabag and nightmarish trip to Kokopo leaving his family behind in shock.

'If I had gotten that K10million, I would not be here. Our submission for damages had not been tried yet. I wonder how police drew their conclusions,' he said.

He had suffered for representing a client. I am now wondering if lawyers should not be representing their clients anymore.'

No doubt, the State was indeed losing money to lawsuits in millions every year. Justin Issack was mistreated by his employer, Enga Provincial Government. He was never compensated for the mistreatment he received in the line of his duties as a lawyer for the provincial government.

Justin Issack was never compensated by the State for unlawful arrest and malicious prosecution while working as a lawyer for a client in the normal performance of his duty as a lawyer.

He says, he forgave all the people behind all the nightmare and started his law firm – Lawama Lawyers in 2013 in Port Moresby. He was into his 13 years of private practice operating on the 8th Floor of one of PNG's oldest buildings – the iconic ANG House in downtown Port Moresby. It was the only tall building in the country when independence was gained 50 years ago.

He had four lawyers and had a sizeable client base and did not regret any more. He said that it was good to forgive because the Good Lord opens another door of opportunity when you forgive those who wrong you.

I could relate to Justin Issack and agreed with what he said because forgiving one another was the key to peace and unity in Enga province.

There was another serious threat which kept disturbing the peace in the province, a threat that was destroying the economy and compromised the security and stability of the country's progress. That was tribal warfare induced by politics. Leaders were suspected to be deeply involved supplying the sophisticated weaponry to simple villagers.

Late Dr Samson Amean rang me from the Gateway Hotel in Port Moresby to go with him to Kandep and stop a tribal war involving Don Polye's Kambrip tribe and Alfred Manase's Akulya tribe.

He knew I was an unattached officer. Why he asked me instead of other journalists in his administration was baffling. I was a humiliated public servant and, maybe, he wanted to uphold the Public Service Commission instruction to reinstate me.

But I decided to go with him to demonstrate that it was better to forgive than hold grudges against people. And record the milestone event for future generations to understand that fighting brought nothing but death and destruction.

I have maternal blood ties with both the Kambrip and Akulya tribes. I did not like my uncles and cousins dying in a tribal war for power and prestige, an unnecessary conflict for just one man to enjoy the perks and privileges that came with the blood, tears and suffering of the ordinary people. It had already claimed over 100 lives.

The real heroes of all conflicts were those who advocated for peace. People like late Anderson Aipit was a real peace maker. I had gone with him to stop tribal wars in many parts of Enga province when he was in office. I decided, I might as well go with Dr Samson Amean too.

I am glad I went with him because I recorded everything he did and said when he stopped the fight between my maternal uncles – the Akulya and Kambrip tribesman.

Sadly, Dr Samson Amean, the peacemaker and longest serving provincial administrator of Enga province died nine years later.

5

"HAPPY ARE THE PEACE MAKERS…"

'Happy are the peace makers for they shall be called sons of God"
Mathew 5:9

Dr Samson Amean: Death of a Peacemaker

I was in the company of another peace-maker Chief Sir Paul Kurai when we received the sad news in a poignant text message that Dr Samson Amean had just died.

We were in the Ambum Valley trying to talk with the Kombane tribesman to stop a politically-induced tribal war in the area and to get them to lay down their arms.

"He breathed his last, just now," said Robin Wintawae. He was by his side in the Intensive Care Unit, ICU at the Port Moresby General Hospital on Sunday afternoon at about 2.30pm on 9th October, 2022.

Chief Sir Paul Kurai and the delegation were trying to meet the Kombane people to talk to them again to stop involving themselves in the prolonged tribal war in the Ambum Kompiam electorate. But the people were nowhere to be seen. Their village had been wiped out by their enemy.

During a previous visit, Kombane leaders asked him to stop the fight that had spread all over the Ambum Valley. But now their village and property had been completely destroyed. It was a sad sight to behold. With a heavy heart, Sir Paul Kurai and the peace delegation drove back to Wabag.

Just as we left the deserted village and turned a corner, the text came advising of Dr Amean's death. It seemed to me that of the few peacemakers I had accompanied on previous peace missions into tribal war zones, only Chief Sir Paul Kurai seemed the only one left.

Late Dr Samson Amean had remembered Sir Paul before he was medically evacuated to Port Moresby. He had asked his staff members to find out how much he owed Ribito Hotel. When he was told the amount, he took out his personal cheque book and wrote a cheque for K7,000.

Then he had searched his wardrobe and took out one of his suits, packed it neatly and left it for Chief Sir Paul Kurai. He had also signed a cheque for K70,000 through the government accounts to settle outstanding debts incurred during official functions hosted at Sir Paul's hotel.

After that he was taken to Wapenamanda airport and flown to Port Moresby on a charted aircraft. Sometime later, the news of the heart wrenching death of Dr Amean came in that text message as we were heading back to Wabag.

Dr Amean together with Governor Sir Peter Ipatas had progressed Enga, a back-water province, to modernity in the last thirty years of his distinguished service to the province and country. They had accomplished many impact projects.

Dr Amean was the key figure, the driver of modern Enga. His efforts were marred only by tribal warfare and bad politics which impeded the smooth flow of service, progress, stability and lasting peace.

He operated from both his office at the B Wing top floor of the Ipatas Center and his home a couple of minutes-walk away at Sangurap. A stream of public servants was always seen going there to receive directives or discuss work-related issues with their boss. He was sociable, simple and flexible but always kept himself busy with work.

"My brothers never went to his house. I used to force myself in. He was always with his public servants. He never went for leave or anything. He never rested. His number one priority was work,' said Robin Amean, his brother.

Robin said this in front of acting Provincial Administrator, Sandis Tsaka, members of the top management team and other public servants at the funeral home at late Dr Amean's town residence on Monday afternoon, 10th October.

He requested Sandis Tsaka and the top management team to enable representatives from the Irapun tribe to go down to Port Moresby and accompany Governor Ipatas back to Wabag with the body.

Dr Samson Amean had been sick for some time and when his condition worsened, he was taken to Port Moresby for treatment where he died.

Volumes would be written about his distinguished service to the people of Enga and PNG in the 30 years he worked in the public service, 20 of those as Provincial Administrator.

But something that stood out in all his work, apart from the multi-million-kina impact projects, were his attempts to bring peace to the province.

He knew that the people of Enga must live in peace to benefit more from the impact projects the provincial government was establishing and aimed to drive the province forward and cement the new name tag the province had earned – Modern Enga. Dr Amean died at a sad moment in Enga's history when the province was gripped in election-related tribal warfare resulting in much death and destruction. There was widespread fear and uncertainty in almost every part of the province.

There was intense on-going tribal war in four districts – Kompiam Ambum, Kandep, the new Laiagam district and the new Porgera Paiela district. Although not election- related, the new mining district of Porgera Paiela where Dr Amean grew up continued to be engulfed in social turmoil. It had turned into a killing field.

In this state of affairs, it was fitting to recall some enduring words of late Dr Amean when he was deeply involved in stopping a guerrilla-type tribal war between Alfred Manase's Akula tribe and Don Pomb Polye's Kambrip tribe following the 2012 national elections in Kandep.

It was hoped the words he spoke might influence some leaders involved in election-related tribal wars at the time in the four districts to lay down their arms, respect government and try to live in harmony with each other.

The fighting continued in many parts of the province and became out of control. But the two tribes from Kandep – Kambrip and Akulya tribe had been honest with Dr Samson Amean when they promised never to fight again.

'I am Crying for Your Children'

The fight in Kandep had lasted for over a year. It had claimed over 100 lives and destruction to much property running into millions of kinas.

Saturday 20th April, 2013.will always be remembered by the Akula and Kambrip tribesman as the day their fight was stopped by late Dr Samson Amean, new Provincial Police Commander at the time, Supt Philip Weila, Director Law and Order, Nelson Leia, acting District Administrator, Ben Besawe, police operations commander, Senior Inspector Martin Keliee, senior public servants and police.

Emotion overtook Dr Amean on that day when he saw all the wholesale destruction and obvious suffering on the faces of women and children as soon as we landed at Pura village on a chopper.

He took off his glasses and wept openly in front of these people with the serene Lake Papale stretched out silently in the background where fish swam freely in the clear pristine waters. But the ducks that flocked the waterways here had long disappeared.

Dr Amean cried some more on the steps of the Kandep District office in front of Kambrip tribesmen. He had wept on the same steps in the previous month on his first peace mission to Kandep, on Monday 11th March, 2013. Today, he repeated somber words he had spoken on that first visit.

"Today you see me crying. I am crying for your children. Your children will suffer if you continue to fight. I live in a good comfortable house and my children have a choice to go to nearby schools if the Elementary School at Amala village near Wabag town was full.

"You must think of your children. Bougainville[7] was destroyed due to problems that started like this. Twenty years of conflict there has seen a whole generation of people deprived of formal education. Many people were killed in that conflict and all services stopped. You must be warned, the same thing can happen here in Kandep if you resort to violence again."

These words touched the Akul and Kambrip tribesmen immensely. In a light-hearted approach to ending a serious tribal conflict – government authorities and war-hardened tribal warriors mingled together in a show of unity. They held hands, laughed, sang songs and danced around until sweat ran dry on their painted faces.

Dr Samson Amean was in the thick of it all, enjoying every moment. As a formality, the two tribes and supporters were issued with Preventive Orders to stop them from engaging in further fights. Some of the people were relieved. They wanted to return immediately to their forlorn villages, build houses, make gardens and reset their lives.

But police stopped them.

They were warned to wait patiently for a further two weeks when the Akulya and Kambrip tribes would be brought together – this time to stand face to face on Saturday 11th May in Wabag to sign a Memorandum of Understanding or MoU to permanently stop their fight.

They were to sign the MoU in front of the Police Commissioner, Tom Kulunga, all politicians from Enga province especially Grand Chief Governor Sir Peter Ipatas, Treasury Minister and member for Kandep, Don Polye and prominent lawyer, Alfred Manase.

Provincial Police Commander, Supt Philip Weila said it was important for leaders from Enga to be present at the signing of the MoU because they have a mandated duty to safeguard the welfare of their people and should promptly address underlying social issues that threatened the livelihoods of the common people.

Many key speakers emphasised that the cause of the fight was political in nature and two key figures who had to be present on the 11th of May were Don Polye and Alfred Manase who were viewed as enjoying modern comforts in Port Moresby while their people suffered.

---

7 - Bougainville Crisis 1988-1998; now know as The Autonomous Region of Bougainville.

But in actual fact the two men were also locked in a battle of their own – in the court of Disputed Returns where the latter was challenging the 2012 election win of the former. It was for this reason that their tribesmen and political supporters took on each other, resulting in many deaths and destruction to property worth millions of kinas.

The whole peace process, up to that point, was initiated by Amean, Weila, Keliee, Leia, Besawe, their staff members and local leaders – but none of the leaders who were expected to be present when the peace agreement was signed later.

The only time any politician stepped into the picture was when Ipatas approached Prime Minister Peter O'Neill for help. The PM promptly provided K250,000 as his contribution towards restoration of peace and services in Kandep.

According to official figures the death toll was about 72. But it was estimated that over one hundred lives had been lost. Property worth millions had been reduced to rubble including the multi-million kina, Kandep High Altitude Rice project funded by the Chinese government.

After the two weeks buffer period lapsed on 11th May, the Akulya and Kambrip tribesmen were driven up to Wabag at government expense. They saw each other – face to face, for the first time in front of the police station and agreed to stop fighting.

"Our coming here and talking like this is a sign that we want to stop our fight. We are the ones who are dying and suffer so much," they said.

Dr Amean told them that they would begin restoration work immediately on the two major trunk roads in Mariant. And then would follow rebuilding of schools and health centres that had been destroyed.

"But men killed will never be replaced. No amount of money or pigs will bring those lives back. And this was why the government, the church and law enforcement agencies were stopping the fight to save precious lives," he said.

The Akulya and Kambrip tribes have kept their promise not to fight to this very day after two general elections (2017 & 2022) thanks to late Dr Amean, former Provincial Police Commander, Supt Philip Weila and their team of police and public servants.

The two candidates – Don Polye and Alfred Manase took their election disputes to court. That was the right avenue to resolve election disputes. They had even restrained their supporters from fighting after an election.

Dr Amean would rest easy now that at least some warring tribesmen in Enga and candidates did listen to him and respected his efforts to stop fighting.

When all the good men go one by one, it was a haunting feeling to wonder where Enga would end up if election-related tribal fights remained unresolved.

The onus was definitely on the people – either they died so one man can enjoy power, wealth and prestige or start searching their own hearts for an answer to *how they could make good use of their short life on this earth*. They would also have established a peaceful foundation for their children to prosper in a safe and secure environment. That was more important than short term gain.

Another important person who worked really hard to stop tribal fighting was late Anderson Aipit when he worked briefly as provincial administrator.

But he died too in the prime of his life. If he had been given the chance, he could have done more for the province, in terms of promoting peace and unity among the people.

Only if "Enga Anderson Aipit" Was Given Another Chance

On 12 April, 1993, the Enga Provincial Government under Danely Tindiwi was suspended for a record second time over allegations of gross misconduct in office.

The National Executive Council appointed retired Australian Kiap, Mr Bill Bates as Administrator.

Mr Andersen Aipit had been appointed Acting Secretary on 26th February, 1993 by the Tindiwi government. He had replaced Mr Luke Kembol. When Tindiwi was suspended, Mr. Andersen Aipi also lost his job. But luckily, he became Deputy Administrator.

But Mr. Bates was quite an old man and lacked the vision, drive, strength and tenacity needed to run the affairs of a volatile province like Enga.

When Mr. Andersen Aipit saw these weaknesses, he successfully took out a National Court Order and disqualified Mr Bates and took over as the Enga Administrator by early 1994.

He moved fast to first restore stability in the public service, then removed the expatriate Legal Officer for not providing the right advice to the Enga Provincial Government which resulted in the second suspension.

The legal officer was also removed for allegedly questioning the National Court Order to remove Mr Bill Bates and be replaced by Mr Andersen Aipit.

"The legal Officer was asked to interpret a National Court Order and while everybody else accepted 'Bates out, Aipit in' he went about and questioned the legal order," Mr Aipit wrote to the Enga Employment Authority.

"This in fact divided the public service which could possibly instigate full-scale civil disorder. Enga had gone through hell already and it did not deserve to go through it again the second time. Thus, the decision to sack him is final."

Andersen Aipit also moved fast to gain the trust and confidence of the ordinary people. He personally made it his business to intervene into some seventeen different tribal fights in many parts of the province and successfully negotiated ceasefires leading to peace settlements.

He said lawlessness such as tribal fights existed because leaders failed to act in the initial stages of a conflict. He said this while surrounded by two warring tribal warriors from the Yamaip and Yalipun tribes at Bioko – the place where the colonial government era policeman was killed in the 1960s while they were building a new road to Margarima.

The fight had been raging on for a long time after the alleged rape of a girl.

Andersen Aipit had been accompanied by Provincial Police Commander, Supt Allen Kundi, Provincial Peace and Good Order officer, Mr Andrew Rai and other officers. They had flown into the remote area by chopper. They issued preventive orders to both sides to stop fighting from then onwards. Seven people had died.

The fight started when a councilor's young daughter was allegedly raped by a Yalipun youth when she went to buy soap at Kakaliak in

October, 1993. The girl was in grade 3 at Bioko Community school when the incident took place.

The fight ended on June 1 when the preventative orders were issued to ten leaders from the two warring tribes. Mr Aipit told them that, if they continued to fight, then the ten village court magistrates and councilors would be arrested and put behind bars.

He told them that law and order problems were decreasing and it should be kept that way all over the province.

Lack of law and order, especially tribal war, started because leaders like councilors and village court magistrates failed to do their duties.

"If leaders go in the front and put people at the back then true peace will always be achieved," he told the warriors.

Only one or two people committed the crime and not all of the hundreds of people involved in a war, killing each other and destroying each other's property, should be involved.

"It looks as if you have all gone mad. All of you should have tied up that one man and handed him over to the police," he told the startled people.

People from other provinces talk about Enga in the media as a fighting province. But what critics fail to realise is that Engans can sometimes change their attitudes and live better lives. The power to live good lives is in the villages.

Don't come looking for it in Wabag or Kandep. The councilors and magistrates were given the power to solve your problems here," he said.

Aipit knew that if there was no peace in the province, businessmen would not come to the province to invest. And to encourage business activity, he introduced the popular "Buy in Enga Policy".

This policy stressed that all purchases like blank paper and other consumables made by the Enga Provincial Government and administration had to be done in Enga province.

He noticed that thousands of Kina were spent every year outside the province on such basic items – money which, he felt, could easily end up in the pockets of local businessman.

This policy prompted a handful of local businessmen to set up stationery shops in the small township which still exist from that time onwards.

And to further promote peace and economic activity in the province, he established the foundations of the Enga Cultural Show in 1994 — which has continued to be staged in August of every year. I was appointed a member of that first Enga Cultural Show organising committee. I remember the cascade of people who poured in from all over the province to showcase their culture.

I also saw Mr. Andersen Aipit cry in front of the smoldering ruins of the new Provincial office complex which had been set alight from inside the Bureau of Management Services, which controlled the finances of Enga province.

Mr. Andersen Aipit had come to work in his province as Provincial Planner. Previously, he had held a senior position in the Trade and Industry Department in Port Moresby. He wept openly when the Enga Provincial Headquarters office complex was burnt down by unknown arsonists in May 1993.

It was widely claimed that the fire consumed a lot of evidence that could have been used to prosecute Premier Danely Tindiwi. So, due to a lack of evidence, the Enga Provincial Government was reinstated on June 4th, 1994.

Andersen Aipit, after serving for only about six months handed back power to Tindiwi and the Enga Provincial Assembly at a brief ceremony held at the Amapyaka Lutheran Convention Center on 5th June.

Since Tindiwi had appointed him as the acting Secretary back in February, 1993, Aipit had expected to be given back his job. But, instead, Tau Liu was appointed.

This shocked Dr Samson Amean too because when Andersen Aipit was the Administrator, the National Executive Council had appointed him as the acting Secretary of the Department of Enga.

Late Dr Samson Amean had silently stepped aside. But late Andersen Aipit fought back. He wrote a lengthy letter to Premier Danely Tindiwi questioning him why he had been overlooked after he had done so much for Enga as Administrator in a short space of time. The following is an edited version of the letter.

"The Tindiwi government gave me the acting Secretary position on February 26, 1993 when I least expected it. Unfortunately, Enga Provincial Government was suspended and my dreams were shattered.

"As Administrator, I saved Enga from definite downfall and have come up with specific initiatives that have touched the hearts and minds of almost every Engan."

"I created an office that was second to only a few. In addition, I would love Enga more to act otherwise. The only thing is that I expected you to give me my rightful office – the Office of the Secretary – so I can continue to keep that special relationship with the people."

But certain people whom he termed "leaches" had ensured that Tindiwi did not re-appoint Andersen Aipit to the Secretary's position.

"I call on you to put them aside as they are a liability to you and to our beloved Enga. Let true work be seen by our people rather than allowing yourself to be dragged down by such people who neither have you, your government nor the Enga people in their hearts.

"I now do not have an office and no specific task to perform and I am thus awaiting directions from you. Week No 2 has passed and this has not been done.

"Finally, I have proven to you over and over again that I am your right-hand man to take you and Enga beyond the horizon and even cop the nasty shots every now and then when the going gets tough.

"Those who are mingling around you now were never around you and I doubt whether they would be around you when you ride the rough waves yet again. More likely they will scatter like chickens as they have always done.

"We are supposed to be leaders in our own right, making bold decisions as we have full authority over Enga.

"Instead, you are allowing yourselves to be toyed around like a five-year old child by the so-called leaches as described above.

"The direct consequence is that Enga is and can gradually slip away from your hands. Because of this, my request is simple.

"You will be surprised as to how things can be made simple and effective for the sake of our beloved Enga people and for a long while you can enjoy heading a government that is effective with a public service that is responsive to your vision and people's needs."

But Tindiwi did not respond favorably—and did not even acknowledge receiving Aipit's letter. In disgust, "Enga Andersen Aipit" contested the Premiership race in the 1994 national elections, but lost.

Tindiwi however won back his seat as premier for a third term but never lasted to enjoy perks and privileges that comes with occupying such public office. Andersen Aipit's prediction that Tindiwi would ride 'the rough waves yet again" had been fulfilled.

Andersen Aipit Suddenly Passes on, Danely Tindiwi Loses Power

When an important person from Enga province died, all the people felt the loss. They were the pride of everybody in the province.

When PNG High Commissioner to Fiji, Dennis Kepore died of a heart attack, Enga lost him. So was Riot Squad Commander Inspector Peter Pyaso who was killed by warring tribesmen in Kompiam. Enga province also lost.

Public Service Commissioner Waka Busa who was killed in a traffic accident after a UPNG graduation ceremony. Andersen Aipit joined the list when he suddenly died of a heart attack in his village.

Other Engan public servants died when some politicians manipulated the system and smartly filtered out well-educated and experienced professionals and replaced them with their own cronies.

Only Premier Ned Laina was transparent and remained neutral in public service recruitment matters. He had the guts and foresight to stop a Department of Enga public service staff selection process in early 1989. He asked Personnel Management Secretary, Wep Kanawi to suspend all appointments when he suspected nepotism was involved.

Premier Ned Laina wanted a careful screening of all appointments made to appoint the best people in the various positions in the Department of Enga Administration.

Michael Puio, Luke Kembol, Philip Kikala, Andersen Aipit, Dr Samson Amean, Tau Liu and a long list of others were well qualified. They had all gone through the rigorous and strict colonial administration structured education system to go to High School, university and finally to work their way to senior levels. But some of these top names disappeared into thin air.

Mr. Luke Kembol was first a Deputy Secretary before he became Secretary. But he was dumped by Premier Ned Laina. He favored Michael Puio a top planner with the National Planning Office in Waigani.

Michael Puio left the scene when Danely Tindiwi came in as Premier of Enga and took on Luke Kembol again only to be dumped shortly thereafter. He was replaced by Mr. Andersen Aipit after some sort of an argument. Mr. Andersen Aipit was in office for two weeks only when the Enga Provincial Government was suspended a second time.

However, Mr. Aipit was appointed Deputy Administrator. But after a hard legal battle, he took over from Bill Bates as Administrator. At the time National Executive Council, NEC appointed Dr Samson Amean as Acting Secretary of the Department of Enga. For five months these two young men were working very closely together.

On June 5th, however, Andersen Aipit handed power back to Danely Tindiwi whose government had been reinstated. Enga people were now in a guessing game as to who would be the next Secretary. There were many names floating around. Would it be Andersen Aipit or Dr Samson Amean? If it was somebody else, would Mr Aipit and Dr Amean disappear from the public scene like some of their predecessors?

In all respects, Andersen Aipit and Dr Samson Amean had worked with a common interest to serve the people of Enga in one accord. They had the same vision, and the same genuine desire to get Enga moving forward.

Some of the new initiatives like the Buy in Enga policy, and the Enga Show were effective and people generally accepted them outright and were the subjects of discussion in many a *hausman* across the province.

What decision Premier Tindiwi made to accept the initiatives and policies set down by Andersen Aipit and Dr Samson Amean or to reject them would be the deciding factor of his own future political career.

Premier Tindiwi had to realise that it was not a good idea to bring in somebody from outside to be Department Secretary. He had to seek from within. Either he confirmed Dr Amean or re-appointed Andersen Aipit.

People in power in free democracies anywhere in the world often made decisions in line with public opinion. Tindiwi had to make appointments in line with whom Enga people wished to have. Tindiwi's choice was exceptional, but a surprise pick.

He brought in Tau Liu. He was the Director Human Resource Development in the Department of Enga Administration.

Under the new reforms that followed after the elections, Premier Danely Tindiwi became deputy Governor to Jeffery Balakau. But when he was dismissed from office, Tindiwi automatically became acting governor.

For his deputy, Danely Tindiwi appointed Provincial Assembly member and Wabag Local Level Council president, Cr Peter Ipatas. But he very easily sidestepped Tindiwi through a successful court order and took over as Governor of the province, a position he has held onto since. He won his first election in 1997.

Late Andersen Aipit had been hoping to nominate in the 2007 national elections. But he died suddenly from a suspected heart attack on 29th December, 2006. He had been attending a Christian Apostolic Fellowship (CAF) church National Youth Conference in Porgera.

Andersen Aipit went home to Kaipale village in Laiagam when he suddenly collapsed near the highway. He was rushed to Wabag General Hospital, but doctors pronounced him dead on arrival.

That day, many people were in Wabag town when the new People's Party of Governor Peter Ipatas was being launched. The sad news of Aipit's death spread fast and shocked everyone.

Although the program still continued as planned, an electric band that was ready to entertain the crowds did not perform in respect of late Andersen Aipit.

His body was held at the Wabag General Hospital morgue for a few more days because of the launch and New Year celebrations. Thousands of mourners poured in for the funeral at Kaipale, his village. They included Deputy Prime Minister, Don Polye, Inter-Government Relations Minister, Sam Abal, local MP, Kappa Yarka, provincial government member, Lukas Yalipin, senior public servants from the area – Philip Kikala, David Lambu, Patrick Nasa, public servants and others attended his funeral.

Former Lagaip Porgera MP, Waitea Magnolias said, that Anderson Aipit was a true campaigner against corruption and good material for top government jobs but had been overlooked.

National Alliance Enga Branch President, Cr Paul Kurai, on behalf of his party, contributed three large pigs, food items and K10,000 in cash towards funeral expenses.

Late Aipit was survived by three sons and three daughters and his wife of mixed parentage of Madang and Enga. All the children were in school except one girl who was working in Port Moresby.

"I have proven to you over and over again that I am your right-hand man to take you and Enga beyond the horizon," Aipit had written to Premier Danely Tindiwi when he requested him to reappoint him as Secretary of the Department of Enga in 1994.

"We are supposed to be leaders on our own right, making bold decisions as we have full authority over Enga province and its people. Instead, you are allowing yourself to be toyed around like a five-year old child," he wrote.

Tindiwi did not give Andersen Aipit the Secretary's job. But the work Aipit did and the things he said in the short period he was in office were words that should be etched in gold.

He was buried at Kaipale village beside the national highway. He was a high-caliber elite with great potential. But the government did not recognise him. The people also rejected him at the polls. But the love and commitment he had for his beloved province was real. Maybe he loved it too much!

Anderson Aipit's legacy will be the Enga Show, the Buy in Enga policy and his involvement in stopping seventeen tribal wars in the province. It is a long lasting legacy!!

6

ACTING ON IMPULSE, CONTROLLED BY EMOTION

"When humanity dwells in the souls of leaders, the nation and citizens remain preciously in their hearts,"

Mr. Kang in Quora, 6th March, 2025

Jacob Luke Found Dead in The Jungle; Nine Women Tortured

Jacob Luke, another iconic figure, who equally loved his province and lived among his people was found dead alone in the jungle a day after of his return from America.

The multi – millionaire, owner of Mapai Transport was never expected to die in such a manner a short distance from his mansion at Lakolam village after arriving from the US – in July, 2022.

Jacob Luke was physically fit, healthy and of sound mind. How could he just walk into the bush alone and die – to be found the next day?

These kinds of provocative questions may have influenced relatives to round up nine women from the vicinity and torture them in the most heinous manner possible. These innocent women were blamed for killing Jacob Luke through *sanguma* or sorcery.

Jacob Luke's people knew he was a Christian and staunch supporter of the Lutheran church of which his father was a pastor. Late Luke himself had been a product of St Paul's Lutheran High School. How could relatives jump to these conclusions and tarnish the family name?

Late Jacob possessed a loving 'Spirit to Serve', the motto he adopted for his transport company to serve people with love, respect, dignity and understanding

But sadly, his people had acted on impulse controlled by emotion to accuse nine innocent women of killing him through *Sanguma* or sorcery. How was this possible?

Before I relate some details of the cruel act, let me first relate how late Jacob Luke's body was found and trace his last movements in PNG since arriving from America.

His body was found by Digicel PNG technicians who used their GPS tracking devices to pinpoint the exact location from where he had made his last phone call 24 hours earlier.

They had taken a photo of the location in the jungle some distance from his new Mukeres home at Lakolam on the Highlands Highway to Porgera. The relatives enlarged the photograph to pinpoint where Jacob's body was.

He had died sitting upright dressed in a grey sweatshirt with a hood. He had his gum boots on. One of his mobile phones and a bush knife he had taken along lay beside him.

He hadn't struggled. No suffering, no surprise, no regret nor was there fear or terror written on his face. His facial expression was one of peace and calm said Jacob's second brother, Kayto Lesan Luke.

Jacob Luke was humble and kind. He was slow to anger and lived a normal, ordinary life. He never acted like a multi-millionaire who owned Mapai Transport a large trucking company that was contracted to major resource projects on the coast and in the highlands.

At some stage when Jacob was still in America, he rang his best friend and brother-in-law Chief Sir Paul Kurai. He told him how he and a group of twelve friends and relatives were visiting fourteen states in a private jet belonging to an American business associate.

On Sunday 17th July 2022, Jacob rang him from Lae to tell him that he was back in the country and was preparing to drive up to Wabag in Enga province.

But Chief Sir Paul Kurai asked him to delay his trip. He needed somebody to pick him and three friends up from Nadzab Airport on Monday 18th July.

"I had to stay back because you are important to me" Jacob Luke told Paul Kurai as he and his three friends seated themselves in his latest model V8 wagon.

'Thank you for waiting. You can be my driver today," Chief Sir Paul Kurai recalls jokingly saying to Jacob. They both laughed as Jacob steered the powerful vehicle out from the parking lot towards Lae International Hotel.

Before Jacob left them at the hotel to settle down, he gave Paul Kurai the keys to a vehicle for use during their stay in Lae. That was the very last time Chief Sir Paul Kurai saw his best friend in person. His next telephone call was from Kassam Pass telling him that he was now headed to Wabag.

That was on Tuesday morning. In the afternoon Jacob called again, this time from Ribito Hotel in Wabag town.

Jacob Luke apologised and made one request. He asked Paul Kurai to go to his residence in Lae and pick up his passport which he had forgotten and take it with him to Port Moresby.

They had made arrangements to travel to Manila in the Philippines on Sunday 24th July on another business trip.

Jacob did not ring on Wednesday. So, on Thursday, he rang Jacob Luke but there was no answer. He tried several times but still there was no response. He did not suspect anything was wrong with his best friend.

So, Paul Kurai sent a text message explaining he was making his way back to Port Moresby with his passport. He would wait for him there for their planned trip to Manila.

But his text messages remained unanswered. This was uncharacteristic of Jacob Luke.

Then Paul Kurai received two consecutive calls from Luke's brother, Kapili. He ignored the first but answered the second. There was a slight pause on the other end. Then Kapili broke the sad news that his late brother, Jacob Luke had been found dead in the jungle.

It was shocking news. It took some time for reality to finally sink in for Paul Kurai. How could Jacob just die like that?

The saddest part was when the nine women were accused of causing his death through sorcery or sanguma. They were rounded up and tortured in the most heinous manner possible resulting in the death of four within the hour. Five survivors were rescued later.

Houses and property belonging to late Jacob Luke's neighbors at Lakolam were burnt by a mob who came over the mountain range accusing them of not looking after him properly, especially when he chose to go live with them near the Highlands highway.

They should have provided security or at least one of them should have accompanied him into the bush. Jacob Luke was such a big man, hard to replace.

But he always took solitary walks and seemed to enjoy the natural surroundings when he relocated to Lakolam from Monokam, his other village. He didn't need security. He even liked to drive all by himself from Lae to Enga and back.

The last thing he would have liked to see was for his relatives to torture the innocent women. He was a strong Christian, one of the main foundations of the Gutnius Lutheran Church.

He did not only give to the church but to other charity organisations and attended to the needs of his employees and relatives too. Like when he put smiles on the faces of 12 of his close friends by taking them on their first ever overseas trip to America

He loved everybody and liked to make people happy. He gave freely. His company motto is 'Spirit to Serve' and that's what he liked to do – to serve freely and give freely, no matter the cost.

Who in Papua New Guinea ever gave away a nearly million-kina brand new Mack highway truck to a driver?

Only Jacob Luke did – not one but 10 of them. He knew that he made big money through the careful driving and hard work of his drivers.

He gave the brand new Macks to ten senior drivers because that was their reward for working so hard to make Mapai Transport a multi-million-kina enterprise.

Henry Enomb Tanda had been present to capture the moment when Jacob gave the 10 trucks to his drivers. Jacob Luke had emphasised that the drivers should bring along their wives to get the keys from him because, he was giving the new trucks to their families. The wives were part owners.

"Traditionally, we have a saying in Enga. If you give *bilas* or decorations like bird of paradise feathers to a person who doesn't own any, he will not look after it. He will break the headdresses."

Jacob Luke said. "Some of you act like cowboys in my trucks. So now I am giving you *bilas* which you will own and you will look after. It will be yours.

"When you come out to get the keys, I want you to bring your wives with you. I know that when you drive the trucks, many of you will misbehave. Your wives are going to get the keys because the trucks belong to them too."

Each truck was worth about K600,000. In one decision, he created 10 new Papua New Guinean-owned transport companies and passed on the ownership of more than K6million of Mapai assets to his drivers and their families.

"I used to be a driver before and I know. The most important people in a transport company are the drivers. They make the wheels turn. The rest of us are just support staff."

People knew the kind of person Jacob Luke was – a generous, simple, peace-loving citizen. But his good name was tarnished when the nine women were accused of causing his death through witchcraft or *sanguma*.

How can that possibly be? Nine women meeting somewhere in the spirit, all planning to eat the heart of Jacob Luke in the forest! How absurd and demonic a thought.

The innocent women were rounded up and tortured in the most heinous way possible resulting in the death of four. The five women who survived were rescued by police and taken to a safe house.

One of the five survivors told reporters: "We do not know anything about sorcery and yet we were falsely accused and tortured and burnt all over our bodies."

The perpetrators made a metal platform out of roofing iron and used tires to build fires underneath.

The nine women had gone to mourn the death of Jacob Luke but instead they were falsely accused of causing his death through sorcery by people who were not close to Jacob or his family

They were stripped naked and blindfolded and placed on the burning hot platform to helplessly scream in pain as they were repeatedly burnt with scorching red hot bush knives that sliced into their bare skin while the hot roofing iron slow-cooked their bodies.

Other perpetrators used metal rods which were heated in the fire and shoved into their private parts and several of them were unconscious from the pain.

All nine of them were bound together by their wrists and were tortured continuously for almost 12 hours. They were finally released because of the pleading of some of the survivors who knew the tormentors. The five survivors would bear the bad memory and scars on their bodies for the rest of their lives. The perpetrators had undermined Jacob's Christian principles of sharing and giving. He was never a violent person. What a great shame it was!

Signs Accompany the Burial of Jacob Luke & Dr Samson Amean

Believing in dreams and interpreting unusual phenomena or signs that occurred on sad occasions like funerals has always been part of Enga culture.

The signs and dreams influenced the daily lives of relatives so much so that they confessed or stopped negative behavior, particularly if it was to hurt other people. They would also interpret the signs as leading to a brighter future.

When an important person died and if such signs manifested, the stories were retold as folklore in every *akalyanda* & *endanda* or man's and woman's houses, gradually spread by word of mouth. The signs reflected the type of person he or she was in life.

Today, news of such events, whether properly researched or not, traveled much faster on social media using advanced digital technology in an age where everybody seemed to own mobile phones complete with video cameras.

During the week-long funeral program of late Dr Samson Amean, light rain fell at the right moments on three different occasions.

The people interpreted this openly, even by the master of ceremonies over the public address system that it was a sign that Dr Amean himself was crying with the mourners – the people whom he loved and served for more than three decades.

On Monday 17th October, after a touching full military funeral program, fittingly accorded to late Dr Samson Amean, light rain fell towards the end when Governor Sir Peter Ipatas, Porgera Paiela member, late Maso Karipe, assembly members, public servants and family members went to place wreaths and pay their last respects.

When everybody returned to their seats, the light drizzle stopped. The same thing happened on Wednesday 19th October when Dr Amean was laid to rest just when a full military burial program ended. It stopped shortly after and was replaced with fine weather.

Light rain fell yet again on Friday afternoon, 21st October when customary compensation was paid to late Dr Amean's maternal uncles and cousins. Towards the end there was a mighty earth-shattering thunderous roar accompanied by lightning and strong winds.

Town residents could see it coming and worried for a moment how they would cook their evening meals if power supply was disrupted. During such storms, trees would be uprooted and thrust against power lines cutting off the power supply completely.

But there was no thunderstorm, only a light drizzle as on the last two occasions.

While late Dr Amean's funeral program was accompanied by light rain, Jacob Luke's burial was accompanied with a display of colorful lights in the evening sky in July, 2022.

During his burial, the lights appeared and formed an incredible arc resembling the gateway to heaven. Even the image of a sheep was seen lying down in front of the arc.

Everybody who had cameras and mobile phones took multiple shots of the phenomena and uploaded them on social media, which went viral.

The interpretation was that Jacob Luke's relatives had been wrong to brutally torture nine women blaming his death on sorcery.

People felt that the sign also indicated Jacob was in a good place and that forgiveness and peace should prevail in the community and people should continue on with the work Jacob had started at Lakolam village. He had come home to build his home, a church and a school in the village and to live among them. Some Engan businessmen established themselves away from home in fear that their property might be destroyed in never-ending tribal feuds.

Jacob Luke's good name was marred only by the attack on the nine women and burning down of property belonging to their families by some relatives who came across the mountain range.

It appeared that Jacob Luke seemed to know his time was near and went alone into the jungle to die peacefully.

Dr Samson Amean probably knew he might not return when he was medically evacuated to Port Moresby. He had left his suit for Paul Kurai and had paid off his bills.

A new government building was built in his memory, known as the Dr Amean Building beside the provincial headquarters office complex which he had operated from for 30 long years.

He was laid to rest in a plot where three others rested: Enga's first elected premier Danely Tindiwi, first deputy premier and Dr Amean's own dad, Peter Amean, MBE and Enga's first female judge, Regina Sangu.

They were all selfless, humble and peace-loving citizens. They devoted their whole lives to serve Enga and the country. They had given their best to improve social and economic conditions for the common people to live in peace and prosperity.

The province could not afford to lose such men and women so soon. They all had so many years left in them. But the sad reality was that they had died and nothing much could be done about it. That's the reality of life. But everybody in the province, including family members, friends and employees should draw strength and carry on with the work they all started.

But the people in the province were always fighting and that was something businessmen were forced to contend with on a daily basis. The scourge had scared away a lot of potential businessmen to other peaceful locations in the country.

Jacob Luke came home from Lae to build his modern mansion in his village at Lakolam. He named it 'Jacob Luke's Mukeres Home' located right beside the Highlands highway, a couple of kilometers from Wabag town.

Jacob Luke had invited Chief Sir Paul Kurai to the official opening of his new home. He knew it wasn't properly completed so Kurai asked his friend why he was rushing.

"There is no time left," he said bluntly to Sir Paul.

According to Enga culture, if a person spoke like that, it was regarded as abnormal, an indication something drastic might happen to the person. But such thoughts were kept at the back of their minds until it happened.

Perhaps late Jacob Luke felt his time was near and he had to open his home sooner when he did in mid-2022 just before the national elections. After that he went to America with close friends and relatives.

When he returned, he died and his people went berserk, rounded up the women who had gone to his funeral and subjected them to barbaric tortures.

It was a shameful act when people were controlled by their emotions too quickly to burn government property when they, the people themselves, were involved in a conflict.

It was a sad scenario to see public property burnt to ashes and ruins of once thriving hospitals and schools in every part of the province.

There was one such ruin in the Tsak Valley of Wapenamanda. It demonstrated that as much as people had no respect for other people's lives and private properties, they could easily destroy mission or government establishments which provided services for everybody.

Respect For Law, Authority Gone, Tsak Secondary School Gone

As much as people rounded up other people's wives and daughters and accused them of murder through sorcery, the total destruction of Tsak Secondary School in Wapenamanda was a good example of how Enga people did not respect and appreciate government efforts to serve them.

They didn't seem to pause to think for one moment that Tsak Secondary School was benefiting them and their children. That they didn't have to travel long distances to enrol their sons and daughters at such institutions. The population was growing fast and soon there would be no space in the few institutions that continued to operate.

They had to realise that schools and health facilities established by the government, missions or privately established by individuals benefited a lot of people.

The people of Tsak Valley did not seem to appreciate the Enga Provincial government which had established the new secondary school in their area. They burned it to the ground with no second thoughts.

The Enga Provincial Government saw the need to build more high schools including Tsak Secondary, due to a rapid increase in the number of enrolments in primary schools.

This was due mainly to the popular 'Free Education Policy' which Governor Sir Peter Ipatas supported when he was first elected to office during the 1997 general national elections. He even rebuilt the Highlands Lutheran International Secondary School destroyed by arsonists.

Ipatas has continued to establish many other educational learning institutions from primary to colleges in the province too, the most notable being the Innovative Enga University with faculties at Sopas, Irelya and Akom.

Some educated Engans engaged at various levels of government and the private sector were the fruit of the Free Education Policy.

Currently, there are six high schools and six secondary schools as well as colleges. Three more high schools were approved, gazetted and under construction in Kandep. The only high school in Kandep which had been operating for many years was eventually upgraded to secondary school status. There was still need to establish more high schools. Education planners had to cope with a rapidly increasing school-aged youth population.

Tsak High School was established in 2011 to cope with the high demand. But it was totally destroyed during wide-spread fighting in the area.

Many teachers did not want to go and teach at Tsak High School because lots of battles had been fought for many years in the valley. It resulted in the destruction of millions of kina in government and private property – and hundreds of lives lost.

A private high school established by Mr Ben Wia, one of Tsak's first educated elites was one of the institutions destroyed during a previous tribal war.

Ben Wia had been supported by his Yambaren Paus tribe in establishing the private high school. They were the first tribe in the country to be given a licence to run a high school as a nationally recognised agency school in March 1987.

This followed an agreement signed by Premier Ned Laina, Provincial education authorities, representatives of the school board of governors and Ben Wia's people.

Part of the agreement stated that the school was to be jointly run by the provincial government and the Yambaren Pausa tribesman.

But during a tribal conflict with neighbouring tribes the high school went up in smoke. Not only that, the nearby Tsak Pumakos Catholic Mission which had been established by the first missionary to Enga – Fr Jerry Bus, SVD was reduced to ashes as well. Clearly, there was no respect for Mr Ben Wia, Premier Ned Laina and the Catholic church.

Despite the past history of senseless destruction, one teacher – Mr Jerry Nyeta from the Kunalun tribe of Sirunki in Laiagam put up his hand to go to the valley and start the school at Yogos, an abandoned government outpost.

He moved to Yogos with eleven teachers and began developing the three hectares state property which had been vacated by police and Coffee Industry Corporation staff when tribal war persisted for many years.

Mr Nyata and his pioneer teachers moved their families into run-down IMQ houses, renovated some of the vacant buildings as classrooms and established the staff room and headmaster's office in a run-down community hall.

Two hundred and twenty-six Grade 9 students were enrolled immediately dividing them into four classes. Of these pioneer students, 170 completed their Grade 10 education in 2013. Of these, 88 were selected to continue onto grade 11. The following year, 80 more students were selected to do grade 11.

Meanwhile, the school was improving with ample assistance from the Enga Provincial Government. Four double classroom buildings were completed as well as a library building, science laboratory and permanent toilet building.

Five new teacher's houses were under construction at a cost of K270,000. The Enga Provincial Government allocated K500,000 to build a mess and kitchen, one more double classroom and more staff houses.

From that allocation, the school bought a Lucas Mill to mill their own timber. Locally sawn timber was used to build the five teachers houses – which meant that only iron roofing, steel posts, nails were sourced from outside.

Within only five years, the school had improved so much with community support. Impressed with the developments, Education authorities elevated Tsak High School to a secondary school status in 2016.

The year 2017 saw the first intake of Grade 11 students and appointment of two deputy principals while pioneer headmaster, Mr Jerry Nyata was elevated to Principal.

A new four-in-one double classroom at a cost of nearlyK500,000 was built to cater for the four classes of pioneer Grade 11 students enrolled that year.

The 5KV genset used to supply power was inadequate for the expanding school. More funds were going to be secured for a new power generator while construction of five new staff houses began.

Authorities saw that, as Tsak Secondary School progressed, it required more land for more staff houses, classrooms, sports fields, agricultural projects and for student dormitories. At the time, all students in Grade 9, 10 and 11 were day students.

Mr Jerry Nyata liked to teach agriculture at Wabag Secondary School prior to his appointment as principal. He admired the rich state-owned farmland at Yogos, not then being utilised by Department of Primary Industry.

He wished to ask the provincial government to transfer the property to the school because it required more land to expand.

But just when Tsak Secondary School was progressing well, an indication that the Enga Provincial Government' free education policy was bearing fruit, everything was reduced to rubble in renewed tribal warfare in the area. Over 20 years of effort put in by the provincial government had been wasted.

Mulitaka High School was also completely destroyed as soon as it was set up. Many years earlier, Liagam High School had been destroyed. Later it was relocated to the Upper Headwaters of the Lagaip River at Philikambi.

The people seemed to have no respect for government and the efforts it put in to provide vital services like health and education for them in the province.

Conversely, it may appear, as in the escalating crime situation in the golden district of Porgera, that when ordinary people took such extreme measures to disobey laws to burn schools, perhaps they saw that the leaders holding the reins had vested interests in such projects in the country.

Such leaders and individuals who continued to destroy and involved themselves in secretive corrupt government deals and unlawful activities should know history. It reveals that their very own actions would result in reaping what he or she sowed.

History Has Lessons, Criminals & Corrupt Leaders Beware

Leaders must not shout *'prosperity'* and secretly involve themselves in corrupt deals when their constituents suffer from want of basic services. Or when they oppose authority.

Leaders need to exercise caution and conduct public affairs in an honest, fair and transparent manner, especially in this land of a thousand tribes. Elected leaders were from just one of the tribes, and they had to be very cautious in dealing with people from the other tribes.

Elected leaders had to be aware when they were putting a lot of strain on the lives of the ordinary people. What did people think when their loved ones died from curable diseases because there was no medicine, or when the cost of living became unbearable mainly in urban areas?

Were the leaders not aware that the people became angrier every time a million-kina corrupt deal was exposed?

Papua New Guinea has already seen the rise of angry young men like bank robber William Kapris, 'Black Jesus' Steven Tari and 'Robin Hood'

Tommy Barker, whose gang was pursued in once peaceful Milne Bay Province.

Was it not possible angry revolutionaries were being bred in an environment of deep-rooted corruption, bad governance, nepotism and other vices so prevalent in successive governments since independence? A story from the pages of history would hopefully instil some sense in the ruling class.

On 6th September 1901, William McKinley became the third president of the United States of America to be assassinated.

He was shot by shy 28-year-old former steel worker Leon Czolgosz inside the Temple of Music during the Pan-American Exposition in Buffalo, New York.

"Welcome President McKinley, Chief of our Nation and Our Empire," were the welcoming words displayed at the expo. But anarchist Leon Czolgosz had planned to kill McKinley, who was six months into his second term.

Czolgosz had arrived in Buffalo a few days earlier and purchased a .32 calibre Iver Johnson revolver – the same type of weapon that another anarchist had used to assassinate Italian King Umberto I the previous summer.

He waited in the front line with other people inside the Temple of Music to meet and shake the president's hand. When McKinley reached out to shake his hands, Czolgosz shot him twice, with the revolver wrapped in a white handkerchief.

"It was in my heart; there was no escape for me," Czolgosz later said. "All those people seen bowing to the great ruler. I made up my mind to kill that ruler."

On 29th October 1901, Czolgosz was executed in the electric chair at New York's Auburn Prison.

"I killed the president for the good of the labouring people, the good people," he said in the moments before the sentence was carried out. "I am not sorry for my crime."

What is the significance of this story in today's PNG where so called 'die hard supporters' who hid behind fake names heap praise on certain leaders by giving them all sorts of uncanny titles like King, Queen, Chief, Leader, One and Only to name a few?

The rural masses may be ignorant but the educated few who live in the cities could possibly no longer be fooled.

Our leaders must not shout 'prosperity and water down important issues while they are secretly involved in corrupt deals to enrich themselves and their cronies.

Former University of Technology Vice Chancellor, Albert Shram said accepting extractive, corrupted State institutions which benefited only a predatory elite means keeping the whole population hostage in an endless cycle of poverty, ignorance, disease and violence.

Make no mistake – accepting the Chinese development model, means to do away with all democratic niceties and individual rights. Eventually, this predatory elite will be hated by the population at large.

It was disappointing that no serious effort was being made to protect constitutional rights and those essential institutions for an open, free and democratic society, such as a free press, independent universities, an independent judiciary, police, etc. PNG inherited these institutions from the colonial times, but then failed to exhibit collectively the behaviour required to sustain a democratic society.

Making inclusive, democratic institutions function in PNG was never going to be easy. It was hoped that politically motivated murders won't be necessary in the future.

But a new dangerous trend was beginning to take root. It was politically-induced tribal warfare.

7

CELEBRATING AMIDST NEW TRIBAL WARFARE TRENDS

Every day there was gunfire in Enga Province. Constant reports of death and destruction poured in from almost every district. Property valued at millions went up in smoke – shops, homes, schools, health facilities, all gone

– Author

Celebrating 75 Years of Mission Work, First Local Bishop Arnold Orowae Dies

Like a tree, the Catholic Church had grown strong to maturity but, sadly, it was slowly destroyed at the roots by politically motivated tribal warfare, sorcery-related killings and deep-rooted corruption.

This was the message veteran missionary, Archbishop Bishop Douglas Young SVD brought across to thousands of Catholic faithful who celebrated the arrival of the first missionaries to Enga, 75 years ago.

Bishop Young had been celebrating different stages of growth of the church – 25 years, 50 years and now 75 years later the bishop was proud to celebrate with two local bishops from Enga, local priests and thousands of Catholics from throughout the province.

But on the other hand, the progress of church work was hindered by a new trend of politically-induced tribal warfare involving sophisticated high-powered guns and sorcery.

In olden times, although bad, it was understandable why people fought over land or women as this was part of tradition. But politically-induced tribal warfare and sorcery-related killings were very dangerous new trends that needed to be stopped immediately.

"It's not part of our culture. It wasn't here before and it must be stopped," Bishop Young SVD said. He had come to Enga as a deacon and worked in the province for many years before moving to Mt Hagen.

He wondered where Enga would end up in the next 75 years if people didn't realise that bad politics and sorcery- related killings could gradually destroy Christian values and beliefs planted as seeds by early missionaries like Fr Jerry Bus, SVD.

Chief Sir Paul Kurai also gave a speech at the celebrations and told people to heed Bishop Young's warning and stop the slaughter. He had been trying very hard to stop an on-going tribal fight in the Kompiam-Ambum electorate and the celebrations provided the opportunity for him to speak to the thousands of Christians, urging them not to fight – starting from that day onwards.

"Right now, as I stand here and speak, two of my Kamainwan tribesmen have been killed at Kasi in the Ambum Valley. I told my people to stay away from the fighting area. They should listen to me.

"People should know that their lives are special – gifts from God. They should respect themselves and enjoy the short time all of us have on this earth"

Similar messages were delivered by speakers during the action-packed golden jubilee celebrations as the fighting continued in the Kompiam Ambum electorate.

Archbishop Douglas Young SVD was proud to celebrate with the two local bishops – Bishop Arnold Orowae and Auxiliary Bishop Justine Ain Soongie. They were both from Catholic Mission Tskiro near Kasi village where the election -related tribal war was raging that moment.

Exactly, two years and 25 days later, Bishop Arnold Orowae died on Thursday 27 December, 2024 at the Wabag General Hospital after experiencing a drop in his blood pressure.

The sad news instantly spread to all corners of Enga province thanks to social media, disrupting Christmas and New Year celebrations for the catholic faithful, friends and relatives.

Nobody expected to hear such sad news about a humble down-to-earth man of God like Bishop Arnold Orowae at such a merry moment.

Bishop Arnold had developed a heart problem in 2006 and was taken to Australia for treatment. He did recover fairly well, but not totally. He had been taking medication for 18 years. This enabled him to perform his pastoral duties adequately.

At the time of his death, he complained of the heart symptoms resurfacing. He was taken to Par Health Centre. But a particular drug which could have stabilised his condition was not available.

He had to be referred to Wabag General hospital, but the doctors there could not help either because the drug was not in stock there.

In desperation, Auxiliary Bishop Justine Ain Soongie and his priests had no other option but to airlift Bishop Arnold to Australia. They paid the airline and were ready to go, but he died.

Meanwhile, doctors at Wabag General Hospital had also worked hard to source the particular drug from somewhere. But when it arrived, it was too late by about five minutes.

"Bishop Arnold talked properly. He was normal but died. Shortly after his death, say maybe 5 minutes later, the medicine arrived.' said Fr Philip James. 'But it was too late. But we had done all we could to save our bishop."

As soon as Bishop Arnold died, people began demanding that the Catholic Church arrange a funeral home at Mommers Soccer oval in Wabag town, the venue where he had been ordained as Bishop.

The people pressured the church and said Bishop Arnold was a recognised leader in the province and an open funeral which would allow the public to attend would befit his status. But funeral organisers refused it outright.

Chief Sir Paul Kurai said from Port Moresby that the people were right about Bishop Arnold being a leader. But they failed to understand that he was a church leader.

People should understand that Bishop Arnold was a man of God and earthly practices should not mix with how the church handled the dead bodies of their workers.

Today, funerals are big business in the country which attract cash, cartons of coke, sugarcane, bags of rice, sweet potatoes … everything. But people had to understand that tradition can't mix with religious practices.

Deaths of people had generated so much wealth in Enga province. Take for instance when late Joe Tamalane, Chief Sir Paul's eldest brother died.

"Our relatives and friends wanted us to extend the funeral period when they saw over K200,000 in cash was contributed in just two days of mourning. This was not to mention the pigs, coke and, cooked food, firewood and everything else that was contributed by mourners.

"I had to forcefully stop it. I asked my people why they hadn't gone to visit, late Joe Tamalane when he was in hospital. You see, I visited Bishop Arnold at the hospital before coming to Port Moresby. I gave him some money. And I am satisfied I at least visited him," he said.

People had to respect the Catholic church and other churches too which operated in the province. When any church worker passed on, people had to refrain from holding funerals in the traditional way.

Sir Paul said he knew the Enga culture well and it was okay to receive cash, pigs and food contributed by people who came to mourn when ordinary people died.

But when our bishops, priests, sisters – people who serve the church die, public funerals must not be held.

'Arguments and discontentment set in when maternal uncles and aunties or *'mama lain'* came into the picture. In this case, we do not want to complicate church procedures and hide what Bishop Arnold stood for in his 41 years of priestly life.'

Bishop Arnold Orowae would not have liked a public funeral. He didn't even want to be buried in a fancy grave. He was a simple, humble man who wanted everybody to respect each other's lives and live in peace.

Bishop Arnold Condemns Leaders Involved in Corruption

When he was ordained Bishop of Wabag Diocese in 2008 and when he was elected president of the Catholic Bishops Conference of Papua New Guinea and Solomon Islands in 2014, he spoke out against torture and killing of innocent women accused of *sanguma* or sorcery which was never practised in traditional times.

Bishop Arnold and Axillary Bishop Justine Ain were deeply involved in encouraging young people to surrender and change their lives. They had been involved in torturing nine women after businessman, Jacob Luke was found dead.

The youths were all from around Monokam village in the Ambum Valley. They all surrendered to the church and burned all the weapons and instruments they had used to harm the nine women.

The perpetrators had been under the influence of drugs when they carried out the atrocities, and, at the surrender ceremony, they vowed to give it up. They then erected a steel cross at Monokam beside long serving councilor, late Cr Alois Alapyala Yolape's grave.

Bishop Orowae had opposed the reintroduction of capital punishment when parliament reintroduced it in 1991.

"One reason the government reintroduced it was to punish people to help them change their behavior. But the death penalty did not do this. It kills them," Bishop Arnold had said in a statement.

The death penalty violated the dignity of every human person and the sanctity of human life which are at the center of Gospel teaching. And the life of every person must be respected from conception to death.

"Killing a killer violates the sanctity of every human life. One wrong does not make it right to perpetrate another one. When the death penalty is carried out, the State, in the name of the people, imitates the criminal by itself committing a crime against life,".

Bishop Arnold spoke selflessly against corruption and mismanagement in government. This resulted in the people feeling insecure as they did not prosper in a socio-political scene that wasn't right.

"In God's name we call on the elected leaders of this nation to give priority to the respect for law, the common good and future of our nation," Bishop Arnold said.

In March, 2025 after his death, Cardinal Sir John Ribat, leader of the Catholic Church in Papua New Guinea did not mince his words to say that problems in the country were as a result of deep-rooted corruption. He called on the police to have clear powers to arrest corrupt leaders.

Weak and corrupt governments were the breeding grounds for illegal activities that caused massive suffering for the people said Cardinal Sir John Ribat in a front-page story in the Post Courier on March 11th, 2025.

He called on the government not to interfere with the Law & Order enforcement agencies and said that the heads of the law enforcement agencies should have executive powers and arrest members of parliament without fear or favor.

The fighting in the upper highlands, the killing of policemen, the closure of the Highlands Highway, ethnic tensions, kidnapping, rape, torture, murder of women and abuse of gold miners, were all signs of a society weakened by prolonged corruption

"The government is weak and corrupt in terms of upholding the rule of law and providing services to directly improve the economic livelihood of individuals and families," Cardinal Sir John Ribat said.

Lawlessness also meant telling lies and not being honest by leaders when they were involved in bribery, systematic corruption and stealing of public funds under false pretext, not allocating sufficient funding to programs and projects.

These were tough words that Cardinal Sir John Ribat had never said before but he expressed them when there was lawlessness everywhere in the country like never before just as the country was preparing to celebrate 50 years of independence anniversary.

Parliament was in session that week but no leader stood up to counter the cardinal's accusations.

Bishop Arnold Orowae went to Rome when Pope Benedict XVI was in charge to attend the Synodical Assembly and delivered a homily in front of more than 2000 bishops from around the world.

He focused on the family as the place where most people come to know Christ and learn to be members of His church. The family unit was where parents took seriously their God- given responsibilities to nurture and support, teach and guide, protect and defend their children to be good members of the church and society at large.

That was what he tried to promote at home too – that the family unit had to be intact for children to grow up in a caring and loving environment.

If there was anybody who knew more about late Bishop Arnold Orowae, then it had to be Chief Sir Paul Kurai. The two of them had attended Tskiro Primary school and Fatima High School together.

After they completed their high school education, they went their separate ways – one trained to be a catholic priest, the other trained as a Kiap at the Administrative College in Port Moresby. He later became a businessman after resigning from the public service.

They didn't know but in God's Divine plan, it was decreed that Chief Sir Paul Kurai would help the Catholic church in a big way after the expatriate missionaries retired.

Bishop Arnold had loved his parents very much. After school, and even when he went home from seminary, Bishop Arnold used to collect a lot of firewood for his parents and stock-piled it in every space available in their house. He wanted his parents to use the firewood when he was away in school. Both his parents used walking sticks to move around. He never felt tired to help them.

On Sundays and during school, Arnold had always dressed up well by wearing fresh *tanget* leaves all the time with a neat little apron made of string in front.

Bishop Arnold Orowae died at 8:30 pm at Wabag General Hospital. That night the body was taken straight to Sangurap Cathedral Church. Next morning it was driven down to the Kenmix Funeral Home in Mt Hagen. The management kindly declined to take any form of payment and offered to help in the funeral arrangements free of charge, including transportation of the casket to Wabag.

On Wednesday 1 January, 2025, the casket was moved to St Paul's Parish organised by Mt Hagen Archdiocese. Next day, Holy Mass was celebrated at St Paul's Parish and Archbishop Douglas Young SVD handed the casket over to be taken to Enga province.

In Wabag, the convoy drove around the town streets, up to Sangurap Catholic headquarters and then proceeded to Tskiro parish, late Bishop Arnold's village where he used to collect firewood for his parents. A funeral was conducted there to enable friends, relatives and people in the Ambum Valley to pay their last respects.

On Saturday at 10 am a Funeral Mass was celebrated by Archbishop Douglas Young SVD at Par Catholic mission. Then finally, after a long journey in life, late Bishop Arnold Orowae was laid to rest beside other missionaries who had gone before him.

Tribal Warfare & Sorcery Related Killings Continued

It cannot be denied that tribal warfare persisted in almost all parts of the province immediately after independence, when the tough Australian colonial administration had departed, leaving the country to Papua New Guineans to manage. But there seemed no end to the scourge. The work begun by the church many years ago was affected by the dangerous new trends.

As the catholic faithful were celebrating at Pompabus, there were on-going election-related tribal wars in three electorates – Kompiam-Ambum, Laiagam and Kandep. There were, also, sorcery-related killings still happening in some parts of the province.

Chief Sir Paul Kurai called upon all Catholics in the province to refrain from taking part in any tribal fight from the time they were celebrating the 75 years anniversary onwards stressing that their lives were precious.

Even minutes before he spoke, news spread that two of his Kamainwan villagers had been killed at Kasi village in an ongoing tribal war wich had started during the 2022 national elections in the Kompiam-Ambum electorate.

Chief Sir Paul Kurai had been trying to stop this fight appealing to both parties to lay down their arms. But the warriors kept fighting. Up to 80 young men had been killed at that point. Much property costing millions of kina including the Kasi Health Center went up in flames. It will take many years to replace the properties. But the lives lost will never reappear.

Countless innocent men, women and children were the victims of much destruction, crime, violence, heinous atrocities and human rights violations during the worst ever general elections conducted in 2022.

The torture of the nine women at Lakolam after the death of Jacob Luke was committed during this violent period.

I was one of many public servants living in Wabag town who asked our relatives to come and provide security for our families. There was no safety and security any more. The under-resourced police were over-stretched. They would never turn up if anything happened to us.

People were aware that the morale of the police men and women had sunk to the bottom of the Lai River years ago. The perpetrators took advantage of this degeneration of the once proud Royal Papua New Constabulary.

But yet some policemen seemed ready and available to provide security for members of parliament or foreign businessman.

Every day, from the day nominations opened, there were gun shots in Enga province. Constant reports of death and destruction kept pouring in from almost every district.

Powerful international TV networks like Aljazeera reported on the bush-knife wielding thoughtless tribesmen who caused mayhem and inflicted gross human rights violations in the province

Not to mention local TV news channels, daily newspapers and social media screaming with such negative stories regularly. The election-related death toll kept climbing towards the 200 mark. Why should people die for one person to occupy a seat in parliament for only five years?

Some deaths and destruction were caused by sitting MPs, others by new aspiring candidates. And still others were instigated by supporters without the knowledge and approval of the poor candidate they were trying to elevate as a national leader. This gave rise to serious questions.

Just where was Enga and PNG headed?

My 2017 Election Diary Points to Where PNG Was Headed

My beloved country, the country where my umbilical cord was buried, the country I saw gain its independence without bloodshed was headed in the wrong direction.

I saw Danely Tindiwi's provincial government suspended three times for minor problems – unlike today when millions were deliberately squandered, stolen and nobody got jail terms or the provincial government suspended.

Governor Jeffery Balakau was dismissed from office for a minor incident. Yet hardly any governor was dismissed or his government suspended after the reforms were introduced.

His brother Malipu Balakau was assassinated in front of his Mt Hagen home. The suspects have never been caught.

Budding young Engan businessman, Seth Timinao was shot dead at a roadblock in the early hours at Tomba for no apparent reason. The suspects were never caught.

Inspector Peter Pyaso was shot dead when he went to stop a tribal war at Lapalama in the Kompiam district. His cold-blooded killers were never arrested or compensated by Lakain tribesmen following traditional custom.

I got suspended and demoted for a truthful piece of information that people had the right to know. No attempt was made to revive the provincial paper – Enga Nius. It provided practical experience to trainee journalists from the province. Freedom of speech was teetering on the verge of total suppression.

Then my property was destroyed for no apparent reason a year after the 2022 national elections – the year my freedom was taken away from voting for a candidate of my choice. Supporters took our freedom when they ticked the ballot papers for many senior public servants in our polling booth right in town.

With what I saw and experienced during the 2022 general elections the future looked grim. In fact, problems had really started during the 2017 general national elections.

I had kept a diary and published it in PNG Attitude, extracts of which I would like to share here.

First, I had to apologise to organisers of the Sunshine Coast International Readers and Writers Festival in Australia to which I had been invited. I had to explain that the situation was getting out of hand. It was happening in the provincial capital – the seat of power, where security forces were concentrated.

My family and I were confined to our house for the last few days due to shocking election-related violence, death and destruction in Wabag town in mid-July.

The violent scenes I witnessed many years previously and described in one of my books was played out again in Wabag on Saturday 22 July, 2017.

Three political supporters and two policemen were shot dead. A third policeman was airlifted to Port Moresby for treatment. The Assistant Returning Officer for Kandep and two other people were in critical condition in the Hospital.

Returning Officer, Ben Besawe narrowly escaped death when the vehicle he was travelling in was sprayed with bullets. We saw it happen in the distance on Lankep street from the Premier Hill which overlooks most parts of the township. The gunshots reverberated all around town.

There had been continuous gunshots for the last few days as security forces and supporters of some Kandep candidates exchanged fire.

I saw social media images of a gunman shot dead and lying in a ditch after he had reportedly killed three men. Later I found out that two policemen had been shot dead, and another mobile squad member had been injured. They were staying at Kids Inn at Sangrap.

I saw smoke billowing from burning shops and cars and people running for cover in the small township.

Yesterday, Monday 17 July, police commissioner Gary Baki flew in with reinforcements bringing some normalcy to the town and allowing people to breathe easier.

He enforced a lockdown, restricting movement of traffic and people until Friday when all ballot boxes would have been counted for the Enga regional seat and the Wabag, Wapenamanda and Laiagam seats.

The Kompiam-Ambum electorate saw John Pundari win back the seat. Kandep counting had been suspended indefinitely.

This following record of events is from my diary:

Wednesday 19 July: Heard about 12 gunshots early this morning. Heard 21 remaining ballot boxes for Kandep had been tampered with last night. Right now, Alfred is leading with more than 15,000 votes followed by Don Polye on 11,000 votes. Don Polye's base vote boxes have reportedly not been counted yet. Went into town at about midday. I took a short cut up a steep gradient. But police and soldiers at the top turned me back. They said Wabag town was shut down due to last night's problems. I turned back, walked up to the Porgera bus stop and turned right towards the BSP Bank. Everything was closed. Wabag was a ghost town.

Thursday 20 July: Yesterday there were gunshots. But today security forces have secured the town. Some services like the bank, shops and post office are open again.

Friday 21 July: There is dancing in the street. I hear John Pundari has been re-elected to the Kompiam Ambum seat. The ballot boxes for Kandep are still disputed, not counted yet. Wonder what Ben Besawe is doing? I am sure he will be neutral and think about people's lives first. Many have suffered and over 100 people died in the 2012 election violence. That wasn't long ago.

Saturday 22 July: Julie has just told me about a bad dream she had last night. I decided if I should go home to Kandep today. But she said I must wait till next week. Lucky, I didn't go. Between 7am – 8am there were many gunshots coming from the Lankep area to the north. It seemed as if there was a war on. Soon there were reports of casualties. There were reports that Ben Besawe, Kandep returning officer, his assistant George Marke and a couple of others in their car had been ambushed outside their hotel and shot dead. They were travelling in a ten-seater to Wabag Primary School to resume counting. Supporters of Don Polye were said to be responsible.

A while later there were more shots. This time in the direction of Sangurap to the west. Soon there were reports of casualties. Two supporters of Alfred Manase were shot dead by police. One of them had shot dead three policemen before he was killed. The same gunman had first shot dead one of Don Polye's supporters. Then police had shot off one of his legs. While bleeding in a storm water drain opposite the Kids Inn, he shot the three policemen perhaps to avenge himself before he died. A little later I heard George Marke was still in critical condition but not dead as reported earlier. And Ben Besawe was lucky to be alive after he missed a bullet aimed at him.

Heard more gun shots. Heard of two men lying dead in a drain at Sangurap. Saw pictures on Facebook of them lying there. Terrible, sad day for Enga. I see police choppers hovering in the air. I saw the car used to attack Ben Besawe and George burn on Lankep Street. It had been abandoned on the street and the assailants had escaped into the notorious Kop Creek gorges. Then I hear two policemen had been shot dead by a gunman. A third was fighting for his life. Why kill policemen who come to protect us to conduct our stupid election in safety?

I am always upset when people kill policemen. Why kill them when they try to maintain peace? I saw several police cars travelling in a convoy to remove bodies from the morgue and take them to Mommers Soccer oval. Saw chopper take the bodies away towards Mt Hagen. Very sad sight.

Later in the afternoon, heard gun shots very near my house. I cannot count how many shots were fired. All my family crammed into one room terrified. A few of us ventured outside minutes later. I saw dark brownish smoke bellowing into the air. People said two of Alfred Manase's cars and two others belonging to the local Apiap tribesmen were burning. A store belonging to a young Apiap man was also burning. Very sad.

"It takes a long time to make a man. Why shoot policemen down like this," a policeman was heard saying in between tears while mourning his colleague's deaths. How true, why all this wanton killing? At 6pm, I saw a news bulletin on EMTV news confirming that the two policemen killed were from Special Operations Mobile police based in Mt Hagen. A third had been airlifted to Port Moresby for treatment. I saw Don Polye condemning the carnage on EMTV news that same evening.

It's a sad, sad day indeed.

Sunday 23 July: I hear police commissioner Gary Baki will come to Wabag tomorrow. At 3am heard more gunshots – about 6-10 in all. People attempting to destroy ballot papers? Attempting to take revenge? Fed up hearing gunshots. By daybreak, I hear birds singing as sweetly as ever, as if nothing happened yesterday. Life goes on?

Monday 24 July: Saw a lone chopper flying in. Gary Baki must be coming. I have been at home all day today and during the weekend. With the police commissioner here in Wabag, I feel enlightened.

He is encouraging his men to complete the task at hand – which is complete providing security so counting can be completed despite losing two of their number and one fighting for his life. I must applaud the police, brave and committed.

Normalcy returned to the small township of Wabag after a ceasefire was imposed over a week ago. Students returned to school at Kopen Secondary School and Sir Tei Abal Secondary School.

But then on **Tuesday 22nd August**, at about 4:30 pm, I heard gunshots. Election violence had resumed. Next day at 5am rapid gunfire was heard echoing across the small township. Later that morning a death was reported.

Wabag townsfolk experienced one of the most frightening, most violent times since Enga Province severed ties with the Western Highlands to assume its own political and administrative responsibilities in 1974.

The situation was made difficult for relatives when a young pilot, Sano Peter Mendai from the Lankep tribe died unexpectedly. He was to have graduated from a flying school in New Zealand that same month.

Late Sano Mendai had come to Port Moresby to witness the graduation of his wife, Jane Kipok, from the University of Papua New Guinea. They had planned to get married in Wabag, then fly to New Zealand for Mr Mendai's own graduation. But he died in August during the election violence. His relatives who live on the edge of Wabag town could not hold a proper funeral.

Nor did they properly celebrate the election victory of their tribesman, Dr Lino Jeremiah Tom, who toppled PNC strongman Robert Ganim in the Wabag Open seat.

Jane Kipok's relatives from Kandep could not go to the funeral either because of election violence between Kandepen supporters of Alfred Manase and Don Polye.

The other heart-wrenching tale in Wabag was the death in a fire of a Bangladeshi businessman.

Four of his colleagues escaped to the police station with no possessions, not even their passports. They lost everything including much cash in the fire that started from a faulty gas stove.

The men had moved to Wabag from Manus that year and rented a new property to establish a store.

I live near the premises and heard the screams of the victim very early in the morning. I rushed down, as well as many others to find the fire had already spread. Nobody could do anything, but stood and watched the fire do its destructive work. It was still spewing smoke into the next day. Only the ashes of the unfortunate man were found.

In the election violence, over 30 people had been killed including two mobile squad policeman and three babies in incubators at the Wabag General Hospital.

Many more people had been injured, some seriously, including a policeman from the Mt Hagen based mobile squad. He was in critical condition in a hospital in Port Moresby.

It seemed the weak and innocent people would continue to suffer in Enga province. I related some very sad incidents in one of my books *'Survivor: Alive in Mum's Loving Arms'*, which was published as fighting continued here early this month. The book features a young woman whose parents were both killed together with her brother when she was just nine months old. She was found alive in her mum's loving arms. Her parents had been ambushed in a revenge attack after two university students had been killed in an equally vicious attack which had happened in Lae a year previously.

Nobody, not even the police could provide just how many people were dying and suffering in the rural areas in this province as election related violence continued unabated.

Those were very sad times indeed.

I was interviewed by Johnny Blades of Radio New Zealand when news of the 2017 election violence had spread all over the world.

Fighting for Uncounted Boxes

Finally, Wabag town residents, business houses and the general public were able to resume normal life.

The post-election warfare officially ceased on a Wednesday under a heavy police and army presence. More than 30 people had died in the violence, including four killed in the week I kept the diary.

Provincial Police Commander Supt George Kakas said the Kii and Kala tribes had wrongly allowed former opposition leader Don Polye and civil aviation minister and member for Kandep, Alfred Manase to exploit them to stage three weeks of killing and destruction in town.

The two tribes had agreed to stop fighting and accepted conditions of a preventative order which restrained them from further violence.

"Leaders named in the preventative order documents will be arrested," Supt Kakas warned, adding that police and army personnel would remain until normalcy returned to the small town. The guerrilla-style tribal war claimed very many lives and caused property destruction valued at millions of kina.

Sophisticated modern assault weapons like M16s and Russian-made AK47s had been used in the fighting which raged on the edge of Wabag town after Kandep returning officer Ben Besawe and other election officials were shot at on Saturday 22 July, 2017.

Of the many election-related violence incidents, three babies died in incubators and a fourth was stillborn after the mother fled Wabag General Hospital when it was attacked after Governor Peter Ipatas was declared winner of the regional seat.

The hospital suffered much destruction and was closed for a week before it reopened. Two patients, had fled to safety to be cared for by relatives. They were Kandep assistant returning officer George Marke and Tauwale Kondal who had been attacked on their way to resume counting.

In a separate incident, a Grade 11 student from Kopen Secondary School was killed in Wabag town as looters tried to destroy an Asian shop. He had arrived from Sirunki with his mother to withdraw from studies but was caught in the melee.

Supt Kakas said a post-mortem would be conducted to determine if police-issued firearms had been used to shoot the student.

The student's parents claimed a policeman had shot him and this would be determined after proper investigations and ballistics tests.

According to Supt George Kakas, Mr Polye's supporters may have been forced to fight after it was alleged seven boxes of ballot papers expected to favour Mr Polye had been set aside. It was understood that a directive from electoral commissioner Patiliu Gamato had been sent to returning officers to count all boxes so results could be disputed in court later.

Mr Polye's supporters were advised to go home and it was said the former Opposition leader should apply to the Court of Disputed Returns to settle outstanding matters.

"I told them if they kept on fighting, more deaths and destruction would occur and nobody would achieve anything," he said.

He would keep the seven ballot boxes in a safe location until a decision was made by the court. He warned that leaders named on the preventive order documents would be arrested if people continued to harbour political supporters of Don Polye and Alfred Manase.

At the time, one educated elite from Kandep, Sakias Tameo personally felt counting should be suspended for the good of all village people until 2022.

He said the governor and administrator of the province could run the affairs of the unfortunate district for the next five years. He felt the people did not seem deserving of a representative in parliament.

Five years before over 100 people had lost their lives following the 2012 national elections. Sakias Tameo made the statement in 2017 when it looked like more people would die if counting was continued and a winner was declared. An indefinite suspension of counting would satisfy all parties.

Our people could choose whoever they wanted as their leader without intimidation. Intending or serving leaders had to respect the wishes of the people. They had to accept the outcome of any election through free and fair elections. It was unlawful to manipulate the electoral system and other illegal means to steal the leadership of Kandep.

"These are my thoughts towards addressing the main cause of the killings and destruction that Kandep is currently going through. But every Kandepen is entitled to his/her own views," he said on 30th July, 2017.

However, Don Polye took the case to the Court of Disputed Returns and won the case for a by-election which he won too.

Earlier that month on 12 August, the son of former Administrator Darren Talyaga expressed how sad it was for Wabag to burn due to the 2017 Elections. It was a case of traditional loyal ideologies meeting modern democracy. We will learn one day, or lose because no one wins in a fight.

Darren expressed his thoughts after I published the election violence in the popular blog, PNG Attitude.

"If King Solomon was here, he'd divide Kandep in two. One empire for Alfred Manaseh, the other for Don Polye. Because the Kandep people die for them, that is how it can be solved, unless one or both give away the Kandep Open Seat.

"The Kandep people either go for one or the other. They don't like more than two options and could organise and act upon to stand for their choice. So it seems.

"Wish they fought for an agenda rather than two people. They die for it and don't speak a word about it. Loyalty and democracy – old and modern – it was the era and times.

We blame them. But it is the times, the crossroads where they and we learn to change – change for the better. It's the laws of physics. It takes a greater force to bring upon a change.

"One day, we'll visit Kandep, a land of legends where they say from Tundak where the world's ends meet, where Hela gave birth to his 5 children, there will come a change. This is the beginning for them for, through pain, new lives are born.

"Keep your strategy to have one option – but for a good agenda, and stand for them – but without guns!"

I had to respond to Darren's brilliant observation. Most Kandep people voted either for Alfred Manase or Don Polye. The conclusion of all elections was a court battle and a tribal war at home.

But the situation was never like that when three elected leaders were in charge of Kandep when Don Polye and Alfred Manase were still in school.

Nenk Pasul MBE was the first elected member for Kandep. He served for just one term. John Yaka who defeated him served two terms and Jimson Sauk served for three terms. Each term was for five years.

These three men didn't know anything about maths so they kept Kandep as a whole for 30 years. John Yaka was an apostolic pastor. Jimson Sauk was a committed Christian Apostolic Fellowship church elder. They both knew about King Solomon.

Nenk Pasul was an atheist, but a powerful traditional leader. He was not as wise as King Solomon. But some of his predictions have been fulfilled in modern times.

I still remember one statement he made at Kombolos village: "People will fight their tribal wars, settle their differences and live in peace again. But if something happens down there (parliament), nobody will live here (villages). Educated people, when they fight, their fight will be more destructive, not before seen by our ancestors. This place (Kandep) will not be as it is today, it will be gone."

Darren was right about Tundak. It had a legend which some people believed would be fulfilled. And when you look at all the tribes in Enga they are all intertwined – some have links to Kandep.

Look at all the tribes surrounding Wabag town as an example. My advice to Kandep people was by way of using a line from Darren's words that it takes a 'greater force to bring upon a change.'

They must now begin to explore this 'greater force' that is capable of changing their individual lives.

People must forget Tundak because whatever they believed in won't happen in our lifetime. In any case, doesn't the name sound like 'tudak'in Tok Pisin – (night, dark, chaos, confusion, corruption, crime etc)?

People should change their own individual lives, seek peace and enjoy their brief lives on this earth.

Terrible Dreams: Maybe My Brain Recorded Too Much Violence

After the violent elections, I flew to Port Moresby to recuperate. I ended up having some terrible dreams, some so scary they made me sweat. Maybe my poor brain had recorded so much destruction, crime, violence, atrocities and human rights violations that the events kept resurfacing in my sleep.

My family and thousands of other peace-loving Enga folk lived through hell during the worst general election Papua New Guinea had ever experienced. The terrible events caused a terror that could still be felt as a subsiding tremor.

I had to ask 10 relatives to come to Wabag to provide some form of security so I and my family could feel a little safe. The police normally turned up only after a crime had been committed – or they never came at all. There were just not enough of them. And they were poorly resourced. All the people knew how police morale had sunk to the bottom of the Lai River a long time ago.

Perpetrators knew they could take advantage of the once proud Royal Papua New Guinea Constabulary. Yet, it's a shame to see that some policemen still seemed ready and able to provide security for members of parliament or unscrupulous foreign businessmen.

Every day from the day nominations opened there was gunfire in Enga Province. Constant reports of death and destruction poured in from almost every district. Property valued at millions of kina went up in smoke – shops, homes, schools, health facilities.

International TV networks like Aljazeera reported on the thoughtless bush-knife wielding tribesmen causing mayhem and inflicting gross human rights violations throughout the province.

Then there were the local TV news channels, newspapers and social media screaming with negative stories each day as the election-related death toll climbed upwards.

Why should 100 people die for close to the same number of seats for somebody to occupy in parliament for just five years?

Some death and destruction were caused by sitting MPs, some by new aspiring candidates and others by supporters without the knowledge or approval of the poor candidate they were trying to elevate as a national leader.

On a Friday night, I had one of those nightmares in which I found myself attending the funeral of one of my relatives. Next day I received the devastating news from home that one of my brothers-in-law had been killed in an election-related tribal war in the Lower Wage area of Kandep.

Why he had gone there to die, I was not sure because he was from the Mariant area where many candidates had nominated. He must have cast his vote for one of them in the race for the Kandep open seat.

Two of his brothers were at my house in Wabag and they had to go home for the funeral. I had to restrain them on the phone to not go to the tribal war zone to seek revenge. I pointed out their own lives were special. They must not throw them away unnecessarily. Their brother was gone for good, never to come back to help them. But I wasn't sure if they would heed my words. Today's youth were different.

Two of the worst non-election related acts of violence in Enga was an event in which up to 30 people were killed and then the abduction of a girl believed raped and killed in an ongoing tribal feud in the mining township of Porgera.

Maybe the warring tribesman on both sides should lay down their arms, get down on their knees, start to negotiate peace, pay compensation for all the deaths and destruction, come to their senses and realise they cannot allow innocent women and children to suffer like this, and so often.

The two sides had to realise they had a new member in parliament now in Maso Karipe, a man to whom they could take their grievances and during whose term of office they could try to live in peace. The Porgera gold mine would reopen soon and everybody should look forward to that occasion.

The other non-election related violence occurred immediately after Engan trucking tycoon, Jacob Luke, was found dead in the jungle. The subsequent torture of nine women that followed resulting in the death of four innocent women.

I had another dream last Saturday during an afternoon nap. I dreamt I was trying to shoot two kingfishers using a slingshot. They were feeding and one came towards me. I aimed to shoot it but the bird was too close. I could have reached out and caught it with my hands.

But the instant I put out my hand, the bird transformed into a handsome young boy. He looked like an African child and he was with an elder, maybe his father or uncle.

The young boy looked up at me and smiled. That instant I woke up.

I don't know what this means. But I can guess two scenarios. Maybe somebody will offer me a baby boy to adopt.

Or maybe Enga Province and PNG will discard all that was weighing them down – corruption, crime, tribal warfare, poor governance, mismanagement and sorcery-accusation-related violence and learn to change.

And regenerate to become a peaceful nation filled with happy smiling people just like the smiling African boy in my dream.

No, my beloved country did not regenerate but regressed. The 2022 national elections were far worse. I lost my property on the Kandep government station as I've related in the first chapter of this book.

When friends read about my loss, many of them felt for me. Of all the advice, friends offered me, there was one that provoked me into action. He lived in Kandep but I never had the chance to meet him. His name was Kevin O'Regan.

"So sorry Daniel as these continuing events solve nothing. I lived in Kandep probably close to a year based at Sawi (a former mission station of some sort).

"We worked on forming a track – across the outlet of the big swamp – on the Kandap Margarima road.

"Enga Engineering was our supervisor. But work petered off because of compensation delays and funding restraints. As big as Daniel's problem, *Attitude* published an excellent article about the late Malipu Balakau's assassination and the need for a visionary leader to step up.

"I have been waiting with bated breath for some comments on Daniel's recent thought-provoking article to no avail. Does the whole province just no longer care, have they become mute or too scared to speak?

"It is hard to 'care' any more. I mean really care! Amazingly many of us still do. My thoughts are with Daniel. Keep writing bud, please."

I followed Keven's advice to keep writing. I mean, I have always been writing as a journalist. But I had to join a special group of writers – poets, essayists, novelists and authors, people who wrote books for posterity.

8

JOINING WRITERS TO PROMOTE LITERATURE

"If you find a book, you really want to read but it hasn't been written yet, then you must write it."

Toni Morrison, 6th August, 2019.

Starting to Publish Books for Posterity

My former councillor of the Aimbarep Pumbuti tribe, Cr Samson Pelata advised me to resign from the Department of Enga Administration and seek a job elsewhere in Papua New Guinea. He didn't like the excessive punishment dished out to me. But I could have been working elsewhere already.

Former Editor of the Post Courier, Oseah Philemon remarked one day that I was 'wasting national talent' in Enga province indicating he wouldn't mind me working for the oldest newspaper in the country.

Former Provincial Secretary, late Kundapen Talyaga had wanted me to work with him in the Public Affairs Department of the giant Porgera Gold Mine. He wanted me to head the Media Unit of the Public Affairs department. Yet I had declined to pursue these new possibilities. There was nothing attractive about Enga province. But I decided to remain in the department as an unattached officer.

I did not see from the perspective of these important people who thought I was wasting my time occupying a lowly paid job breaking my back doing a lot of work to promote the province.

My good friends didn't know I could have joined them if I were a single man. When I weighed the situation, the lives of my large family members would be affected. All the amenities were right there on the doorstep – the many shops, the market and Wabag general hospital were very close. Some of the doctors were family friends and some of our relatives worked there too. The service provided at the hospital was really good, except that it had regular power failures that made it difficult for staff. Or when the hospital experienced a shortage of drugs, like the time when Bishop Arnold Orowae died for lack of a particular medicine that was not in stock.

All my children were in school – Wabag primary school, Kopen Secondary School and Sir Tei Secondary School were all very close. Even St Paul's Lutheran High School, Sirunki High School were not that far. If I moved, my children's education would be affected. On top of that it would be costly to move my family and settle them in a new location.

I was suspended but still drew my fortnightly salary. Above all, I loved my province and felt it better to remain and promote Enga province on my own initiative through media coverage.

I missed my public service privileges like the use of a car, housing allowance and annual gratuity payments as Director of Media and Information Services. But I reasoned that money was not everything – job satisfaction was. The fact that I was not actively engaged meant that I had a lot of free time to write. But writing books was not in my mind yet.

The first thing I did was to take copies of all the issues of Enga Nius I had published to the National Library in Port Moresby. I handed them over to the women at the PNG Section of the National Library for the benefit of future generations.

Then the idea hit me to compile two books, one consisting of all the published short stories written by Engans in various publications and a collection of poems, satire and essays by Engan authors and people living in the province. I placed copies of the two separate books – *Remember Me* & *Can't Sleep* in the National Library. I was happy that at last all these important stories were compiled in book form for posterity, that future generations might read them.

Then I published *I Can See My Country Clearly Now* based on my travels to the United Kingdom, United States of America and Mexico. In that book, I was able to compare my experiences and observations with the situation as it was in my country.

In America, I met one African student named Massamba Sonko from Senegal whose country had been under French colonial rule for over 300 years before they got independence, a stark contrast to PNG. Sonko was a fashion designer trying to further his education at an American university.

At a national convention of black journalists, I came across some Africans arguing over democracy whether it was good or bad. They nearly came to blows. I was glad PNG had always been free from the olden days to the time we attained independence. We had always been free to hunt, garden, fish, raise children, fight, pay compensation and lived in peace again in a free environment.

I got the greatest satisfaction when I helped Tony Sulupin publish his book. Tony is from Wanepap village in Laiagam. He was a university graduate but had been paralysed from the waist down and spent his days sitting in a wheel chair. But he had written a book. He didn't know how to get it published. Easy. We got it published through the same process – through Pukpuk Publications set up by former Kiap – Philip Fitzpatrick. Tony Sulupin was also involved in farming, trying to get his people to stop tribal warfare and involve themselves in planting cash crops.

The other person I assisted and whose book I co-authored – 'Legend of The Miok Egg' was late Johanes Kundal from Wapenamanda. The book was about their only son Ismael. Johanes and his wife Rose tried their utmost best to unite him with his wife from Kerema on the coast. But Ismael was defiant. He wanted to marry a second wife from the highlands.

My latest book 'The Old Man's Dilemma' was based on several experiences. First, I created the main character – Akali Wakane – The Old Man, when I noticed that many charity organisations, I benefited from to travel around the world had been started by selfless, kind-hearted and committed men who wished for people to live in freedom. Journalists were the people who could promote freedom and be the voice for the voiceless around the world.

I greatly benefitted from four generous organisations spread across the world. I either met the founders or their siblings who were passionately running the organisations to help foreign journalists attain new skills and expose them to the wider world.

I visited the United Kingdom where Queen Elizabeth II lived and even saw her in person across the street visiting a hospital in London in 1989. My trip was made possible by The Thomson Foundation based in Cardiff, Wales in the UK. It had been started by a Canadian businessman, Lord Thomson of Fleet.

In Mexico City, I met Bob Meyers, then president of The Washington DC-based National Press Foundation in 2008. They sponsored me to attend the 17th International Aids Conference in Mexico City.

Back in 1991, I had met Jonathan Friendly and his late mum Jean Friendly in Washington DC. I had won a scholarship to their country made possible by the Alfred Friendly Press Foundation.

Jonathan's dad, late Alfred Friendly had created it in 1984. He was a Pulitzer Prize-winning reporter and former managing editor of the Washington Post. It has now been renamed Alfred Friendly Press Partners.

Back home in September, 2016, we met the CEO of Paga Hill Development Company, Gudmundur Fridriksson and Lawyer Stanley Liria who is an accomplished author in Port Moresby.

They had partnered with, Professor Ken McKinnon to establish the McKinnon-Paga Hill Fellowship Scheme to sponsor wheel-chair bound writer, late Francis Nii, Martyn Namarong and myself to attend the 2016 Brisbane Writers Festival. Professor Ken McKinnon was the first director of Education during the Australian colonial administration period.

All these individuals had established these organisations with foresight to enable journalists and writers from emerging nations to learn skills that would benefit people back in their own countries.

I decided the main character in the story; The Old Man should be somebody like these generous men with warm hearts to give freely to humanity.

"More chapters will be written about the work started by The Old Man as his love for humanity continues to flow 'like a river down in the valley' keeping the vegetation lush and green as it makes its way over and beyond the horizon."

I wrote this line with the generous gentleman who set up those organisations in mind.

My other book 'Survivor: Alive in Mum's Loving Arms' was dedicated to all women past and present who died or live with regrets in their hearts due to circumstances beyond their control.

The girl on the cover is Tuman Kende Apulu, daughter of Engan father Leo Kende and Samoan mother Fa'ala'ula'u Apulu, who were both murdered in PNG when Tuman was just a few months old.

Tuman, now a New Zealand citizen, had a miraculous escape, apparently saved by her mother.

My wife Julie's story is also in the book. She, like Tuman, grew up having lost her mum who was stabbed by her father's third wife. She came with us to Brisbane to attend the festival.

We returned home via Cairns. Just before we departed the next day, she asked me to write an article to thank everybody who had been involved to make her feel welcome to her first trip overseas.

My Wife thanks Australia for Treating Her as One of The Writers

I had been listening to my wife, Julie's daily prayers to God in the Enga language in the privacy of our hotel rooms in Noosa, Brisbane, Sydney and Cairns over the action-packed two weeks we were in Australia.

One morning in Brisbane, I heard Julie plead with God to make Keith Jackson's spinal operation successful and when we heard in Sydney that it had indeed gone well and that Keith was ready to go back to Noosa, Julie was elated and thanked God again that night.

"Thank you, Lord for making Keith Jackson's operation successful," Julie prayed.

"I ask you, oh Lord, to please bless him and keep him strong with good health as well as all the other lovely silver-haired men and women so they can live longer and continue to help more writers from PNG.

"I thank you Lord Jesus for making it possible for me to come here to this beautiful country. Amen."

I thought that was thought-provoking and I decided to interview her on Saturday before we departed for Wabag in the highlands.

I talked to Julie in our room at the Bellview Motel on The Esplanade in Cairns. I knew she would find the words to relate her experiences here in Australia but was surprised at how she poured out her thoughts without any hesitation, like a spring.

What follows is the word for word transcript:

> *Before leaving my highlands home at Wabag in Papua New Guinea's Enga Province just over two weeks ago, I was wondering what kind of place I was going to.*
>
> *Having seen some action movies about Australia in PNG, I thought I would see violence and rough people on the streets, especially in cities like Brisbane and Sydney.*
>
> *But there was none of it. I think action movies are an illusion that gives a bad image of peace-loving Australians.*
>
> *As soon as I landed at Brisbane International Airport, I saw that Australia was beautiful. I also saw that the people were humble and kind. The coach driver was very helpful. He handled our bags with care and spoke to us with kind words.*
>
> *A lady in Noosa offered to take my photo in front of the Noosa Blue Resort where we stayed. She told me her dad had fought in New Guinea during the war and that she was happy to meet me.*
>
> *I was made to feel welcome on the Qantas flight to Sydney when one of the cabin crew brought me three bottles of water and spoke to me in Pidgin English, saying he had grown up in Rabaul.*
>
> *I have seen clean streets, beautiful parks and even saw a lady walking her dog in a public place in Noosa and picking up its excrement using a plastic bag and dumping it in a rubbish bin provided by the local council.*

Australians know how to enjoy life. They create heaven on earth and I think many of them will go to heaven. They are so kind, happy and willing to help each other.

I think they live less stressful lives and that's why they live longer. I could not believe that Professor Ken McKinnon, our Sydney host, was 85. I am sure he and his lovely wife, Sue, will live to be 100 and I told him so in his apartment where we had dinner with two other guests.

He took us to his secret place, a small beach where he swims every morning and has been doing this for many years. I wish buai chewing, cigarette smoking, boozing Papua New Guineans would follow his example and learn to live quality lives. I think lifestyle diseases are destroying many of our people in PNG.

I went into many Australian homes, ate with them and shared jokes with those who could speak Pidgin. I sensed that I was accepted as I was — an illiterate woman from a remote province up in the highlands of PNG who was on her first trip overseas.

If I struggled with my fork and knife and ate with my hands, they didn't seem to mind or notice. These gestures comforted me. I mixed with them as if I had known them before.

Something I noticed in the shops, train stations, hotels and public transport systems is that everywhere there are people ready to help.

I went shopping on my own in Brisbane and Sydney and, when people realised I was new to the place and gave only one-word answers, they simplified everything for me. I was able to understand much better and felt at ease.

The streets are designed with everybody in mind — the mother with a baby in a pram, the old men, a person in a wheelchair. That's why we were able to take our wheelchair writer Francis Nii to many interesting locations in Brisbane.

I wish our towns and cities in PNG could be designed in such a manner so people can enjoy themselves. Francis Nii was even booked into hotel rooms, like at Noosa Blue, especially designed for wheelchair guests.

I will take many memories with me back to PNG but the one that stands out is me standing beside my husband to give presents at the Jackson's home in Treasure Cove to Hon Glen Elmes MP, Noosa Mayor Cr Tony Wellington, Deputy Mayor Cr Frank Wilkie, Cr Ingrid Jackson and many Australian friends including the youngest of all, three-year old Leilani.

And finally, I thank Paga Hill Development Company, Keith Jackson and Professor Ken McKinnon, Ben Jackson and organisers of the Brisbane Writers Festival for treating me as an equal to the PNG writers – Francis Nii, Martyn Namorong, Rashmii Bell and my husband Daniel Kumbon.

I received the same treatment and I thank you all for your generosity and foresight.

I am a mother of five children and what I will do now is to encourage my children to read and write more.

I know the problems my children's schools face – no libraries, no books, not many properly trained English teachers and so on. But, despite the odds, it is my duty as a parent to encourage them to read and write more.

And maybe one day they can follow in the footsteps of their illiterate mother to Australia.

Back in the country, I soon got to know many of the writers and we all decided that the government must recognise and help PNG writers. Three of us, Caroline Evari and Betty Wakia got together at Vision City in Port Moresby to draft a letter to Prime Minister James Marape.

A Project for Our Children & PM James Marape Draws Fire

During one of our meetings to prepare for our much hoped for presentation to prime minister James Marape, writer Caroline Evari's two young children joined us.

I don't know what they thought of their mother, Betty Wakia and I working on our letter to Mr Marape but, when they grow up, I believe they will know their mother was doing this for them and thousands of others like them in Papua New Guinea.

I have spent some months away from home working on this project to put our home-grown literature somewhere near the front and centre of our Papua New Guinean culture.

Over that time, I know my family have missed me. My grandson Clinton will be three months old when I see him for the first time.

Two of my children did their Grade 12 national examinations while I have been in Port Moresby on this mission for literature.

I have reminded them that, when I did my own Form 4 final exams here in Port Moresby, my parents were way up in the mountains in their bush material home in the village.

So, the next generation also sat for examinations without a parent around.

But it is worth it. So many people signed the petition to make our literature strong. We all know literature is so important for our country.

We also know that 80% of the population in PNG is illiterate. We, the literate people, are in the privileged group who have had benefited from our access to health and education services. Imagine a child born right this second in the isolated jungle between Enga and East Sepik.

There's a place there I know, Penale. I flew there with Premier Ned Laina in a chopper many years ago. The Penale people, who had so little, asked for a school and a health centre. I am not sure if another Premier or national leader has ever visited them again.

As a gift, they gave us bundles of sago. I later gave the sago to a lady from the coast to cook – and I tasted sago for the first time.

How will the children in the jungle villages feel as they sit in a classroom for the first time if a school was finally built at Penale?

Will the teacher use the internet to teach them? Will they have books to enjoy? Will the books excite them because they're about their own country and people?

Meanwhile, here in Port Moresby, we three – Caroline, Betty and I – are struggling to tell our prime minister that literature is very important for our country.

If our approach fails, and we cannot get to see Mr Marape, we will try to find another way to meet him. Perhaps we can invite him to the 2019 Crocodile Prize presentations.

Mr Marape has attended international rugby league fixtures, the recent fashion week grand finale and other similar events. I don't think he would decline our invitation.

But if he still didn't come, we writers can draw some conclusions and go our own way.

We as writers did not see Prime minister James Marape together as a group of PNG writers but saw him when I was part of another group of writers – journalists. I pointed out to him how important it was to support PNG literature pointing out that the building we were sitting in will one day be replaced with a much better architectural design. But the words in books will stay written.

Then in February, 2021 Prime Minister James Marape provoked some of us PNG writers with words he published in the press telling children to have hope. These were his exact words:

"To all my children across our beautiful and blessed country, have hope and faith that you too can make it in life and make use of your time and talents by working hard wherever God has placed you in our diverse and blessed land of PNG" – James Marape.

I had to immediately respond from Wabag. "You know Prime Minister that your words are gold for children of this country. Your direct message can impact their lives at an early age. Your words can get them off Facebook and get them into a library full of books.

All it required was to support Papua New Guinean writers, who are writing the books – but the books are not finding libraries.

There are so many unsung heroes of modern PNG literature. Our country should be proud of them – and encourage them.

Our country is blessed with a thousand cultures, all different from the other but none more valuable than the other. All unique to this world.

Our *bilas*, our songs, our legends, our way of dress, our methods of cooking and so many more elements of our culture are the very things that give us our identity – they are the heartbeat of PNG.

As far as I know, you are the only prime minister who has proudly worn our *bilas* for the world to see. That is why I placed a photograph of you in traditional Huli-Opene attire in my recent book *'Victory Song of Pingeta's Daughter'*.

Our culture is truly unique and we need to preserve it. I am sure you know that our writers are helping to do that. I am sure you know they need more support to do it so effectively that our children will learn and understand just who we are as a people.

Then Michael Dom wrote from Lae: 'Mr Marape, your message to our children was really some good encouragement.'

'I assume you have had a good reading experience through your life to afford you a strong and cultured intelligence.'

'And I think those young folks you are encouraging could use some reading books.'

'It would be doubly encouraging to read books written by fellow Papua Niuginans.'

'As you know, out there in the sticks a hard copy book is what is most useful.'

'So, here's an idea: why don't you support PNG authors?'

'We've got some ideas, which we would like to share with you.

'About a lasting legacy you can leave this country, a legacy which not even Somare could achieve.'

Then AG Satori congratulated me for having produced the book in which I published the photo of the Prime Minister James Marape in Huli traditional dress.

"I want to congratulate Daniel Kumbon for his magnificent historical book, *'Victory Song of Pingeta's Daughter'*.

'This is a landmark book for Enga and for PNG. It is a book from Enga. But it tells a story all Papua New Guineans can relate to.

"It is a book about us and what we were and what we have become. Our individual experiences may not have been as big and heroic as Paul Kurai's, but the impact of colonisation affected each one of us."

"Daniel's book is something that we Papua New Guineans should treasure and try to emulate – to record our history in our own words."

"History can be big or small, but we need to have its stories recorded.

"Daniel mentions that writers will always continue to write. We know that the dawn of PNG's written literature came about with the advent of Ulli Beier at the University of PNG. After he was gone there was a hiatus until along came the Crocodile Prize."

"Unfortunately, most of our work is self-published. It is difficult for most PNG authors to get their books published and to gain support and recognition for this."

"I applaud the tenacity of our writers to continue to publish their work despite these difficult conditions."

"There have been three very recent books (and probably 60-70 over the last few years) and I hope that more will join them even if Amazon's Bezos goes to Mars."

"So, congratulations to Daniel and all of PNG's writers for their resolute focus in keeping the flame of literature alive with little money and without government help."

Promoting Home-grown literature in PNG Schools

An assignment given to first year trainees at Enga Teachers College about literature and its importance for primary school children prompted me to reflect on the literary tour of Australia I took with my three colleagues – late Francis Nii, Martyn Namarong, Rashmii Bell and my wife who tagged along.

Enga Teachers College was doing its rightful duty to train future teachers who must know from the very beginning that reading and writing was important for children.

I wondered if teachers already working in the field were promoting literature. Did they have access to proper libraries stocked with reading books which could be easily understood?

The PNG government was paying millions of kina through its tuition-free education policy every year. It was also concentrating on supporting sports, music and other major events. It was building modern stadiums, training facilities and provided cash incentives for athletes who won gold at venues like the Commonwealth and the Olympic Games.

The PNG Hunters continued to lift the rugby League profile on the international stage following the team's inclusion in the Queensland Intrust Super Cup competition. Many players kept signing lucrative contracts with the NRL and Super League.

EMTV's Vocal Fusion continued to captivate audiences nationwide as a new wave of sophisticated young men and women exploded onto the silver screen. They won cars and hard cash through their singing prowess and signed contracts to produce albums. This was all very good since it portrays PNG as a successful emerging nation in the region.

But the government seemed ill advised to understand that its writers – poets, journalists, essayists, authors etc can also promote unity and help to change the mindsets of people. All citizens with skill and knowledge should be treated equally to achieve the government's ambitious Vision 50 development plan which aimed to include PNG in the top 50 Human Development Index (HDI) rankings by 2050.

The government hoped PNG would be a prosperous middle-income country by 2030 through its medium-term Development Strategic Plan (DSP) and a world leader in the promotion and establishment of responsible sustainable development.

Literature had the potential to play an important part to achieve these government objectives in terms of quality education, improved communication and preservation of PNG's rich cultural heritage.

While some people aspired to be professional singers, good sportsmen or women, businessman or be successful in the professions, others strive to be successful writers. However, the writers seem only to have been supported by the Crocodile Prize organization and the McKinnon – Paga Hill Development Company Fellowship scheme.

Former PNG residents – Keith Jackson and Phil Fitzpatrick established the Crocodile Prize in 2011 and the fellowship scheme was established by PNG's first education director – Professor Ken McKinnon and Paga Hill Development Company.

Other generous sponsors were OK Tedi Mining Ltd, Kina Securities, PNG Chamber of Mines and Petroleum, PNG Ministry of Tourism, Arts and Culture, Paga Hill Development Company, SP Brewery, The Cleland Family, PNG Association of Australia, individuals like Roxanne Martens and others.

My spirits lifted when I won a prize in the Crocodile Prize competition and went on the literary tour of Australia in 2016 with three colleagues – Francis Nii, Martyn Namorong and Rashmii Bell. We attended the annual Brisbane Writer's Festival, met Australian politicians, authors, media personalities and visited organisations like the New South Wales Writers Centre in Sydney.

The Crocodile Prize has exposed raw talent from most parts of PNG since its inception in 2011. Generous cash prizes of K5,000 have been paid to winners for different categories of writing. The depth of talent was evident in six thick anthologies of essays, poems and short stories.

Several books, including three remarkable novels – Fitman, Rightman, Crooks and Cooks, Man of Caliber and Sibona have been written by Francis Nii, Baka Bina and Emmanuel Peni. Rashmii Bell wrote My Walk to Equality and I wrote Survivor-Alive in Mum's Loving Arms immediately after our Australian tour.

Many Papua New Guineans have the potential to write but a major obstacle was the English language itself. I believe if people could master the English language they could read and write much better. Right now, the state of PNG literature is poor. Not many people can read or write. Few schools have libraries let alone public libraries in our main towns and cities. University students struggle to write essays.

During my Australian tour, I made a proposal in an ABC radio interview about how the Australian government could help improve and lift the standard of English in PNG through its Australian Aid investment.

At the 22nd Papua New Guinea–Australia Ministerial Forum on 11 December 2013, Australian and Papua New Guinean Ministers agreed that Australia would undertake an assessment of its aid investment in PNG.

They hoped this assessment would better align Australia's aid with both Governments' priorities and position the aid program to address key constraints to sustainable economic growth and equitable development in PNG.

It was noted that even though PNG's economy has grown strongly, the resources boom had not led to sustained development outcomes – PNG was not on track to meet any of the Millennium Development Goals, and was placed 156th out of 187 countries in the composite UN Human Development Index.

Australia knew that PNG's population was growing rapidly. It lacked proper infrastructure. Its health, education and law and justice sector services were poor – which hindered long-term economic development and social stability in the country.

For economic growth and stability to take root in PNG, infrastructure development which would involve good road networks and education must come first. A well-educated population would thoroughly understand and manage economic affairs and address social issues properly.

I suggested during the ABC interview that, through its annual aid package, Australia could consider improving the literacy skills of Papua New Guineans by recruiting Australian English teachers and lecturers both as contract officers or volunteers and place them in Upper Primary, High schools, Secondary schools and Universities.

How could a teacher who could not comprehend the English language himself teach the subject to students in educational institutions in the country? That was the dilemma confronting PNG in most schools.

A recommendation made at the 22nd Ministerial Forum in 2012 stated that Australia should focus its investments in literacy, technical skills, better quality tertiary institutions and an enhanced teaching and healthy workforce.

"Australian Aid should support improvements in the quality of education by investing in teachers and school infrastructure enabling more school leavers to be literate and capable of engagement in the cash economy," it said.

Taking this recommendation into consideration, would it be hard for Australia to recruit English teachers from its own country and place them in PNG schools? Their pay could be drawn from its annual aid funds intended for 'literacy and quality tertiary institutions development' in the country.

Good English teachers and well stocked libraries were what PNG students urgently needed. If they could master the English language, students could read and write more fluently and perhaps write more books later in adult life.

UNESCO says that books published was an important index of the standard of living, education and a country's self-awareness. But there were no current records to show how many books PNG had published. However, I knew that over 40 titles had been published through Pukpuk Publications.

Now, I am the author of ten books available on line at First Nations Writers Festival website, Amazon.com and other online book dealers throughout the world. If one or two copies were bought by somebody out there in the world, it gave me great pleasure, a sense of having produced something worthy. But nobody here in PNG seemed interested. Only the UPNG Bookshop sold copies of my books. Perhaps students were reading them. I realised one could not make a living from writing, in a country where the literacy rate was far too low, where there was barely any reading culture at all.

I never launched three of my books. My first book, 'Remember Me' was officially launched by Education Secretary, Dr Uke. Kombra in Kundiawa during a Crocodile Prize presentation. I believe some PNG-authored books were perfect reading material for schools. One of my books, 'I Can See My Country Clearly Now' was about my journey from birth to independence and my travels and experiences in many countries around the world.

I would encourage the government to buy such books written by local authors and place them in all educational institutions throughout the country. Books promote intellectual development, entertainment and social cohesion.

The Enga Teachers College was fully supporting the number one priority of the Enga Provincial Government headed by Grand Chief Sir Peter Ipatas who had been promoting education since he was elected into office in 1997.

Education was indeed important and Enga Teachers College must continue its good work to pass on important knowledge emphasising that literature was key to the success of children in adult life.

Perhaps Enga Teachers College – which is part of the now Faculty of Education of the new Innovative Enga University, and other educational institutions in the country should consider stocking their libraries with suitable PNG authored books. Books written in earlier times by Vincent Eri, Michael Somare, Josephin Abaija, Albert Maori Kiki had been bought by the government and placed in PNG schools.

Why can't it be done now? Or is it too big an ask from Papua New Guinean authors?

I had just published my last book with Amazon with assistance from Phil Fitzpatrick who had started Pukpuk Publications in early 2025. He had said he didn't want to involve himself in publishing but helped me anyway because I was operating in a most difficult province up in the highlands of Papua New Guinea.

But I or other writers in Papua New Guinea wished to keep self-publishing our books. But with Pukpuk Publishing gone they desperately needed other publishers who could publish their work.

Then I Found First Nations Writers Festival and Anna Borzi AM

When all seemed grim for PNG Writers, the First Nations Writers Festival appeared on the scene.

My unexpected meeting with Richard Napam a budding writer and an economist working with the Bank of Papua New Guinea sort of introduced First Nations Writers Festival International, FNWF, to me a year later.

FNWF is a charity organisation which captures the rich cultures, intellect and story heritage of First Nations peoples in the Greater Pacific and beyond. It published books written by writers from indigenous people in the region.

Richard Napam contacted me to announce that his book 'Stunned by Light' had just been published by First Nations Writers Festival in 2023. The first lot of over 100 copies had all been sold in a matter of days. I read the autographed copy he gave me at Rainbow Estate in Port Moresby. I enjoyed it straight away. The book had that international appeal. Those who had read The Crocodile by Vincent Ere could enjoy this one.

The year before, in 2022, when I was at a table waiting for my food to arrive at the Ribito Grill and Restaurant in Port Moresby, there was a light tug on my shoulder. It was one of the waitresses.

"Uncle, this man wants to see you,' she said.

As I turned, I saw this young man grinning at me. He was Richard Napam. He asked if I had the time to read one chapter from a book he was writing. That was no problem. I could go through it. I was no expert. But he needed moral support and encouragement. He had read most of my books as well as books by other PNG authors. Here was a young man who wanted to join a new generation of PNG writers scattered across the country. I had to help him.

I asked him to remain at the restaurant while I went to the lodge at Rainbow Estate to get him a copy of my latest book which I had co-authored with late Johannes Kundal – *The Legend of the Miok Egg.*

I signed the book and gave it to him. He later sent me a copy of the first chapter of his book to comment on. I gave him the best advice I could offer. I repeated to him the fine words of Dr Greg Murphy, Director of the Madang University Center.

"Write in the early hours of the morning when your body is rested and mind refreshed, ready to process new information. The ideas will flow,' he told us at a writer's workshop. It had been organised in collaboration with Kristen Press. I had travelled all the way down from Wabag to attend it.

When Richard sent me the chapter, it was well thought out, well written and presented very well. There was no room for critique. I sent it back wishing him well.

When he next rang me, Richard said he had published his book with First Nations Writers Festival. The novel he had been working on for four long years had finally been published. Thus, the copy he gave me in Port Moresby, was my introduction to First Nations Writers Festival.

I immediately wanted FNWF to republish my first novel 'The Old Man's Dilemma' as a 2nd edition. But they could not, for obvious reasons.

I had self-published the novel with Amazon in 2011, the same year FNWF had been established. I regretted I had missed the opportunity. In my novel I talked about First Nations people of Papua struggling for freedom, how blood was shed in Bougainville, how First Nations people of Australia had been mistreated and not recognised even today by people who controlled the government whose parents had arrived there as settlers or spend time in penal colonies.

First Nations Writers had been started as a charity organisation in 2011. They had 300 or so different outlets throughout the world and books they published received wider publicity.

In 2023, five titles had been published by writers from Papua New Guinea. That was really encouraging to see. Here was an organisation that would help Papua New Guineans publish their works for some time to come.

The two people I had assisted to get their books published

– Tony Sulupin and late Johannes Kundal didn't know how or where to get their books published. I introduced them to PNG Attitude, the Crocodile Prize and Pukpuk publications.

After Pukpuk Publishing shut down, there seemed no hope for PNG writers once again. But hope had been restored. First Nations Writers Festival was available to publish suitable books by Papua New Guineans and other first nations writers from the region.

First, there was Ulli Beier who started to develop literature at the University of Papua New Guinea out of which came famous novels like The Crocodile written by Vincent Eri. After Ulli's departure, everything went quiet.

Then an attempt was made to resurrect it at the university in mid 1980s by the Language and Literature Department. I published poems and an extract of a novel in Ondobondo and PNG Writer. I noticed other Engans were contributing poems and short stories there and to our own Enga Students Association Year books.

Then there was a break till 2011 when former radio broadcaster and journalist, Keith Jackson established the popular blog, PNG Attitude. He, in conjunction with former Kiap, Phil Fitzpatrick started the Crocodile Prize.

The Crocodile Prize drew a lot of writers from all over the country. Over 40 titles were published through Pukpuk Publications. It was a major feat. Two of the first books I published with Pukpuk Publications were 'Remember Me' and 'Can't Sleep'. These were in fact collections of short stories, poems, satire and essays by Engans at UPNG and items from Enga Nius. I published four more books immediately after that.

I was reviewing 'Victory Song of Pingeta's Daughter' when The Crocodile Prize competition folded and no longer would Pukpuk Publications publish books. They had to shut down, understandably so, because old-age was catching up with two *wantoks* – Keith Jackson and Philip Fitzpatrick.

The professional that he was and the immense love he had for literature and himself a published author, Philip Fitzpatrick helped me publish my last book 'Chief Sir Paul Kurai: In My Father's Footsteps', a revised version of 'Victory Song of Pingeta's Daughter.'

Ples Singsing started by Dr Michael Dom, Caroline Evari and Betty Wakia assumed the role of the Crocodile Prize. I encouraged Chief Sir Paul Kurai to make a donation. He generously presented K5,000 to help them in their work. But writing and maintaining a blog is a lot of work. But yet the blog continues to operate with not much support from anybody.

The only book that ever made me some money was a tiny pamphlet titled 'Climbing Mountains, published by Oxford university Press. I kept getting cheques – my royalty payments made from sales. But this flow of royalty payments stopped when my story was published in a collection. That small pamphlet was the first book and successful book I ever published. I never received any royalty payments from my multiple other books I self-published with Amazon.

The University of Papua New Guinea Bookshop offer to sell copies of my books made me some money. As well as copies I sold to friends and interested readers. But soon I realised no author in PNG could ever dream to make a living through writing. That would be possible, only if PNG had a literate population and a supportive government.

But I decided to keep on writing. I was born into a primitive world. My culture was rich and still the best. There was no other culture in the world that was superior to mine. My unique culture gave me my identity. I could not afford to see it lost to the fast-moving technological world.

Some of our cultural artefacts were lost to tribal warfare – human hair wigs, kundu drums, aprons, grass skirts, bilums or string bags, birds of paradise feathers, gourds of tree oil, ceremonial stone axes, kina shells were burned or lost when inhabitants fled for safety to neighboring villages or to urban centers. I have yet to see anybody making a kundu drum or human hair wigs in the villages.

But I could write about some aspects of my culture as I related earlier about that poor pig which had to be sacrificed hoping I would recover from an illness.

I am sure fellow citizens from the 860 other different cultures that make up our united nation had the same view and love for our cultural diversity. We should all sit down and record our family histories, ways of cooking, story- telling, making canoes, paying compensation, marriage ceremonies and our personal experiences in the modern era and record them in books.

Make no mistake, as much as we want to preserve it, there were people in the wider world who were interested to read something about our country, its rich cultural diversity and problems we face.

I am thankful First Nations Writers Festival voted me 'Living Treasure' in 2024. Some of us deserve that feel good emotion to surge through our souls to keep writing before our cultural heritage was trodden on and forgotten for good.

I wish to now share one cultural practice from the East Sepik province. I read about it in our 1975 Port Moresby Technical College Year Book. That era of my student life was the beginning of finding out about the rich cultural diversity of my beloved province and country.

Discovering Cultural Diversity of My Country – PNG

Although we speak the same language, the pronunciation of words, way of traditional dressing and other aspects of the Enga culture vary. I noticed it when I first travelled out of Kandep to do Form One at St Paul's Lutheran High School in Wapenamanda.

I could easily identify which district the students came from based on their attire and way of dance styles during a mini–Cultural Show on the school grounds. We students from Kandep staged one of our own. Those students from Mid-Whagi, Western Highlands and Southern Highlands added color with their beautiful headdresses of Birds of Paradise feathers and colorful body paint.

A staff member had recorded the event in a video which was later screened in the dining hall. I saw myself dancing in my group, my first appearance in a moving video.

I saw more cultural diversity at the world-famous Mt Hagen Cultural Show that same year. I kept close to where people from Kandep had camped in case I got lost in the huge crowds from every district in the Highlands region. It was in Mt Hagen that I saw and touched the thick hide of my first elephant. Its name was Jumbo. I was amazed at its enormous strength when it pulled huge logs in the main arena.

After two years at Pausa, I transferred to Lae Technical College in 1974. There I saw students from virtually every corner of PNG. Jet black students from Bougainville, light skinned students from Central, blonde-haired students from Rabaul, very tall students from Kerema or Daru and stocky highlanders and many other groups of students. The Morobe Agricultural Show presented more cultural diversity. It was here I saw local cowboys on horseback for the first time.

In 1975, we students who took electrical as a trade subject were transferred to Port Moresby Technical College. We had no technical instructors. I was soon exposed to more of my country's cultural diversity – at the college, on the streets of Port Moresby and the Cultural Show at Moitaka near the police training college at Bomana. The delicately clad Mekeo dancers and Milne Bay *Tapioka* dancers were my favorite groups to watch.

Nearby at the amphitheater, I saw my first American Indians, a father and daughter team who came all the way to perform several unique cultural dances. They had drawn a very large crowd. I didn't know from which state or which tribal group they belonged but I was intrigued just the same to see native Americans after watching them many times on cowboy movies.

What I couldn't see in Mt Hagen, Lae or in Port Moresby was the diversity of PNG's cultural beliefs and practices – rituals, ways of preparing food, courting sessions, marriage ceremonies or youth initiation ceremonies. But I began to read about them in books. I read about one such ritual, a painful youth initiation ceremony from the Sepik published in our 1975 College Yearbook. I hope the Form 4 student who wrote it, Thomas Kapai and his children could read about this ancient ritual, unique to their area.

I republished the story with my own classmate in mind, late Martin Trei from East Sepik province. I mentioned about his death earlier. I think he had scars on his body, an indication that he had undergone the youth initiation ceremony Thomas wrote about that year.

Five of us from our class went up to Port Moresby General Hospital to wrap his body in some sheets we took along and placed our friend's body in the morgue before it was evacuated home for burial.

We walked away from the hospital to the bus stop, hopped on the big PMV bus that operated from Hanuabada village. When it dropped us off at the big village, we walked the short distance to our college to resume classes without our friend Martin.

Now after fifty years, I do not know if the initiation ritual is still practiced but thanks to Thomas, he wrote it down.

The Initiation

Papua New Guinea is composed of hundreds of villages. Almost every village has its own customs. A number of villages speak the same language and these villages have the same customs in common, as in my area's case, which I would like to discuss. In my area there are about forty villages which speak the same language and most of our customs are very similar. We have a custom which is entirely different from all of the villages in PNG. It is an initiation ceremony, unlike all other initiation ceremonies conducted in this country.

In this ceremony it is the duty of the boy's uncles to look after the well-being of the boys. Before the boys can be taken into the *haus tambaran* or spirit home, permission must be obtained from the boy's fathers because this ceremony involves lots of hard work and these days, lots of money.

When the permission is given the boys can be taken into the *haus tamberan*. Inside the boys are then laid on their stomachs on the bottom of canoes. Then two poles are put on each boy, one across his neck and one across his legs and four men sit on each end of the poles. This is to prevent the boys from jumping up and down while the initiation is carried on.

When the boys are firmly held the initiation starts by shaving the boy's hair off. Then the real thing begins with three to four men at a boy with brand new razor blades. These men must have at least two packets of razor blades because they have to change the blades every now and then.

In the olden days, they used sharp pieces of bamboo. The maximum depth of the cuts is about one and a half centimeters and the length one centimeter. The men who do the job usually put their blades three times in the same place so that when the sore dries up the mark will be very firm.

While the cutting is going on all the people inside the *haus tambaran* make tremendous noises to drown the cries of the boys. If anybody dies during the ceremony it will be a very big secret until the day they are released. On that day of release the first boy in the line will carry the unfortunate one's head on a tray.

By the time the dreadful business is over the boys are almost dead. They lie there like logs covered with sticky blood. The cutting normally goes on for thirty to forty minutes. Then the boys are lifted onto their uncles' shoulders and are carried to a creek or a river. When the boys are being carried to the water, women and uninitiated are forbidden to see the boys. If anyone is caught spying, he or she will be in serious trouble.

When the boys hit the water, they come to life again. The blood is then thoroughly washed away and the boys are taken back to the *haus tambaran* where they stay awake all night. For a couple of days, the boys do not eat very much but after a week they are expected to eat as much as they like.

The miraculous thing is that the sore usually dries up in about two weeks. Some of you might think that some sort of medicine is being used to cure the sore but nothing is used except red clay and a black liquid that comes out of a certain tree.

They do not release the boys as soon as their sores are dry. They usually keep them for another three weeks or so. In the olden days they usually kept them up to two years.

From the time the boys enter the *haus tambaran* until about three months after, the boys are not allowed to sleep on their backs. Every morning the boys are inspected to see that no boys have slept on their backs.

During the initiation period the boys wear nothing, they walk naked, sleep naked. From the day the boys enter the *haus tambaran*, they are in the custody of their uncles until the day they are released.

When the boys are released, they can get married anytime they want. Now they are regarded as men and not boys anymore.

In conclusion, I would like to say that readers might say that this is more than an initiation, but to us it's just the same as any other initiations. It is also another way of finding out who is brave and who is a coward and also the only way we can prove that we are men and not boys – Thomas Kapai, 4F, Port Moresby Technical College, 1975.

A clear message emerges in this painful traditional practice. Like the young men, PNG was initiated on December 1, 1973 for self-government and declared a man two years later on 16 September, 1975 on Independence Day.

How we have conducted the affairs of our country rests squarely with the menfolk of this country! Have we proven ourselves that we are men and not boys?

CONCLUSION

CHALLENGE FOR PNG'S MENFOLK IN THE NEXT 50 YEARS

"As you know, human history is full of evil deeds, and maybe we ought to think of them with tears, not fascination."
– Elizabeth Kostova, The Historian

I couldn't avoid recounting experiences in my life any other way than as I have presented here. Except the Bougainville crisis, I am happy, my country has managed to survive as a nation. The people have been resilient to deal with some of the most trying times as described in this book.

I did enjoy some moments of happiness as a student during the colonial administration period and when I went on trips overseas. But back home, it was full of constant drama, pain and suffering.

I have related my experiences from the day I demanded to be carried to that first census in 1958, witnessing my country gain independence and experiences during my working life – through my own and the lives and actions of others I came in contact with in the last 50 years. It's been rough and tough for countless families throughout the province. They have seen, felt and lived through the trauma of losing property, the agony of losing relatives in never-ending tribal warfare, fear of getting robbed or killed at road-blocks, struggled to adapt to the high cost of living due to a failing economy.

Our society has become self-centered and violent. Many people in this country didn't seem to care about other people's rights, freedom of choice, their lives or their properties. Ballot boxes were constantly hijacked during national general elections. People had developed an attitude problem against fellow human beings.

It looked like they needed psychiatrists to examine their troubled minds. The constant public rhetoric that Engans were generous and kind must stop. If there were any good people who ever lived in the province, they had to be our fathers and their fathers. They were wiser, smarter and made wise decisions for the welfare of the whole tribe. Not this new generation of lip-serving leaders and violent people. Our forefathers had fought tribal wars but never killed many people or destroyed whole villages. There is much hatred and disdain among people today.

I can't make the same comparison for other provinces. But the type of life Enga people experienced in the last couple of years has been like the untamed American wild west of the 18th century. That period in American history was marked by Indians, cowboys, outlaws, pioneers and gunslingers who had come together through expansion, reinvention, greed and defence. This information is available at Wild West: Military Odyssey. People need to read to understand.

As a student, I hated people who described the western part of my province as the 'wild west'. Now, the description fits the entire province. They are all destroying each other.

The province was at its wildest when the gold rush started at Mt Kare in 1988 to 1994 and the closure and reopening of the Porgera gold mine in April, 2020 onwards. There was confusion, crime, tribal war, illegal miners, death and destruction everywhere. Politically-induced tribal wars and sorcery related killings added to the mayhem. As seen in wild west American movies, law enforcement agencies and illegal miners openly exchanged gunfire resulting in deaths like never before.

The people were already experiencing the times Justice Moses Jalina warned about 18 years ago during the legal year celebrations in Wabag town.

In 2024, Chief Justice Sir Gibbs Salika sounded the same alarm bells. He said in a video recording that went viral on social media that the country was not progressing as it should. Because politicians had taken over the role of public servants.

The Chief Justice blamed public servants for creating the mess by allowing politicians to run the show. It was the traditional role of the public service to deliver services.

"Next year, we are celebrating our 50 years of independence, but I don't know, the country is regressing, going downwards, not upwards. We were better off in the earlier days, but not now. The country is crying; the country is crying but we are not listening to the cries."

The Chief Justice, Sir Gibbs Salika said government workers should work extra hard to serve the people. The role of politicians was different, they are decision makers, they make laws, not perform public service duties.

"It is so entrenched in the administration today, we allowed politicians to run rings around us, us public servants. No, that should never be the case," the Chief Justice said.

But politicians, government workers and the people did not seem to heed the warnings of our top judges and church leaders.

In May, just four months away from celebrating 50 years of independence, there was ethnic violence between Engans and Goilalas residing in Port Moresby. Four men died in that clash. One man was caught and burned alive at the Waigani market. How disturbing!

I have related in this book how I. an Engan from Kandep district and a Goilala man, Perai Manai from Tapini in Central province climbed the Empire State Building in America, two Papua New Guineans exploring the city together, side by side delighting in the sights of New York. But here some Engans and Goilalas were fighting in the nation's capital as if they were still living in the Dark Ages killing each other and burning people at the stake.

If authorities remained indifferent to such gruesome atrocities right on the doorstep of government power, the country will gradually plunge deeper into the endless abyss beyond recovery. Prophet of Doom you can call me but this country desperately needs urgent repair.

I emphasise again that the situation required intervention by the International Red Cross to establish rehabilitation centers on a big scale to provide professional counselling to the traumatised masses – people who saw their family members and relatives murdered, husbands and sons who saw their wives, mothers, sisters and daughters tortured, accusing them of sorcery, women raped and killed during tribal warfare, people who saw gory images of faceless corpses, homes burned with people inside and so forth.

Mercenary fighters or 'Hire man' also known as 'Rambos' needed professional counselling to help them realise their own lives were precious too. A lot of work really needed to be done to instill sanity and order in the communities.

In Enga province, all the women and children should be relocated to rehabilitation centers, isolate them from their menfolk who needed them for comfort and to cook for them when they were out fighting. Engans were never afraid to die – but scared stiff of getting caught and put in prison.

Elected members of parliament had to demonstrate leadership and initiate peace plans. Nobody else will solve our social problems. The vicious circle of death and destruction had to stop somewhere. Fifty years of independence, all the talking and where is Enga province and PNG at?

Many people are sick and tired of selfish, boastful attitudes of some of the leaders. They were sick of the person who stood up and said the people were progressing when they were destroying each other as innocent women and children suffered silently. They were sick of Christian church leaders praying for corrupt leaders when they should be rebuking them publicly. The people are sick of leaders who unfairly distributed the millions of Provincial & District Services Improvement Program funds, DSIP only to loyal supporters and relatives, causing animosity, inequality, envy, greed and lawlessness.

The people are sick of the disciplinary forces who failed to make arrests of corrupt leaders or raided areas where guns and criminals were hiding in known locations. The people are sick of the government not providing enough funds to complete the National Identity Project or NID which was key to running fair, free and peaceful elections. The people are sick of the government compromising the law when they entertained lawbreakers in hotel rooms. They wondered what happened to the once proud Royal Papua New Guinea Constabulary?

The laws of the land had to be respected, protected and upheld by every citizen. Nobody is above the law. People want to see justice prevail in the land. If it is in a peaceful transparent environment, Enga province and PNG would have progressed enormously.

Imagine all the private, mission and public property like Laiagam High School, Tsak Secondary school and Mulitaka High School, Kasi Health Center, Tsak Pumakos Catholic Mission, Marara Primary School, Pina Catholic mission, Pina Primary School and all the other thousands of unaccounted for public and private properties that went up in flames in the last fifty years!

How advanced would the living conditions of people in Enga province and PNG be today?

Elected leaders must learn to say enough is enough and relax their habitual involvement in deep-rooted corruption. They must remember that nobody takes anything along to the next life. They must provide fair and transparent leadership. It looks like some leaders have another agenda based on their actions.

Let the people be people. Supporters and non-supporters must be treated equally. All people bleed the same blood, have the same structure, the same needs and wants and shed the same tears. They are all equal.

Look at the young man who displayed the Papua New Guinea flag far away on Times Square in New York City during one Independence Day celebration.

The choice words he used to express his genuine love for this country were truly touching. And he was a foreign national. The young man stood alone, boldly displaying the flag as cars and people passed unaware of the emotions surging through his mind.

"Nothing makes me happier than to lift up the glorious flag of a thousand tribes here in the heart of NYC, at the iconic Times Square. My deep and abiding love for PNG has defined the core purpose of my life. PNG yu lewa bilong mi. (You are in my heart or I love you)– Rev SML."

These were the enduring words that accompanied the photo, shared by one Faime Ambaiarr on popular social media sites on 16 September.

If foreigners, former Kiaps, missionaries, businessman and their siblings could continue to love and have concern for this country, why can't we ourselves change our attitudes, have respect for one another and live in peace?

America experienced tough times in the 18th century but look where it is today. Papua New Guinea cannot possibly become as powerful or rich as the USA.

But we have an abundance of natural resources, that, if managed properly in a transparent manner, could transform

our country to be the richest, black Christian nation, we aspire it to be.

Look at all the election violence, tribal warfare, revenge killings, sorcery related violence against women and deep-rooted corruption in government. Who were the perpetrators of these vicious criminal acts?

They were mostly perpetrated by the menfolk of this country. They are like the uncles performing the initiation ceremony – cutting deep into the flesh of young initiates.

Yes, you heard that right. Men were the main cause of all the pain, death and destruction, holding this bountiful country hostage – suffocating it from ever progressing.

Let the wounds heal like the scars on the bodies of the young men who underwent the bloody, painful and dangerous initiation ritual.

Let all menfolk bow their heads low in shame, search their hearts this anniversary year, be thankful to the fertile soil on which we stand on, breathe in the fresh air and choose what is right for ourselves, our children, our women and the wellbeing of our beloved country.

Let every man stand up and speak peace and unity. We must establish a solid foundation based on love and respect. Let us declare peace and prosperity to be our goal in the next 50 years and beyond.

If not, the climax, a culmination of everything bad that is happening will gradually bring this country down. The unity, peace and freedom we once used to know will be no more.

THE END

ACKNOWLEDGEMENTS

I wish to thank former Kiap, Jim Fenton for releasing to me his precious patrol reports from Kandep patrol post for the first time. He exhibited strength and energy to tirelessly write the Foreword and read through the manuscript to ensure the information was accurate. Most elderly people of advanced age in my province would just waste away. But not Jim, he was still the Kiap in control, even taking his wife Rita 87 to hospital when she was ill.

I also thank Ed Brumby for his never-ending encouragement and briefly reading through the manuscript in the initial stages to keep me on the right track.

This book is a compilation of notes from my diaries, interviews, commentaries, conversations, experiences and published excerpts from various avenues – The Post Courier, The National, PNG Attitude blog, Paradise In-flight magazine, Sunday Chronical and Enga Nius, the people's paper which I edited that was extinguished like a fire, stopping it from recording Enga's contemporary history.

I thank them all for publishing my stories which formed the basis of this book which tells my story and experiences in my beloved province and my country.

I am grateful to my family members, my children and my many grandchildren for staying quiet when I am writing in my room in the house.

Finally, I am forever indebted to my best friend, Grand Chief Sir Paul Kurai and management of Ribito Hotel for allowing me the use of Room 9 during never-ending power blackouts in Wabag town to complete this project in comfort and with peace of mind.

Thank you

BIOGRAPHY

Daniel Kumbon studied Journalism and Media Studies at the University of Papua New Guinea. In 1983, he helped to establish Enga Nius under the Communications Development Component of the over-all Provincial Development Program called 'Enga Yakaa Laseamana or EYL for short. The five-year project was a national government initiative facilitated by a K8million loan from the World Bank.

Daniel started his career in the media industry with the National Broadcasting Commission in 1977. Then he worked as Director Media and information Technology in the department of Enga Administration. He also edited the popular provincial newspaper Enga Nius until 2008. He has won many international scholarships over the years.

He has published several books. Included are a small supplementary reader 'Climbing Mountains' and his first novel 'The Old Man's Dilemma'. This book: Choosing Peace is his 10th book.

He is married with eleven children and 22 grandchildren. He currently lives in retirement in Wabag, Enga province. As a professional journalist, he continues to contribute to the two daily newspapers as a freelance writer.

www.ingramcontent.com/pod-product-compliance
Lightning Source LLC
Chambersburg PA
CBHW060352080526
44583CB00012B/285